Two week
loan

Please return on or before the last
date stamped below.
Charges are made for late return.

6 DEC 2001		
14 DEC 2001		
WITHDRAWN		

de Gruyter Studies in Organization 48

Euro-Manager or Splendid Isolation?

de Gruyter Studies in Organization

Organizational Theory and Research

This de Gruyter Series aims at publishing theoretical and methodological studies of organizations as well as research findings, which yield insight into and knowledge about organizations. The whole spectrum of perspectives will be considered: organizational analyses rooted in the sociological as well as the economic tradition, from a socio-psychological or a political science angle, mainstream as well as critical or ethnomethodological contributions. Equally, all kinds of organizations will be considered: firms, public agencies, non-profit institutions, voluntary associations, inter-organizational networks, supra-national organizations etc.

Emphasis is on publication of *new* contributions, or significant revisions of existing approaches. However, summaries or critical reflections on current thinking and research will also be considered.

This series represents an effort to advance the social scientific study of organizations across national boundaries and academic disciplines. An Advisory Board consisting of representatives of a variety of perspectives and from different cultural areas is responsible for achieving this task.

This series addresses organization researchers within and outside universities, but also practitioners who have an interest in grounding their work on recent social scientific knowledge and insights.

Editors:

Prof. Dr. Alfred Kieser, Universität Mannheim, Mannheim, Germany
Prof. Dr. Cornelis Lammers, FSW Rijksuniversiteit Leiden, Leiden, The Netherlands

Advisory Board:

Prof. Anna Grandori, CRORA, Università Commerciale Luigi Bocconi, Milano, Italy
Prof. Dr. Marshall W. Meyer, The Wharton School, University of Pennsylvania, Philadelphia, U.S.A.
Prof. Jean-Claude Thoenig, Université de Paris I, Paris, France
Prof. Dr. Barry A. Turner, Middlesex Business School, London, GB
Prof. Mayer F. Zald, The University of Michigan, Ann Arbor, U.S.A.

Wilhelm Eberwein · Jochen Tholen

Euro-Manager or Splendid Isolation?

International Management —
An Anglo-German Comparison

Walter de Gruyter · Berlin · New York 1993

658·18   E

Dr. Wilhelm Eberwein
Dr. Jochen Tholen
Universität Bremen, Bremen, Germany

With 4 tables

Library of Congress Cataloging-in-Publication Data

Eberwein, Wilhelm, 1947—
    Euro-manager or splendid isolation? ; international man-
agement, an anglo-german comparison / Wilhelm Eberwein,
Jochen Tholen.
        p.   cm. — (De Gruyter studies in organization ; 48)
    Includes bibliographical references.
    ISBN 3-11-013481-0
    1. Management — Germany. 2. Management — Great
Britain. 3. Executives — Germany. 4. Executives — Great
Britain. 5. Corporate culture — Germany. 6. Corporate
culture — Great Britain. I. Tholen, Jochen, 1948—   .
II. Title. III. Series.
HD70.G2E23   1993
658′.049′0941—dc20   92-45753
                                                    CIP

Die Deutsche Bibliothek — Cataloging-in-Publication Data

Eberwein, Wilhelm:
Euro-manager or splendid isolation ; international manage-
ment — an Anglo-German comparison / Wilhelm Eberwein ;
Jochen Tholen. — Berlin ; New York : de Gruyter, 1993
    (De Gruyter studies in organization ; 48)
    ISBN 3-11-013481-0
NE: Tholen, Jochen ; GT

Typesetting: Converted by Knipp Satz und Bild digital, Dortmund — Printing:
Karl Gerike GmbH, Berlin. — Binding: Lüderitz & Bauer GmbH, Berlin. — Cover
Design: Johannes Rother, Berlin.

Acknowledgements

The book in hand forms the second part of a total of three greater works dealing with the working and professional situation of top managers in industry. The first part, which refers exclusively to Germany has been available for some time (Eberwein, Tholen: 1990). The second part – a comparison of English and German top managers – will be presented with this book. The third book – a comparison of the working and professional situation of managers in Russia and the Federal Republic of Germany is intended to come out next year.

Such a comprehensive examination, which has been carried out at the University of Bremen over the last years, is only possible with the help and support of many people and institutions whom we are obliged to thank sincerely.

In particular, we would like to thank the following persons and institutions for the help with the Anglo-German comparative study:

- the managers in England and Germany for their willingness to speak to us and for their great hospitality;
- Ute Last, Sibilla Trost, Klaus Hißenkemper, Walter Gröh, Andreas Gelbert and Ulf Schnars for their literature researches;
- Sigrid Hirschhausen, who, with others, looked after the project regarding organization;
- Denise Winkler, for the difficult task of translating the text into English;
- the Deutsche Forschungsgemeinschaft and the British Council for their financial support;
- the University of Nottingham for their hospitality during the examinations in England;
- our friend, Dick Whitehurst (+), who helped us in every way during our stays in England with his advice.

However, we must give particular thanks to our friend and colleague, Ivor Moon, without whose committed support the empirical examination in England could never have taken place.

Bremen, August 1992   W. Eberwein, J. Tholen

Contents

Preface
International management in the light of the European Union

In the face of the planned completion of the European market in 1993 the theme "International Management" seems to be there for the picking and needs no actual reasoning or explanation. Furthermore the appropriate management magazines (and not only the magazines) – according to whatever opinion – are absolutely flowing over with either hopeful or pessimistic forecasts regarding the economic, social and political effects of the common market. Thus, in the meantime, there is a wealth of qualification profiles for the future 'Euro-manager', naturally as a rule from an economic point of view and of a normative intention[1].

Therefore it is even more amazing to discover that in this situation there are hardly any cross-national (industrial) sociological examinations, not even a sociological stock-taking of the work and occupational situation of managers in those countries of the future market which will be to a greater or lesser extent uniform. The following book is concerned with filling (at least partly) this very wide gap. In doing so, we will see that apart from a few exceptions there is practically hardly any connection between German and British management and/or industrial sociology. Whilst at least parts of British or rather Anglo-American discussions are adopted in Germany, German work in England, when it is not translated, is not even taken note of.

In order to lay the foundation for a possible and necessary cooperation we would firstly like to give a general view of the present state of research and discussion in both countries.

---

1   One exception is the comparative study recently edited by R. Calori and P. Lawrence (1991).

1 Regarding the research and conception of the examination

1.1 The sociology of management in Great Britain and Germany – with reference to research and the social discussion

Before comparing industrial management in Great Britain and Germany we should like to start with a comparison of the sociology of management, that is to say to a certain degree a comparison of our 'guild'. This does not involve the question as to whether the level of research possibly correlates positively or negatively to the 'quality' of management in the countries compared. On the contrary, one of the main reasons for carrying out an examination of the working and professional situation of managers was to close a gap in industrial-sociological research which for its part contributes to a discussion, which is ideologized to a lesser or greater degree, about management in our society. There we must first of all proceed from and take stock of the level of research and we must refer at least in a general way to the social discussion in both countries[1].

Let us begin by presenting the German landscape of research. In the last 10 years of industrial-sociological research company employment politics and staff politics in general have appeared and have been taken note of everywhere as considerable factors in placement and organization in different areas such as in the very intensive research of the labour market, humanization research, crisis research and research of technological development (automatic machines, microelectronics, robots etc.).

It appears to us that by doing this, processes of work and companies are in principle regarded as the causes which produce certain working situations which must be dealt with in one way or another subjectively.

---

1 As a matter of necessity we limit ourselves here to a selection of literature most important for our purposes. Those examinations which are concerned with comparative management research internationally will be introduced for pragmatic reasons in the following section. Furthermore we will take into consideration a multitude of individual findings from further examinations in the corresponding sections.

Nevertheless there are only few pieces of work which may be seen sociologically as referring to the tradition of industrial sociology, which are concerned with the method of industrial sociology regarding the working situation and only few which dealt systematically with top industrial management.

This stands in apparently strange contrast to today's almost immeasurable amount of literature on the theme of management. The discrepancy between the multitude of publications and the rather deficient level of knowledge about management problems can be explained by the considerably normative or objective character of the majority of management literature which in Germany is primarily but not only represented by the science of business management.

If we proceed from the "dispositive factor" of Gutenberg (Gutenberg: 1958, p 27), business management literature deals in many variations with the question of optimalization of "company management, planning and company organization".

Additionally a large part of management literature which is directed in a rather organizational-sociological way remains on a more normative and/or simply formal level insofar as it proceeds from an instrumental conception of organization. According to this literature management as leaders of organization are given the task to set the organizational company targets which with the help of bureaucratic structures of instruction should be reached and carried out (cf. e.g. Büschges: 1976).

This characterization of business management and organizational-sociological management research and literature is without doubt extremely global[2]; in our opinion, however, it describes quite appropriately the fundamental intentions according to which a multitude of management models and instructions for best possible management action are designed.

It is obvious that this kind of management literature in its formality and normativity promises little practical information about the working and professional situation of managers.

Apart from this, there is in the meantime a branch of management research for Germany that deals with the themes and forms of managerial occupation under the title "The daily situation of managers" (e.g. Müller-Böling et al.: 1989). However industrial management – that is our impression – continues to remain 'blank' in the industrial-sociological landscape of research.

---

2   See for the multitude of different approaches e.g. Grochla (1972); Staehle (1980a, 1989a).

In the actual industrial-sociological approaches themselves company management is as a rule seen as an abstract authority under the spell of an abstract power (of capital) so that it is only emphasized as an objective company strategy and the underlying subjective carrying out of the managerial situation resulting from the position of company management is neglected because it is not conceived as part of a social connection. Prominent examples of this are the "Munich company approach" (see e.g. Bechtle: 1980) and the "Frankfurt production and time economic approach" (see e.g. Schmiede, Schudlich: 1978). Without doubt these approaches are suitable instruments of analysis within the framework of those questions asked and of those interests in knowledge but the final recourse towards the motive of profit maximization appears to us too global to make sufficient differentiated analyses of management possible.

Therefore there is often a mythologization or "implicit heroization of management precisely as a result of many critical analyses which interpret management strategies generally as of superior interest" (Weltz, Lullies: 1984, p 168).

Ultimately the current industrial-sociological approaches of explanation provide "no satisfactory solution to the difficult problem of conveying management concepts and actions and to the problem of actually carrying out strategies of capital utilization" (Düll: 1985, p 142). Instead (in the worst case unasked) the strategies propagated by management are often accepted, perhaps given a 'negative' sign and considered to be the true picture of management practice.

On the other hand, precisely as a result of industrial-sociological research there are scopes of action and options of behaviour of management that are confirmed and emphasized (as e.g. by Kern, Schumann: 1984). However these are seldom with a systematic explanation of the conditions, limits and possibilities connected to them. In relation to this, Kern and Schumann complain themselves that "developed sociology of management" is still "a desideratum of industrial sociology" (p 26) and they point additionally to the fact that

> different positional, functional and professional layers of interest … have just as much significance in this process of searching, trying out and generalizing (of new conversions of the processing premise) as specific differences in experience according to the generation and differing 'philosophies' (p 27).

To follow we would briefly like to concern ourselves with some selected industrial-sociological approaches of explanation which are possibly in the position to contribute to closing the gaps of the mentioned deficiencies in research.

The so-called "Labour Process Debate" that arose in the Anglo-Saxon sphere in conclusion to Braverman (1977) and which was mainly carried out there, caused management to be focused on in the Federal Republic of Germany to an ever-increasing degree as an acting subject. Yet the strategies of control of management in comparison to the strategies of planning and leadership are put very definitely to the fore. In our opinion the complex mediation between management conceptions and their implementation in the company remains for the most part unsettled.

However the critics of Braverman deserve well for the fact that company strategies of action of management and the fundamental complexity of the decision-making situation have at least been dealt with as themes in a more differentiated way than has usually been the case. Accordingly the functions and norms of managerial action are no longer considered to be given facts but are seen to be problematical and are made to a theme of research with broader connections.

In the German discussion the Labour Process Debate found expression in particular in different pieces of work of the Wissenschaftszentrum Berlin on questions of labour politics (cf. e.g. the corresponding contributions in Jürgens, Naschold: 1984; and Naschold: 1985).

On the whole, however, such a "management control approach" is not sufficient for a sociological analysis of the working and professional situation of managers.

Above all it seems to us that the focusing of the research's intentions on the aspect of management control obstructs the possibility of being able to analyse adequately enough the way the manager copes and deals with his situation. Thus the direct working situation of the managers in this research direction only plays a minor role and the explanation of the strategies of action and forms of coping with the managerial situation is in danger of being reduced to a specialized strategy of control which cannot do justice to the complexity of the managerial decision-making situations.

It is precisely this complexity which stands at the centre of two industrial-sociological approaches of research which, as far as we know, have scarcely been admitted into the current discussion so far: the concepts of the "internal company constellation of action" (innerbetriebliche Handlungskonstellation) (Weltz: 1988; Weltz, Lullies: 1984) or rather the "conception-competition" (Konzeptionskonkurrenz) (Wiedemann: 1971).

Following Parsons, Wiedemann sees the enterprise as a specifically structured social system which in order to reach its economic aim, is continually forced to adapt to its environment and must functionally be in permanent dynamic development. There arises a "dialectic" between formal hierarchy and a partially hierarchical structure whose conceptualization in the sense of the most favourable management according to the company's aim Wiedemann sees as the real task of managers. Hereby there are on different management levels different types of competition running vertically, horizontally or in both directions for the optimum conception. Neither these nor the partial undermining of hierarchy may be seen as obstructions in the way the company is run but as long as they remain controllable and this is the task of the next level of hierarchy, they are functional for the company's aim and the necessary processes of adaptation.

This approach and the approach of Weltz of "internal company constellation of action" looks more closely at the differentiation of company processes of implementation. The internal company constellation of action is made up of a complex working together of different influences. Internal company mechanisms of mediation take their force from the constellation of partial interests, competencies and real possibilities of influence, from the conflicts, alliances and competition arising from these and from the necessity to maintain and to legitimate one's authority. By these the abstract level of interest for the whole company is converted into the concrete company workings.

According to Weltz and Lullies the internal company constellation of action and the mechanisms which arise out of it do not naturally counterbalance the effectiveness of the general company requirements for action as of course the internal company pluralism of interests does not neutralize the fundamental contrast of interests between capital and labour. Nevertheless they determine – perhaps we can say at an angle to these – the modes of behaviour of the members of company management in a manifold and subtle way.

The great merit of the two approaches of research which we have lastly mentioned, that is to say the consideration of specific company requirements, harbours weaknesses too. We may ask for example about its analytical capacity or range. Are they only applicable to the respective company management situation or do they allow summarizing and generalizing findings? And to what extent are "conception-competition" and the "internal company constellation of action" the results of general company framework conditions?

An excellent field of management literature, under the heading "the separation of property and control" concerns itself in Germany with the much-discussed division of the real function of the entrepreneur of property to the means of production and the transference of this function to employed managers who receive a previously defined 'salary' for their occupation[3].

---

3   Parsons made this change in structure to a central point of departure of his system-

The effects of this division have been analysed by a whole line of authors under varying aspects. As a rule they are concerned with questions of a specific investment behaviour of the managers, with their basis of legitimation in the face of owners and with their attitude to the capitalist economic system (revolution of the managers etc.)? The examination of H. Pross (1965) which is indeed a little older but still directive in its way is representative of the abundance of works on this theme.

The study of H. Hartmann from 1959 and thus also a little older, is particularly concerned with the legitimation of entrepreneurial authority whereby private ownership is only treated as one of several fundamentals of this authority.

A number of examinations deal with questions of qualification, origin and recruitment, of career paths etc. of top managers as for example Zapf (1965); Pross, Boetticher (1971); Kruk (1972); Bleuel (1976) as well as the historically proceeding study of Berghahn (1987).

Furthermore in the meantime there are a whole number of examinations and surveys about general orientations, norms and values of company managers. In particular there are some theoretically more demanding examinations to be mentioned as for example Gabele et al. (1977); Pross (1973); and Pross, Boetticher (1971) which particularly go into managers' political attitudes.

At last our own examination, whose first results have recently appeared (Eberwein, Tholen: 1990) offers an explicit analysis of the working and professional situation of industrial company managers. The study is especially directed towards the concrete working situation and examines the working and professional capacity, the company and market relation and the political and social understanding of members of the two top levels of management. The findings and results of other examinations, in particular of Anglo-American management literature are systematically taken into consideration. With this we hope to be able to make a contribution to the scientific realization of the possibilities and limits of management action and thus make the first step towards a sociological theory of management action. However, a more theoretical locating and integrating of our findings is still outstanding.

Our conclusion up to now is that on the whole the level of research of the 'German sociology of management' remains deficient even if, as we have

---

atic theoretical analysis of the economic process, cf. T. Parsons, N.J. Smelser (1969).

described above, there are attempts and approaches to close the present gaps[4]. Now there is the question of the situation in Great Britain.

It appears at first glance that extensive management research has been established in the Anglo-American sphere and in particular in the USA and that quite a lively practice of publication has developed, as e.g. the bibliography by R. Stout covering the ten year period between 1969 and 1979 shows (Stout: 1980a). But Stout too came to the conclusion that "we still do not fully understand what managers do" (Stout: 1980b, p 54). And after working on management literature H. Mintzberg concluded: "Although an enormous amount of material has been published on the manager's job, we continue to know very little about it" (Mintzberg: 1973, p 7). The following characterization of the state of research is formulated here in a very drastic and exaggerated way by the British scientists Beishon and Palmer: "It seems that today we know more about the behaviour of a typical mountain gorilla than we do of a typical ... manager" (Beishon, Palmer: 1979, p 183).

As far as the British scene is concerned this statement must in our opinion be strongly relativized. Here there are a considerable number of sociologically orientated examinations[5] of substantial range but of differing quality. Those thematic areas, publications and researchers which appear most important to us will be consequently introduced in a general way[6].

Let us continue from Mintzberg's comment: An established branch of management research in Great Britain deals under the heading: "What do managers (really) do?" explicitly with the forms, themes and content of managerial occupation, that is to say with the 'job' of the manager.

Colin Hales (1986) gave a summarizing literature report on this theme whose argumentation we will follow in more detail[7]. With his critical assessment of the works of Mintzberg (1973) and Stewart (1983) Hales wishes to go beyond those works which had in their way given a general view of the state of

---

4   On the other hand Schienstock (1991, p 366) has recently taken the view that there is more a confusing plurality than a lack of theoretical approaches in the analysis of management processes.

5   In Great Britain there exists a real flood of business administrative management literature, as for example a glance in the catalogues of relevant publishers clearly shows. We will not go into these in any detail here.

6   We will restrict ourselves here, as for German literature, to that literature which is most relevant to our purposes and intentions. More British management literature is listed in the following paragraphs regarding international comparative studies as well as in corresponding thematic connections of the present examination.

7   A comprehensive discussion may be found in Eberwein, Tholen (1990, pp 124-164); see also paragraph 2.5 of the present report.

research. He describes five different areas, which are dealt with in the respective studies:

1.   The substantive elements of managerial work (What do managers do?);
2.   The distribution of managers' time between work elements (How do managers work?);
3.   Interactions: With whom managers work (With whom do managers work?);
4.   Informal elements of managerial work (What else do managers do?);
5.   Themes which pervade managerial work (What qualities does managerial work have?) (Hales: 1986, p 90).

After going through the empirical examinations on management work[8] which have appeared since the 1950s, Hales then makes the attempt to find out the common findings of the examinations which can be identified as general characteristics of management work:

1.   Acting as figurehead and leader of an organizational unit;
2.   Liaison: the formation and maintenance of contacts;
3.   Monitoring, filtering and disseminating information;
4.   Allocating resources;
5.   Handling disturbances and maintaining work flows;
6.   Negotiating;
7.   Innovating;
8.   Planning;
9.   Controlling and directing subordinates (Hales: 1986, p 95).

Proceeding from this Hales also summarizes the well-known features of managerial work:

1.   It combines a specialist/professional element and a general, 'managerial' element;
2.   The substantive elements involve, essentially, liaison, man-management and responsibility for a work process, beneath which are subsumed more detailed work elements;
3.   The character of work elements varies by duration, time span, recurrence, unexpectedness and source;
4.   Much time is spent in day-to-day trouble shooting and ad hoc problems of organization and regulation;
5.   Much managerial activity consists of asking or persuading others to do things, involving the manager in face-to-face verbal communication of limited duration;

---

8   See here the very informative tabulated view by Hales (1986, pp 91-92).

6. Patterns of communication vary in terms of what the communication is about and with whom the communication is made;
7. Little time is spent on any one particular activity and, in particular, on the conscious, systematic formulation of plans. Planning and decision making tend to take place in the course of other activity;
8. Managers spend a lot of time accounting for and explaining what they do, in informal relationships and in "politicking";
9. Managerial activities are driven by contradicitions, cross-pressures and conflicts. Much managerial work involves coping with and reconciling social and technical conflict;
10. There is considerable choice in terms of what is done and how: part of managerial work is setting the boundaries of and negotiating that work itself" (Hales: 1986, p 104).

The British (or rather: Anglo-American) literature regarding the theme "What do managers do?" offers quite a wealthy and differentiated picture of the managerial occupation and is in this area far ahead of the German state of research. But two critical comments must be made here.

First of all and mainly as a result of Mintzberg's works (1973, 1975) a way of looking at management has been established that sees it as a non-rational occupation without any recognizable rules and structures. Indeed it is correct that the traditional picture of the science of managers, namely that of rationality, of planning action, of strict following of organizational aims is no longer true (Stewart: 1983).

But to see management as an anomic process would be like throwing the baby out with the bathwater. Carroll and Gillen (1987) emphasized that the classical management functions of planning, deciding, organizing, of leadership, co-ordination and control are indeed all constituents of the managerial occupation. They reproach Mintzberg for not being able to recognize the managerial functions in their essence since his examination only applied to visible activities. Managers work mentally and not physically. In an examination of physical activities conversations are seen to be physical work too. But in the managers' case it is important to abstract the conversations from their physical form and to look for the content substrate of the conversation. If we proceed in this way then we may confirm that conversations are only visible forms of a mental occupation. It is not the fact that conversations are carried out which is important but the meaning of the conversations which stand behind the managers' intentions (Carroll, Gillen: 1987, p 43).

A second weakness of British research presented here may be put forward here, namely a lack of historical and theoretical integration and location of most of the examinations of managerial activities (Willmott: 1987), a lack that applies to an even higher degree for the few German examinations on this theme.

One example of management research which includes a historical dimension is the work by Anthony (1986), *The Foundation of Management*[9]. Similarly there is the older but still very informative examination by Bendix (1956, 1975) which puts its emphasis on the historical development of management ideologies as well as Wiener's *English Culture and the Decline of the Industrial Spirit 1850-1980* (1981), in which he traces back the present weakness of British industry to its cultural-historical development.

Anthony also sees the lacking strength of British industry based to a lesser degree on the structural inadequacies of the British social system than on managerial misbehaviour itself (this is of course socially determined for its part). His thesis says that British management in industry has withdrawn more and more from the responsibility for control and leadership and that to the same extent has denied complete social responsibility. But Anthony sees the essential legitimation of managerial action precisely in the obligation of managerial action towards social welfare demands and in the conscious connection between simply economic action and the social consequences arising from this.

This legitimacy which is based primarily on moral and less on economic grounds is for him the central question from which other dimensions – as for example the organization of industrial relations in the company, market behaviour etc. – may be traced. According to Anthony there are here considerable deficiencies in British management which are based on the historically developed current system of norms of the individual manager and industrial management on the whole. To what extent this view is supported by other findings from other examinations and whether German conditions are similar or rather contrary will be dealt with at a later stage in this report.

To follow we will look in more detail and to a certain extent exemplarily at two examinations which have set as their aim the theoretical establishment and penetration of a sociology of management, namely Storey's *Managerial Prerogative and the Question of Control* (1985) and Reed's (nomen est omen) *The Sociology of Management* (1989).

At this point we will quite consciously do without the inclusion of more organizational-sociologically orientated approaches as they are embodied quite particularly but not only in the different works of John Child (e.g. 1977). But

---

9   For Germany, see here the somewhat older study by Kocka (1969) as well as Braun, Eberwein, Tholen (1992).

this direction of research finds, of course, due consideration in the following paragraphs.

But first to Storey's examination: Following Bravermann (1977) and the subsequent 'second generation' of examinations and theories on the capitalist production process (Labour Process Debate) Storey carries out a theoretical observation of the leadership and control situation of management. He is of the opinion that for a long time the theme of managerial control of work has been remarkably neglected in the Marxist as well as non-Marxist theory. Therefore in his work he is particularly concerned with the question of whether management has lost prerogatives, in particular the prerogative of control, whether management can equate with strategic control and how rational managerial action really is and so finally he is concerned with the structural relationship between capital (management) and labour (staff).

The great value of Storey's analysis lies in the systematic summary of relevant management literature which not only refers to theoretical but also practical aspects of research.

Thus he is concerned with the relationship of society in which the control of the labour process is incorporated (Storey: 1985, pp 54-74). Here he divides the literature into two kinds: Firstly authors, who proceed from authority as their central category (in particular structure functionalists like Parsons [e.g. Parsons, Smelser: 1969]) and secondly authors who proceed from leadership as a pre-condition for the existence of authority (Marxists like Clegg: 1989; and conflict theorists like Giddens: 1979a).

The social basis for the relationship of management and staff is for management the objective-specialist founded division and differentiation of functions which on the one hand must be planned and co-ordinated and on the other hand must be carried out. From this way of looking at things authority is therefore rationally founded. For the representatives of the second kind, the forming of authority is based on the fact that the capitalist society is a class society and as such produces a contrast of interests between capital and work which unavoidably leads to conflicts. Since management could monopolize all means of power in this society, it is – according to the representatives of this direction – in the position to find supporters for the given instructions, also regardless of specialized and objectively based authority (whose recognition differs in degrees within this direction). Storey amongst others concludes from the discussion of these different views: organizational aims can neither be defined one-sidedly, only as contributions of the company for the satisfaction of social needs nor can they be seen solely as the aims of management and other control groups. On the contrary we are talking about a complex organization in the case of the modern company in which the interests of the individual members can achieve their own significance in the sense of the

modern sociology of organization. Proceeding from this and with consideration of the relevant literature Storey concerns himself with managerial
behaviour (Storey: 1985, pp 75-97). Firstly he states that there are good
reasons for examining managerial behaviour even if we must proceed from the
viewpoint that this is stipulated in a purely structural way, that is to say
determined by the existence of the capitalist market because:

–   Market constraints must be recognized and interpreted as such by
    managers;
–   Even if managers recognize these market constraints correctly it must be
    analysed how they can make use of them within the company;
–   It must be examined how managers justify their superior position;
–   The degree of determination of managerial action must be contrasted with
    the possibilities of the autonomy of decision-making.

After going over empirical management examinations Storey comes to the
conclusion that a theoretical concept must eclectically consist of empirical
findings and varying theoretical perspectives. Although he accepts the many
subtleties of these empirical studies (cultural, organizational, personality
differences etc. in the analysis of management work), he still views the control
of the production process as the most important and characteristic task and
performance of management. However the manager's actual strategies of
control neither depend one-sidedly on the free will of every manager nor are
they solely determined in a structural way by the market (Storey: 1985,
pp 123-156). On the contrary, different factors contribute to their concrete
form as:

–   structural constraints;
–   the development of technology;
–   social and political developments;
–   class relations;
–   preferences of management.

Although Storey differentiates the control aspect of management completely
and tries to grasp it in its complexity, in our opinion in his over-emphasis of
this view lies also a weakness of his work since the functions of leadership and
control in management are inevitably and according to tendency neglected.
However Storey's analysis gives us valuable insight on the way to a sociology
of management action.

In his results he states that the managerial situation is much more complex and
uncertain than was previously presumed in the theoretical approaches, in
particular in those Marxist-orientated approaches and subsequently in those of
the Labour Process Debate. Hence management is not only a function but also

a professional group. As such it demonstrates common features with 'wage labour' as well as elements which may antagonistically be classified to this.

If we say that the working and professional situation of managers has been touched upon here and that theoretical definition of this has been started we must continue that M. Reed (1989) tries explicitly to work on a sociology of management.

Here he wishes to integrate three theories or rather conceptions of management into his perspectives, namely (Reed: 1989, pp 1-32):

1. The so-called technocratic way of proceeding which views management simply from its functions and therefore fundamentally and primarily as politically neutral. From this point of view the task of management is seen to be in satisfying the functional system requirements. Such a way of proceeding has as its aim the normative requirement to maximize managerial and organizational standards of rationality;

2. The theory of pluralism (conflict theory, political theory) sees management as one of several groups within and outside the company that makes demands and follows its own interests which as a course of their nature conflict. All groups have the aim to achieve as many of their objectives as possible via institutionalized channels. The aim of this approach is to find out how conflicts may be solved and for which reasons the strategies for solving the conflicts are successful;

3. The class-theoretical way of proceeding (theories about the production and labour process, as they are represented above all in the Labour Process Debate) looks to define management in its nature according to class positions in order to trace from this aims, structures of consciousness and ways of behaviour of management.

To continue on from this differentiation, Reed confirms four problems which remain unsolved by all theoretical approaches:

1. There exists no integrating analysis which includes the currently competing approaches;

2. There exists a tendency in every approach to either over-emphasize objective (structural determination) or subjective (strategic management decisions) factors;

3. As a consequence of what has just been said managers are viewed as being either conscious subjects of action who may create and change structures according to their interests or as being will-less puppets of deeper-lying structures;

4. The embedding of management in its cultural, historical and worldly context is lacking and this leads to the fact that rationality potentials of

managerial action are always seen from the point of view of the organization and class interests and are therefore often over-rated.

Precisely these unsolved problems are the starting point of Reed's own concept of "management as a social practice".

Reed thinks that management must be examined to a higher degree with the inclusion of the totality of its social relations. For this it is necessary to include company as well as complete social levels in the analysis. Accordingly management must be understood as a process of social practice, defined as actions in a situational context. Reed is aware of the fact that the situational context does not simply exist a priori but is given by society which in its turn can be influenced by management itself. The consequence for the research approach arising from this brings different competing perspectives together:

The basic hypothesis is therefore that structural framework conditions are given to management (critical perspectives) and within this framework they have to functionally make use of structural free spaces in the most effective way possible (technical perspectives) and must overcome those problems which arise in negotiations (political perspectives).

The differences between the various theoretical approaches become clear for example in the question of control. Whilst the technical perspective in looking at the control of the labour process puts its emphasis on increasing the effectiveness of organizations, the political perspective takes on a virtual neutral position in which it has as its aim the settlement of conflicts of different but principally equal interest groups. The critical perspective emphasizes the class character of control which from this point of view is seen as a means for securing the surplus value.

According to Reed, the concept of management as social practice integrates all these three approaches. Accordingly management sees itself open to different expectations. These go down as aims in managerial strategies of action in as far as they must be fulfilled as unalterable. As a rule problems of settlement arise here because the emphasis of different kinds of expectations is not agreed upon from the very beginning and must first of all be decided by management (e.g. profit versus environmental protection). Once such an evaluation has taken place strategies must be designed in order to fulfil the aims. Here there may arise contrasts of interests (conflicts of aims, conflicts regarding fulfilling such aims practically) and these must be settled in negotiations. This fulfilment on the other hand demands above all technical and business administrative calculation; this is Reed's example for an integration of competing theoretical conceptions of management.

In his observations about the working situation of management Reed points to the fact that the rationality potentials of managerial action in a great part of the relevant literature are over-rated, a realization that was already described above in connection with other examinations. Moreover there have been structural changes in management regarding qualifications, capacities of solving problems and leadership competencies which certainly stand in the face of growing demands on performance as a result of the ever-increasing complexity of the system. To add to this, management of a company is organized and based on the division of labour which finds its analogy in a further hierarchicalization of management itself. This has led to manifold new problems which make a rationalization of managerial working structures more difficult. What is more, precisely here must management be viewed as a professional task that is embedded in an extensive network of social connections and that can only be coped with through socially pragmatic action.

According to Reed it is precisely the hierarchy within management which promotes the differentiation of sub-cultures but which on the other hand are faced by technical, economic, social and political realities of management practice. Reed expresses by this that there is a unity of management as a social group as a result of certain objective requirements necessary for working which are to a certain extent contravened by cultural, personal and subjective contrasts. In daily working life these contrasts must be bridged. How this happens in reality cannot be analysed by orthodox, categorical systems but only by theoretical approaches of action.

On the whole Reed offers a conclusive analysis of essential competing observations (theories would not be suitable here) about management. Many of the questions and themes he has mentioned here have entered into our further considerations during our concrete analysis of empirical material. Reed's own, yet certainly innovative approach of "management as a social practice" would need to be extended though in a more systematic way. In its present state it has rather an additive if not eclectical character as a result of the fundamentally, without doubt necessary integration of contrasting approaches. Possibly the use of more role-theoretical considerations would be suitable as Hales has already suggested (1986). Irrespective of this critical argumentation Reed's work seems to us to be one of the most salient examples of the fact that on the whole the British state of research regarding the sociology of management is considerably further developed than its German equivalent. Our summarizing presentation should have made this clear. Thus, at least it is our opinion that German management research could benefit to a great extent and in many respects from Great Britain. In the following paragraphs of this report we attempt to do this.

1.2   Cross-national management research – Regarding the arrangement, carrying out and objective of the Anglo-German comparison

"Could you imagine yourself working as the manager of a large industrial concern in Leningrad?".

This final question of our interviews with German and English managers came as a surprise for many of our interview partners after they had given information about the work and professional situation as capitalist economic managers for 2 hours and more. Hardly anyone had ever concerned himself with this thought even if questions about international management are not completely unfamiliar to company managers.

But the answers led above all to amazement on our part. Although we had expected that for political-ideological reasons the majority of interviewees would react with a sharp "No" we discovered that in the German as well as in the English sample such an occupation lay within the realm of imagination for more than half the managers we asked even if there were certain limitations and restrictions. But as well as this fundamental mutuality considerable differences between German and English managers became obvious. The following table shows the distribution of answers in the Anglo-German comparison[10]:

If we summarize the positive answers we can see that on the part of the English managers we interviewed there is a greater readiness at least on this more abstract level to embark on the 'Leningrad adventure'. However the difference to the German colleagues is not very great. It becomes interesting if we closely examine the reasons for the reactions of refusal.

Whilst the German managers gave reasons which were related to the system and of a political or economic nature (not sufficient scope for decision-making, necessary party loyalty) their English counterparts gave at the same time reasons of a national-cultural nature (foreign cultural circle, foreign language).

These different points of view may be illustrated by comparing as examples two selected quotes; firstly a German automobile manager:

> I need ... scope to act, I want the risk, I want to be part of determining the objectives and with the exception of laws which apply to everyone I don't want to be directed by functionaries or people unfamiliar with the work. I want to be

---

10   The data of the English sample is marked as B (Britain) and of the German sample as G (Germany) in the tables.

Table 1: Management of an industrial concern in Leningrad*

	Percent	
	B	G
Yes, attractive task	22	23
Yes, similar task	22	16
Yes, under certain conditions	16	13
No, not sufficient scope for decision-making	6	32
No, not in a foreign cultural circle	17	9
No, because a certain loyalty to the party is required	–	4
No, but yes in joint ventures	6	3
No, because of language barrier	11	–
	100	100

* The data of the English investigation are marked as B (Britain) and of the German investigation as G (Germany) in the tables.

creative, to be responsible for social design and that is not possible for me in the system, even in Gorbachev's system as it is presented today (G108, p 35)[11].

In comparison to this the managing director of a small metal processing company:

I think that the first thing for me to work in any other country would be to appreciate the culture. The British are so lazy with the way we tackle language and the way that we are so insular. We are an island still whether anybody likes to admit it or not. ... I think we are not very good at change (B2, p 30).

As for the whole survey these two answers need a differentiated interpretation – above all, in connection with the whole interview which will not be presented at this point. But they raise questions. How can these different answers be explained? Are the English managers more firmly bound to their specifically national culture than the Germans and if so – what significance has this got for their work and professional situation? In contrast, does the German manager think rather in political-economic categories and in which way does this influence his subjective dealing with the situation?

---

11   In the text the English interviews are marked with a B and the German interviews with a G. The numbers following refer to the interview number, the page number and the place in the transcript of the interview.

Such questions and further questions have moved us to expand and then consolidate an industrial-sociological examination (firstly related to Germany) of the work and professional situation of senior managers and executives by a corresponding control study in England.

Thus the theme of the examination is the way top managers cope and deal with their work and professional situation in an industrial enterprise and includes the consequences for the intellectual self-understanding of the managers.

Therefore thematically the examination applies to the work and professional situation because we proceed from the assumption that the social thinking of a social group must first and foremost (but not only) be explained by the experience of its members in the working world[12]. At least this is still the case today to quite a considerable extent for the group of top managers examined by us[13].

The experience made in and through the work and professional situation and the knowledge gained from this is reflected in the present, intellectual self-understanding and social thinking, in the mentality of the company managers. Therefore the objective of the examination is to find out this social self-awareness and its essential objective and subjective conditions.

Now the work and professional situation of the member of the top management level is determined objectively and subjectively by four complexes of requirements relevant to the work and connections which may be attributed in quite a general way to the following dimensions:

a) The dimension of the *relation to the specifically managerial and working capacity* which is determined by the manager's own career and his managerial experience and thus can be seen as a general requirement for the fulfilment of the managerial occupation;

b) The dimension of the direct or indirect *relation to the industrial production company* in so far as this forms the field for the market-related planning and control of production by top management and its expert staff;

c) The dimension of the direct or indirect *relation to the markets relevant to the enterprise*. The possibilities and limits of the markets must no longer be utilized fully by entrepreneurial intuition but also by professionally worked out and systematic concepts;

---

12 Cf. the systematic reasoning of this assumption by S. Braun, J. Fuhrmann (1970: pp 7-22).

13 See S. Braun, W. Eberwein, J. Tholen (1992, pp 436-441) about the discussion of the decline of the structure-forming and socially impressing force of the work and production sphere.

d)   The dimension of the *relation to politics and society*, how on the one hand
     it is expressed in the relationship to State and trade union and on the other
     hand in the economically-conditioned, political self-awareness of top
     management.

From this briefly sketched approach of examination there arise above all the
following sociological questions:

a)   What are the essential qualifications and requirements of knowledge and
     ability necessary in order to be able to fulfil managerial tasks in developed
     industrial enterprises and in order to reach such positions?
b)   What role do the technology of production and organization of work play
     in top management and according to which approach is the internal
     company process of work directed?
c)   In the self-awareness of top management which priority do the external
     developed and creative market relations possess and which consequences
     arise because of this for the securing of the existence and for the politics of
     the enterprise?
d)   In the self-awareness of managers which relationship exists to the political
     framework conditions of company management, internally to the claim by
     the staff for co-determination and externally to the present government
     politics and to the democratic process in general?

The answers to these and other questions will be attempted in the book at hand.
To this theme there is an abundance of empirical material. This is based not
only on the very thorough evaluation of relevant (in particular Anglo-
American) management literature but above all on our own empirical investigations.

Firstly numerous discussions and interviews were held with management
experts, that is to say with representatives of associations, chairmen of works
councils, company consultants, scientists and representatives from government
offices as well as retired managers. Secondly – and this forms the focal point
of the empirical material evaluated here – we held a great number of
qualitative interviews with members of the two top levels of management in
selected companies[14]. In the period between the beginning of 1988 and the
beginning of 1989 a total of 111 managers in 35 companies were interviewed
in Germany. The smaller English control study included 16 interviews in 13
companies which were carried out in May 1990. The conversations lasted
between one and a half and four hours. They were recorded on tape and later
transcribed. Furthermore for each of the included companies we made an
analysis of the current company situation and development. For this we

---

14   For a more precise description of the companies we examined and managers we
     interviewed see 2.1, "The empirical fields in Germany and England".

systematically evaluated internal company sources like business reports, organigramms etc. and data especially prepared for us in the company as well as external sources, in particular relevant magazines and newspapers, company handbooks etc..

What are the particular reasons for us carrying out a control study to make international comparisons and what are the objectives we are following?

In recent years there has been a continually growing need and correspondingly considerable amount of output of research which concerns itself with international comparisons. For example, Keller, in his study which came out in 1981, counted almost 800 publications which solely dealt with management research which made cultural comparisons. The majority of these publications originated from America whilst interest in this research area, particularly in German-speaking areas, seemed to be slight (Keller: 1981, pp 228-229). The reasons for the increase in the significance of research making international comparisons are manifold. Above all they have their roots in external forces and developments which from the outside have effect in the field of sociological research. Else Oyen has systematically summarized these external forces (1990, pp 1-3):

> The major external force is … the growing internationalization and the concomitant export and import of social, cultural and economic manifestations across national borders. … This globalizing trend has changed our cognitive map … .

> The globalization of problems is another key concept. … A national crisis is seldom merely national any more. …

> Also (researchers) … may have vested interests in studies which compare their own country to other countries … (in order) to increase their understanding and mastery of national events.

The internationalization of social, cultural, economic and political relations, the globalization of social problems (best examples are ecology and economy) and the desire to promote understanding of national events by international comparisons are the essential forces for research which is concerned with comparing one country to another.

The complex international links in trade, cooperation and production presuppose cross-cultural interactions between managers. Comparative management studies have shown the significant relations between the general socio-institutional conditions and the specific structures and processes followed by a given organization. In this context managerial behaviour is considered a preferential factor of behaviour within a given network of values, regulations, notions and symbols. Thus comparative research is neither self-purpose nor superfluous luxury. On the contrary we may quote Bechtle and Lutz who say that

> international comparisons ... on the basis of empirically observed and described differences in functionally equivalent structures of two or more industrial nations (can) enable or at least facilitate new access to the understanding of one's own society and to the analysis of fundamental structural connections of modern societies on the whole (Bechtle, Lutz: 1989, p 87; similarly Bechtle: 1991, p 131).

This involves being able to explain the national specificity of empirically observed facts as plausible.

> Thus access to structural connections is possible, which when only observed on a national basis must appear either as a quite obvious (therefore unworthy of examination) component of that what may be called the 'nature' of a modern society or may at least be determined in a speculative ideological way which arises from society's interests to a greater or lesser extent". (Bechtle, Lutz: 1989, p 82).

The objectives and procedure of most of the relevant international comparative studies of questions about industrial management and/or industrial work are directed in this or in a similar way – of course, each study works within the framework of its own field of interest, research hypotheses and questions, mostly in the context of comparative organization research. Heidenreich and Schmidt (1991, pp 7-9) have emphasized the different approaches of this kind of research. They differentiate a total of 6 approaches, firstly those which proceed from organizations imprinted by the culture of society[15]:

1) Every kind of human action is imprinted by culture in some way so that 'culture' cannot be referred to as a differentiating, definable variable, e.g. Sorge, Warner (1986);
2) Social patterns of significance, norms and values influence internally organized and relevant attitudes and modes of behaviour, e.g. Hofstede (1984);
3) Social norms and value systems, which are passed on through socialization and which lead to corresponding patterns of technique, organization and employment materialize within institutions, e.g. Child (1983).

And there are those approaches which proceed from a certain cultural freedom of organizations:

---

15   A representation of these different approaches to research which partly conform to these systematics and on the other hand differ from them may be found by reading Lane (1989, pp 22-38). She identifies a) contingency-theory, b) political-economic, c) cultural and d) institutional methods of approach. See also Smith, Peterson (1988, especially pp 96-112).

4) Political-economic basic structures of capitalist societies lead to comparable technical-organizational structures ("thesis of capitalism"), e.g. Braverman (1977);
5) The logic of development of modern industrial societies leads to comparable technical-organizational structures and attitudes ("thesis of industrialism"), e.g. Harbison, Myers (1959);
6) By comparable situational factors or contingencies may similar structures
be expected ("culture-free thesis"), e.g. Hickson, McMillan (1981).

In the face of such different forms of approach but also and above all in the
face of heterogenous fields of examination there arise extensive methodical
problems when conducting internationally comparative empirical social research. We shall discuss these problems in brief. In the first place there is quite
pragmatically the language problem.

> Language itself presents a key obstacle. Questions can seldom be perfectly
> translated from one language to another and changes in shades (or context) of
> meaning may greatly distort replies and comparability. Subtle attitudinal nuances
> cannot be pursued with crude language translations (Millar: 1979, p 62).

Even the simple translation of the German concept of Beruf into English –
perhaps profession or occupation or job – can possibly cause problems of an
equivalent intersubjectively divided meaning.

Gallie has already pointed to another essential methodological and practical
problem of internationally comparative research (Gallie: 1991, pp 75-77). If
we start by looking at the objective of such research, that is to say "to find out
the discriminating significance of cultural and institutional differences between societies faced with common features" he sees the main difference in the
control of these common variables and the different cultural and/or institutional features. In other words: It may possibly be extremely difficult to
keep relevant variables such as organization structure, technology etc. on a
constant level when comparing internationally and making the comparisons at
the same time. This is, of course, necessary so that specifically national
discriminating features may be identified.

As Bechtle and Lutz rightly stress, this presupposes that the participating
researchers not only possess good knowledge of their own society but of the
society to be compared. This is of two sided relevance. Firstly such knowledge
is necessary in order to be able to judge "what and in which definition and
demarcation in one country or the other may be considered as functionally
equivalent; this is particularly true in the second instance when the point is to
question the very roughly definable macrostructures about what they could
contribute to the explanation of the empirically described differences" (Bechtle, Lutz: 1989, p 86).

Lutz sees the systematic analysis of social micro-macro relations as the adequate way of proceeding to make international comparisons:

> The obvious differences in the impression of essential features of objects which are examined according to the tested process of empirical social research ... give the researcher a kind of search screen with which he can approach the macro-structures in one country or the other. With the aid of this screen the researcher is able to move one by one the certain elements of the macrostructures, like the labour market or educational and vocational training systems, into the centre of analysis without adjusting the view of the project as a whole; the predominant task here is to question the macrostructures about outstanding differences between the countries being compared which correspond so well with the differences already revealed in the micro-structures that they can explain these differences with sufficient plausibility. The task is also to identify those mechanisms which such an explanation may refer to (Lutz: 1991, pp 102-103).

Thus Wiener has already pointed out in his historically proceeding study about the "decline of the industrial spirit" in England that the behaviour of the manager cannot be explained sufficiently without taking the implications of the national education system, national industrial culture etc. into consideration (Wiener: 1981, pp 167-170).

On the other hand John Child points to the fact that the sole observation of the macro level gives no adequate value of explanation, but that the comparison of the micro levels (in his view these are the managers and the company organizations) elucidates those differences and similarities in their social connections (Bate, Child: 1987).

In addition to this, Lutz has also rightly pointed out that the subjectivity of the researcher cannot be completely excluded:

> However it is possible to organize the search for a macro-micro arrangement which is compatible with the available empirical data and is logical in itself without any basic difficulties as an explicit procedure which is subject to the standard rules of scientific argumentation (Lutz: 1991, p 103).

One last problem of method may finally be mentioned here and that is the question of a more quantitative or qualitative approach of examination. The advantages and disadvantages of both these procedures are sufficiently well known in the field of empirical social research. When making comparisons between countries they arise in an intensified form as Mansfield and Poole have stated:

> Provided the concepts can be appropriately defined ... there can be no doubt that ... quantitative techniques provide a much greater precision of description and hence of comparison. They have the added advantage of allowing easy assessments of relationships between variables and hence of comparisons between countries (Mansfield, Poole: 1981, p 55).

It may also be added that as a rule such quantitative techniques offer better possibilities to generalize the findings. The most well-known example of a quantitative approach is that of the study by Hofstede (1984). But this quantitative approach also shows striking disadvantages, especially in the case of comparisons between countries:

> Such quantitave approaches in the field of cross-national studies depend on being able to define and develop ... 'world measures'. ... Obviously the measures must ideally be devised to encompass all the possible divergences between organizations and management operating in different conditions in different countries. The danger is that a vast variety of meaning is lost in the search for dimensions which can be compared across nations. ... There is always a danger with approaches such as this that the essence of the phenomena being studied is lost in a search for universal measures and statistical precision (Mansfield, Poole: 1981, p 56).

Precisely the latter may be avoided by a technique which is more qualitative in its approach:

> The second approach to research using a qualitative technique is likely to have considerable advantages in being more able to represent the essential characteristics of the phenomena in a particular country. ... the reader is given considerable insight not just into the phenomenon in question but also into its context in time and space (Mansfield, Poole: 1981, p 56).

But on the other hand the qualitative approach contains dangers of a difficult objectivity and limited generalization of the findings:

> As the technique requires the researcher to act in a relatively unstructured way he has relatively few obvious checks on the objectivity of his observations. ... The second problem is that the peculiar detail of each individual case may make any realistic sort of comparison difficult (Mansfield, Poole: 1981, p 56).

The examination presented here follows the qualitative approach on the basis of the advantages we have already mentioned. Apart from this a study which compares the working and professional situation of top management has not been presented so far and so we are treading on new "territory". In this respect our examination brings with it explorative features in a certain way and is therefore better suited to a qualitative kind of approach as is commonly accepted within the field of empirical social research.

We have naturally tried to avoid the disadvantages we have just described as far as possible: on the one hand by carefully selecting the managers and companies we interviewed in Germany and England and on the other hand by assessing thoroughly those examinations which have already been carried out and which deal with industrial management in German-Anglo comparisons. The latter of these will be briefly presented here.

In the last decades there has been a whole series of studies that have dealt partly exclusively and partly within the framework of multinationally organized examinations with the comparison of English and German management. Child and Kieser say that one important reason why Anglo-German comparisons are obviously so very popular is:

> The two countries are at approximately the same stage of industrialization and have very similar economic structures … . Economic organizations within the two countries, which are of similar size and other contextual characteristics, should demonstrate no significant differences in structure or in the nature of their approach to management (Child, Kieser: 1975, p 5).

We must add, on the other hand, that it may be assumed for good reason that there are sufficient remarkable differences between the German manager as representative of the 'Continent' and his English colleague as member of the United Kingdom to make a comparison of the two attractive and promising.

David Granick was one of the first to occupy himself with the similarities and differences between German and British (further French and Belgian) managers in his report about a one-year research stay in Europe (Granick: 1962). So he pointed to the comparably low prestige of British industry and described the British industrial manager in particular in comparison to his professional American counterpart as an industrial amateur (pp 265-286). On the other hand he attributed a comparably stronger tendency towards centralized and authoritarian rules and modes of behaviour to German than to British managers.

This last finding was also in the centre of the examination by Haire et al. (1966) and was strengthened by this. After this, e.g. for the German managers, the concept "to direct" had greater significance in contrast to the English managers than the concept "to persuade".

This coincides with a widely spread view that the Germans generally prefer authoritarian relations based on command and obedience rather than participative relations (Child, Kieser: 1975, p 5)[16].

In the later examinations this thought no longer stands in the centre of attention. Indeed some researchers have concerned themselves with the pro and contra of the so-called culture-free-thesis by taking English and German managers as their examples[17]. This is explicitly the case for the work of Child

---

16   A notion, which – as far as the managers are concerned – appears no longer very plausible to us in the face of the arrangement of industrial relations in Germany with its much stronger participative orientation than the industrial relations in Great Britain; see here the observations regarding industrial relations at point 4.2.

17   See here our overall view of the different topics of research above.

and Kieser (1975) which we have already mentioned. Proceeding from extensive empirical examinations in 82 British and 51 West German enterprises they come to the conclusion that:

> There can be no question on the basis of this evidence that, contrary to the view implied in some recent writings, a sociologically valid theory of organization must take cultural settings into account (Child, Kieser: 1975, p 24).

This analysis of the culture-free-thesis was taken up once again in a later work about "Corporate goals, managerial objectives and organizational structures in British and West German companies" in a differentiated form (Budde, Child, Francis, Kieser: 1982, p 1):

> The findings reinforce the view that in capitalist systems high profitability and growth are dominant corporate goals. In some respects, the structure adopted by companies in the two countries appeared to match their contingent conditions, although differences in decision making were consistent with a culturist explanation.

In a detailed and more descriptive orientated comparative study Jean Millar has analysed management and industrial relations of a German and British enterprise. The starting point of her examination was (Millar: 1979, pp 55-56):

> Large discrepancies in performance had been noted between the two similar factories in Germany and the UK in the empirical study. In Germany this was written down to the fact that shop floor workers in the UK performed at only 70 per cent of German workers.

Here only the aspect of management attitudes is put forward out of an abundance of reasons:

1. German management appeared to be more concerned about 'human relations' or 'people' issues than their UK counterparts.
2. German management showed more awareness of the role and significance of genuine participation.
3. The company policy was geared to increasing elimination of differences between shop floor and office workers, in terms of working conditions and privileges.

Thus this stands in complete contrast to the previously mentioned studies which emphasized a greater fixation on authority and less willingness to participate on the part of German management than of English management.

Peter Lawrence (1980) gives a comprehensive picture of German management and its specific differences in particular to Anglo-American management. He constructs his presentation against the background of modern German post-war history and proceeding from this he analyses the structure of German enterprises, the background and character of German management, the role of production management and of the qualified worker as well as the position of industry in Germany. Finally he asks to what extent there could arise from his findings conclusions for British management. He does not consider a simple transfer of German models over to another cultural circle to be possible and meaningful. However, according to Lawrence, it is worth considering in this respect the high level of industrial peace, the emphasis of the product, technology and qualification and finally the reason for the manager's authority as a result of his experience and performance.

The questions about technology and production are at the centre of a series of comparative case studies carried out by Bessant and Grunt (1985) in England and Germany. They particularly examined the question as to which role managers play in the technical process of innovation and whether differences in innovative performance may be traced back to the managers themselves or to the context in which they operate. Their findings point to the fact that cultural factors at the most have a secondary influence on managerial behaviour. If we simplify, they come to the conclusion that 'cultural differences stop at the factory gate' and that differences between English and German management are not to be substantiated on a social-cultural level but mainly lie within the companies themselves independent of their national location.

> In conclusion, we reiterate the point that our sample has shown that it is equally possible to be technically progressive in the UK and in West Germany. Whilst the management cultures at national level may vary and help or hinder this, in the end it is the individual technically progressive manager who is at the centre. Our evidence suggests that such technically progressive managers are to a large extent independent of national culture in their management behaviour. Good managers are made, not born in any particular country; if we are to develop any policy aimed at improving national innovativeness then it should start with this focus (Bessant, Grunt: 1985, pp 329-330).

The questions which Sorge and Warner (1986) examined go in a similar direction. They made several comparisons between German and British companies that were similar in respect of their company size, product, production technology etc.. By analogy with Maurice et al. they make use of the conception of the "societal effect" according to which noticeable connections between social areas (usually seen as being autonomous) exist that show their autonomy as being limited. In this case causal influences do not only go in one direction but there exists certain reciprocity between the areas. If we apply this to our examined question it means that the process of technological development in both countries depends on social, economic and institutional factors. In their results the authors conclude that the system of vocational training and the nature of career and organization within the Federal Republic of Germany obviously makes it easier than in Great Britain to assert oneself with innovative deployment of new techniques on specialized markets.

In her book *Management and Labour in Europe* Christel Lane (1989) published the most recent comparative study of German and English (and French) managers. After a discussion about the different approaches and examinations presented she realizes:

> I do not see one of these … approaches to the cross-national study of organization supersede the others but view them as complimentary, to be used in combination (p 37).

Since Lane takes into consideration the different approaches to research as well as the most important empirical findings of German-English comparative research we would like to deal somewhat more comprehensively with her study at the end of our brief view of the relevant literature. It is the aim of her work to explore the behavioural action of managers. She asks about the constraints which roughly structure the behaviour of industrial management. Apart from traditional procedures (thesis of capitalism and the thesis of industrialism)[18] Lane also tries to include the significance of cultural institutions in her considerations.

The use of a culturalistic perspective allows the emphasis of a specifically national culture and its influences on organizations and patterns of behaviour within organizations. However the researcher should not make the mistake of reinforcing common prejudices – a danger which is particularly prevalent when dealing with cultures which have been submitted to dramatic historical processes of change as it is the case in Germany.

Lane's examination confirms the results of other studies about the comparatively low social prestige of industry in Great Britain. According to her findings British managers are more greatly interested in their income, promotion chances and personal prestige whereas German managers, when asked about the criterion for professional success, refer to the content of their tasks.

Lane therefore contradicts the widespread view (see above) that German managers are more firmly bound to authority than British managers. She sees this as one example of the previously mentioned danger of taking over stereotypes without making any critical examination. She gives us an example that speaks against a comparatively authoritarian German style of management practice by stating that in contrast to Great Britain there is relatively unproblematical solving of industrial conflicts in Germany which supports German managers' ability to carry on dialogues. Lane recapitulates on this

---

18   See here our brief presentation of different topics of research above.

aspect that the assumptions that German standards of production could only be upheld by means of authoritarian leadership whilst democratic leadership, as is practiced in England, would only lead to losses in competition, are prejudices that are based on false hypotheses. Firstly the German managers are not a priori authoritarian in their values and management style and secondly industrial relations in Great Britain are not necessarily more democratic than in Germany.

And in a final summary Lane reaches the conclusion:

> The strengths of German manufacturing enterprises are widely seen to emanate from two core institutional complexes – the system of vocational education and training and the system of industrial relations (Lane: 1989, p 298).

We set about our English comparative study against the background of the findings and results of the Anglo-German examinations which we have presented here.

Our extensive German investigation is the starting point and reference point[19]. In a quite general sense we are above all concerned with consolidating the results of this investigation in regard to the function of company management in order to elucidate realistically and in particular the conditions of the managerial situation. Specific features of German management behaviour in comparable industrial situations are to be made clear by investigations and thorough evaluations of appropriate literature on an international level[20] in order to open up the important possibilities of comparison for the social locating of the results[21]. We hope that at the same time a realistic picture of English management will be presented which could be particularly informative by its contrast to German circumstances, that is to say by identifying differences in the two systems as well as by identifying certain similarities.

We will firstly try to do this by considering the working and professional capacity of German and English managers.

---

19   See Eberwein, Tholen (1990) for the results of this investigation.
20   Apart from the English study, an investigation in Russia was carried out at a later point in time (May 1991).
21   This method of procedure and these intentions allow us to interview a considerably smaller number of managers in England as adequate especially as we have already worked on a large amount of secondary empirical material.

2 The work and professional capacity of German and English managers

The central reference point of the examination is the situation of the individual top-level manager. By observing his role in the top management of an industrial company and by carrying out a corresponding pattern of behaviour he is integrated into a certain management constellation to a greater or lesser extent.

This constellation demands the fulfilment of a certain task which is difficult to define as well as the deployment of certain subjective social skills if a functioning company management is to come into being. For this, training of a specific managerial work and professional capacity is necessary, a capacity which can be seen as a general requirement for the fulfilment of managerial tasks.

We proceed from the working hypothesis that the transition from intuitive managerial behaviour to professional behaviour of a non-owner but (in the words of Marx) 'working' manager is indeed unmistakeable but that precisely on this level strongly personality-related qualities, which are relatively independent of professional qualifications (like the ability to deduct or assert oneself) are still authoritative and set the standard for moving into or staying in such positions.

In the conversations with the members of top management we wished to establish on the one hand the objective-factual and

on the other hand the subjective-social elements of the managerial work and professional capacity.

2.1 The empirical fields in Germany and England

Before we could begin with the interviews (which then took place in Germany from the beginning of 1988 until the beginning of 1989 and in England in May 1990) it was necessary to select the 'right' enterprises and managers, that is to say those managers and enterprises that were comparable in both countries.

After doing this, it was then our task to win our future interview partners, burdened by many business commitments, for our purpose.

In spite of the quite pessimistic forecasts of colleagues and experts, our optimism prevailed: access to the managers was easier than had been expected by many[1].

With a great amount of flexibility and great perseverance on our part we were on the whole able to place the interviews in number and dispersion (according to the size of the branch or enterprise, according to the position and function of the interviewed managers) as we had initially intended in our concept. Firstly we were able to do this because of a differentiated number of ways of reaching the managers and as a result of great support by different mediators. Secondly – at least we hope this is the case – many managers found our questions interesting and our conception convincing so that their willingness to give us information was very great.

Moreover a secondary effect proved to be helpful to us which was clearly evident in the English field as well as in the German field. Firstly we may assume that most of the interview partners took a keen interest in the topic of our examination and in the consequent questions: indeed the matter concerned their own work and professional situation with all its difficulties which, as was often lamented, were otherwise seldom taken note of. In connection with this the interview situation offered many of the managers the opportunity to reflect themselves on their own position and situation, which they are not able to do in their daily business, whether it is simply because the relations of power and competition which exist in tendencies towards team work do not permit such an openness necessary for such critical self-reflection[2]. This points to a lack of possibilities for discursive communication of the managers' own self-awareness within company management so that the possibility of an interview with neutral and informed scientists was judged in a thoroughly positive way.

Proof of this is solely the fact that often considerably more than the planned 2 hours for the interview was organized and the fact that in many cases the interview partners met us with great hospitality.

By and large our experiences in the empirical field in England and Germany were identical. However in England there was one additional feature. Firstly in conversation with foreign scientists who found themselves on 'neutral ground', the English interview partners expressed themselves in a particularly open and

---

1   A comprehensive survey about those practical problems is given by Easterby-Smith et al. (1991) especially in the chapter "The politics of management research" (pp 44-70).

2   Horst Kern and Michael Schumann made similar experiences (1988).

frank way. On the other hand as experts on German management we were asked many questions, mostly with a view to the common European market. This mutual exchange led considerably to the success of the interviews.

2.1.1   Characteristics of the selected enterprises

The definition of the sample is firstly laid down by the theme and questions of the examination.

Since we proceeded from the hypothesis of the examination that a gradual independence of industrial management is achieved as a result of professionalism, organization and "becoming academic" (ultimately so that the picture of a systematically working management is portrayed) there arose a limitation on the size of the enterprise of a lower level: The enterprise had to have at least a rudimentarily developed management with its own relation to the market and circle of customers.

Furthermore the selection of the enterprises had to comply to features of comparison as well as of feasibility.

In the main we restricted ourselves to industry because management in the services sector or bank sector is subject to significantly different conditions than in the technical production companies in industry. Apart from this we assumed that recruitment for industrial management took place mainly within industry itself – an opinion which was made on the basis of interviews with industrial consultants and of a study of the relevant literature. This opinion was then extensively confirmed. Furthermore the emphasis of the German selection of enterprises lay in the industrial centres of North Germany which was supplemented by a much smaller selection of South and West German enterprises and features of particular branches (within industry) were then also taken into consideration.

The much smaller English sample of enterprises was in the main restricted to the region of East Midlands with its centre Nottingham. As a result of its manifold economic structure (there is no dominance of one particular industrial branch or even of one enterprise in particular), this area offered good possibilities for a qualified selection of enterprises which could satisfy features of comparability with the German sample[3].

---

3   There is no uniformity about the East Midlands. ... (This region) has no homogeneity. ... The concomitant ... is a strongly diversified economy. No single sector assumes the importance that, for example, the automotive industry has in the West Midlands. ... No single town dominates the region in the sense that London acts as a focus for the whole of the South East of England or in the sense that Birmingham

Although we did not consider the characteristics of the branch of industry as most important the sample contains the branches above all within the processing industry and permits a comparison between larger and smaller companies.

From the outset our choice of companies was not orientated towards the requirements of statistical representation for reasons of the topic of research, the questions arising from this and the methodical procedures. Instead it was our main concern to achieve a qualified dispersion of companies in respect of certain dimensions – e.g. company size, branch of industry. Furthermore we did not strive for any identity of the German and English sample (which in any case would be impossible to carry out in a research practical way). Within the framework of our qualitatively orientated procedure it was necessary to find the features mentioned in the comparable structures. Therefore the numbers and values which will be recorded should not be seen as unaccountably generalizable information but as a clarifying of similarities and differences according to a tendency, which are illustrated by selected extracts of the interviews.

In total we were able to conduct our examination in 35 German and 13 English companies:

In spite of the smaller number of examples especially in the English sample where some groups are not represented we still feel that the economic group structure is sufficiently manifold for our purposes. The structure of the size of the company is a similar case:

Within this distribution which is sufficient for our theme and questions it was also important for us to take the criterion of company growth into consideration. Indeed recruitment as well as the objective work and professional situation and the subjective coping with this situation by top managers is considerably influenced by the existing (lacking) prosperity of the company in question.

If we take the basis of the last 5 years and if we choose as the criterion for company size the number of its employees then we may say that out of the 35 selected German companies 10 were in a process of recession, 11 companies were stagnating and 14 had grown. The situation in English companies looked less favourable. Only two were in a process of growth; a further two were stagnating. The others found themselves in a process of recession to a greater or lesser extent or had already come through such a process, partly with

---

overshadows the West Midlands. ... Nor do large employers dominate areas (*Financial Times*, 17.12.1990).

Table 2: Distribution of companies within economic groups

Economic Group	No. of enterprises	
	G	B
1. Energy production & distribution	2	0
2. Chemical	6	1
3. Mineral Oil	2	0
4. Metal production	2	1
5. Metal processing	2	1
6. Mechanical engineering	3	0
7. Road vehicle construction	3	2
8. Shipbuilding	3	0
9. Air and space technology	2	0
10. Electrotechnology	2	0
11. Food and luxury food industry	3	4
12. Building trade	2	2
13. Services, transport	3	1
14. Textile industry	0	1
Total	35	13

dramatic dimensions; it is possible to see this as an expression of the generally poorer situation of the British economy.

Processes of decision-making, communication and information depend quite essentially on the formal and informal structures within the companies themselves and these in their turn are impressed by the kind of production, company size, company history, cooperation between staff and management etc.. We got to know the most different forms of organization including the traditional linear type of organization, project and profit-centre organization to name but a few. None were ever found as 'pure cultures' but they always included components or parts of other organization structures. A knowledge of the existing forms of emphasis of the organization – which are the result as

Table 3: Structure of company size

Company size (employees)	No. of companies	
	G	B
Up to 199	5	2
200 - 999	9	2
1,000 - 1,999	6	2
2,000 - 4,999	7	4
5,000 - 9,999	1	2
10,000 - 19,999	4	0
over 20,000	3	1
	34	13

well as the condition for managerial behaviour – is of a significance which must not be underestimated in our interpretation of the interviews.

In the next step we must concern ourselves with marking more closely the structures of the examined management group.

2.1.2   Characteristics of the examined management group

The description of the structures of those enterprises included by us has shown that the choices offer a qualified spectrum of branches of industry, company sizes etc.. We presume that within this spectrum considerable variables of the work and professional situation of top managers are taken into consideration. To follow we give a comparative overall view of the essential structure features of the German and English samples which is to make a classification of the findings to be presented much easier[4].

Position, Status, Scope of occupation, Sex: The first point to be explained is the definition of the group in question, the top manager. Our empirical access was firstly orientated towards the position, that is to say we only asked members of the first and second hierarchical and management level. This

---

4   A differentiated social location of the German sample may be found in Eberwein, Tholen (1990, pp 31-47).

involves e.g. in full public companies the executive board and the level immediately below it, in limited liabilities or joint stock companies this concerns the executive committee and the level beneath it etc.[5].

In total we carried out interviews with 52 members of the first and 59 members of the second hierarchy and management level in Germany. In England 8 managers belonged to the first and 8 to the second level. 3 of those asked and only 2 out of 111 in Germany were owners of the companies. All the others were employed managers; an initial reference to the professionalization of industrial management (which was our assumption), the professionalization resulting from the separation of capital ownership and the actual en-trepreneurial function, at least within larger companies.

Apart from this dimension of the position the functional aspects of industrial management were also taken into consideration. The interview partners in the companies were especially selected in such a way that if possible the central areas of production, distribution, personnel and where available also research and development etc. were represented. In the English sample the industrial relations and personnel manager was greatly represented, a function which does not exist in this form in Germany.

All those asked in Germany were men, women were not only not represented in our sample but were not at all represented in the two top levels of management in the companies we examined. In England – much to our delight – there was one female manager in the group of our examination. However, for reasons which are not to be discussed here, it was to be expected that up to today specifically industrial and technically orientated management still seems to be predominantly a male matter.

Age structure and length of stay in managerial positions: The age structure of our sample is seen in the following overall view:

The central point in the age distribution lies quite clearly between 40 and 59 years of age; approximately 80% of the German and over 60% of the English managers we asked can be classified here. In the English sample the percentage of managers over 59 years of age is clearly much higher than in the German sample.

This is an initial reference to the fact that the way to the two top levels of management is as a rule quite long and that professional experience gained over several years appears to be an essential managerial qualification. "High

---

5   A very helpful explanation of the English and German expressions (which are by no means always identical in their meaning) is given by Lawrence (1980, pp 30-55).

Table 4: Age structure of the managers

Age	No.	No.	Share in percent	
	G	B	G	B
up to 39 years	11	2	10	13
40 - 49 years	47	6	42	37
50 - 59 years	42	4	38	25
60 years & older	11	4	10	25
	111	16	100	100

flyers" as well as "job hoppers" are much more rare in industrial management than is generally assumed in public. The professional and career paths, if not always definitely planned, take a long term, continual course, often in one and the same company as will be shown in detail at a later stage.

The high significance of professional experience for managers is also under-lined by the duration of their stay in their current positions: More than 50% of those asked in both countries have occupied their position for more than 5 years, a quarter (in Germany) and a fifth (in England) for more than 10 years.

Apart from professional experience a corresponding specialist qualification is a necessary – if by no means sufficient – requirement for an occupation in top management.

Qualification structure: Let us first of all turn to the school education of the managers in question.

Almost 80% of the German managers we asked had gained the "Abitur/ Hochschulreife", that is to say the highest school qualification. In contrast only a good 60% of the English managers had gained the corresponding "A" level. Does this point to a comparably lower level of formal education on the part of the English managers? This assumption is reinforced if we follow the education path a little further. The high level of formal education on the part of the German managers is confirmed by the fact that over 80% have had an academic qualification (including "Fachhochschule" qualifications). In con-trast more than half (indeed 9) of our English managers have not studied. If we differentiate the academic training into specialized directions then we have the following picture:

If we divide the specialist subjects into two main groups, the academic education of the German managers is divided equally between economic and law courses of study on one hand, technical and natural science courses of study on the other hand. However the majority of the English managers have taken up the economic direction and only one had completed a technical course of study. Thus a viewpoint which is often presented in the literature is also reflected in our samples – the view that technicians/scientists are much stronger represented in German than in English management (Lawrence: 1980).

But apart from the academic education, the apprenticeship as a form of vocational training also plays a significant role in the case of those managers in question: More than half (55%) of the German sample completed an apprenticeship, of these 55% half a commercial apprenticeship and the others a trade-technical apprenticeship. And in the English group 6 out of 16 managers (almost 40%) had completed an apprenticeship although this kind of training in England is not as widespread by far as it is in Germany. Interestingly enough, those who completed an apprenticeship in England, finished an apprenticeship which was purely of a trade-technical kind; is this perhaps a substitute for the lack of academic technical qualifications?

Those are some of the most distinctive structural features of the German and English groups in our examination. If we go on from the observations we made about the qualification structure we may now give a detailed analysis of the education, recruitment and careers of the English and German managers.

2.2   Training, recruitment and careers of managers in Germany and England

On the one hand training, recruitment and career depend quite essentially on the existing potential but on the other hand on the demands made on managers. These demands for their part are defined by a management situation which nowadays could look considerably different to what it did 20 years ago. All this is embedded in the respective social structures which can be completely different in England and Germany – as for example in the area of education.

2.2.1   The ambivalent development of the management situation

The starting question of the interviews with the managers – also to fulfil the purpose as a warm-up question – was whether it has become more difficult today to work in management, whether the requirements of economic, specialized and social managerial qualifications have increased, whether perhaps the managerial situation has become more difficult and consequently whether other ways of training and career should be entered upon.

The background of this question were book-titles in Germany like *Die Unternehmerlücke* (Hamer: 1984) and *Abschied von den Wunderknaben* (Strasser: 1985). Strasser notes a crisis of German managers and entrepreneurs, also in the face of the Japanese challenge. In Strasser's opinion many German company managers are only "fair weather captains", spoiled by the post-war boom, incapable of reacting to the changed world economy, afraid to take risks and authoritarian. Thus the Federal Republic of Germany is on the right way to becoming a second-class industrial nation.

Interestingly enough a similar discussion in Great Britain has been taking place for over a year also with reference to Japan and the European integration and in fearful expectation of the economic power of the now united Germany. The question arises here as to what extent such assessments of blame of German and English managers as the "repeaters" in the round of international management are perceived by the managers themselves and whether in such perceptions and interpretations national differences become clear.

Firstly regarding this point German as well as English managers have a great deal of openness in common: in their majority they feel that in comparison to former times the management situation has become much more complex.

Only a small minority, namely in England approximately 11% and in Germany 12% see the management situation as unchanged in comparison to 10 years ago. The percentage of managers who see the management situation as having become easier is approximately the same in both countries: in England 22% and in Germany 25%. However the differences become particularly clear when we look at the reasons for their comments.

Whilst in Germany the main reason for the management occupation becoming easier was seen to be the greater liveliness of the managerial occupation (away from the routine) caused by changes of the market, the crisis of the old hierarchies etc., in England the legislation since the beginning of the Thatcher government, since the beginning of the 1980s was primarily quoted as a reason:

> I think it has become easier in the sense that in the last 10 years there have been major changes in industrial relations legislation. … Therefore it has enabled us to talk more with people in our factories with less interference from outside agencies in that sense than the trade unions. We are a total trade union company here. All of our employees, including staff, are in trade unions and we have actively encouraged them to do so. We are not anti-trade union but life has become easier (B1, p 2).

We will discuss at a later stage whether this widely-spread opinion amongst British managers is a typical expression of a secret pleasure in the fact that the

Conservative government 'overcame' the trade unions and thus strengthened the managers' own position. Or whether behind this opinion lies perhaps a deep-lying change in values within English society, away from the unsteered 'Bargaining Process' to more legally defined co-operative structures which are more binding and therefore actionable for all concerned and moreover a change which includes the works council to a greater degree in the workings of the company. A German manager notes this:

> Key word: co-operation with the works council. This takes a burden off me in that I can now put the social concerns into the hands of the works council and have a partner with whom I can negotiate (G77, p 1).

But let us look now at the reasons for the subjectively perceived increase in the difficulties of the managerial situation: in first place in the case of the Germans as well as of the English (25%) there stands the international market which is becoming more and more complex and which necessitates faster reactions of decision-making. However in regard to the English managers there was a somewhat stronger emphasis on home-made difficulties: the high interest rates for credit in Great Britain delay necessary investment and worsen the profit situation.

In second place, but not far behind, were the changed demands in regard to management style stated by managers in Germany: As a result of the higher political-democratic level of claim on the part of the employee the traditional, authoritarian style of management is no longer possible. The prognosis of German sociologists Pross and Boetticher at the beginning of the 1970s was fulfilled by this. They said that the democratic movements in the Federal Republic of Germany in the second half of the 1960s would inevitably lead to a dismissal of personal-paternalistic models of organization and management within the companies (Pross, Boetticher: 1971, p 13).

This can also be a burden as a manager from the automobile branch describes:

> First of all, in regard to technology, everything has become more complex and this means that I need more qualified people. As a rule more qualified people have a higher claim on individual freedom. Even the man at the conveyor belt expects today, as a result of enlightenment through television, educational courses in which he educates himself further or the "A"-level student from a working-class family is treated in quite a different way than to what he was 50 years ago. We have passed through a great development in Germany which perhaps goes to the extreme that we can no longer ask for normal amounts, that we only talk about things. This trend to discussion particularly strikes you when you have been abroad (G102, p 18).

Also the changes in technology as well as through technology (Key word: Third industrial revolution, microelectronics) are seen to be a considerable reason for higher claims on management.

With regard to the English managers it is completely opposite: 22% say that more complex technology is one difficulty but only 11% mention the increased political-democratic level of claim of the employees and with this the crisis of old, authoritarian styles of management.

Does this difference lie within the different levels of coping with the situation?

In comparison to the English the Germans are said to be obsessed with technology so that they cope better with technical demands. On the contrary in England there is the widespread opinion that German management is traditionally more authoritarian than English management (which is stamped by the example of the individual free Englishman) so that higher democratic claims in England are easier to overcome. We cannot explain this difference conclusively either at this stage, it refers closely to the respective, cultural self-understanding. The change of values of the members of staff remains uncontested at home as well as abroad. The personnel manager of a large pharmaceutical company in England told us:

> The key thing about the manager's task is the need to motivate people and that is becoming increasingly difficult because people's commitment is less great than it was. It is becoming more difficult to manage nowadays because change is everincreasing and in my working lifetime of 25 years the change in the last 5 years has been incredible. Managing change is always quite difficult (B17, p 1).

Far down the list (in fact in Germany only every 10th manager stated this and in England only one) were comments and information regarding increased legal publications (labour law, environmental regulations, health protection etc.) as reasons for the management situation becoming more difficult. Firstly there appears to be an inexplicable contrast here between the complaints often in public and presented by associations about too much State interference and the actual perception by those directly concerned, namely the managers. This will be explained in more detail at a later stage.

It seems that the answers regarding the general lack of education and training (as stated by managers) are typical for Great Britain and are considered to be a reason why the managerial situation has become more difficult:

> It is significant and that is a comment about British industry generally: The investment in training and education is really at a very low level (B10, p 6).

On the whole we must note that

a)   only a very small number of German as well as English managers refer to a consistent perception of the situation of the demands of their own professional situation;

b)   the reasons for a changed professional situation in England and Germany are very different; they are – apart from objective-specialized differences – possibly psychological projections of their own difficulties – in England the difficulties to be overcome as a result of the demands of technology and in Germany the difficulties regarding industrial relations;

c) there is no difference in the evaluation of the great significance of the market (external relations) for the management situation. And we think that an English owner-manager (and what he says is applicable to both countries) has stated the requirements for management qualifications arising today:

> I think … managers have got to be more multi-skilled than they were. It is not enough nowadays to have a good engineer. You want your good engineers also to have some people skills. They must be able to get their ideas across to the people who are going to use the tools and implement their ideas. So I think we are looking for more rounded characters than we did 20 years ago (B2, p 2).

2.2.2   Is company management lacking good trainees?

Do the young, that is the management trainees in companies really measure up to this complex task which has become so difficult today? How does the industrial establishment judge the oncoming generation? We assumed before our interviews that above all reasons of competition and conflicts of generations ("The young trainees are no good!") would provoke a negative evaluation of the young managers. In fact this is partly seen in some of the relevant literature (Strasser: 1985, Hamer: 1984). But, at least in Germany, we were surprised: Here almost 60% of those asked thought that there was neither a lack of management quality nor of suitable managerial trainees – the threatening demographic 'time bomb' is defused by some who point to the great yet so far undeveloped potential of women.

The matter looks a little different in Great Britain: Here only approximately a quarter of those asked thought that there was neither a lack of managerial trainees and managerial quality. In contrast to this, approximately three quarters stated some corresponding deficiencies and the reasons for these are given quite a different emphasis to those in Germany. In the case of the German managers who feel that managerial trainees and managerial quality are lacking (40% of the answers) there dominates a kind of self-criticism; in the companies and branches that have reduced their staff numbers and have pointed to a worsening profit situation over several years those measures were first of all cancelled that did not directly promote rentability – as for example the measures regarding recruitment and training. Furthermore gaps were created by dismissals and employment blocks which now, in a more favourable situation, cannot be closed at such short notice.

Some companies have not the courage to entrust young people with the necessary responsibility if young people cannot prove themselves to be top managers. It seems to be safer to employ an 'experienced' manager than to risk giving young people a chance. This was a complaint made by a (younger) manager from the brewery business (G25, p 2). However the fears of competition of older managers who are afraid that younger managers may overshadow them, are more serious because they cannot be solved by programmes or strategies etc..

In England only 12% of the 75% who stated lacks in managerial trainees thought that these deficiencies were caused as a result of missing personality-related qualities and therefore and above all were the faults of the individual. A large number – in total about half – saw that the deficiencies were based on insufficient professional qualifications which can be found in inadequate professional training in Great Britain (and this indeed is the case for the State education system as well as for the commitment of companies regarding company further education). A manager from the Chemical industry described it drastically:

> In the UK we have an undereducated workforce and undereducated management (B17, p 2).

Without checking in any more detail the amount of truth in this statement – which is indeed subjective but based nevertheless on many years experience – the complaints about the low level of education of managers came to no end. Here is the comment made by the personnel manager of a large food company:

> The ideal management trainees should have a good educational background. That is the premise from where we start because the English educational system does not produce people educated to a high enough standard. You have the statistics as we have seen them that we have less people in higher education than most of our competitive countries. The other thing is and this is a criticism of the British educational system, traditionally the British higher educational system has concentrated very largely on the arts than on the sciences (B3, p 3).

And an industrial relations manager continues:

> I think people should be educated towards their career. But they just get a general education. Many of them go into university at 18 and they have no idea what their career is and then when they are in the third year of university they go out on the milk round and they have interviews with a whole range of companies and inevitably they move towards the attractive careers of banking, in finance, in marketing and the best of them go there and we get the rest of them in industry and it is almost a second choice (B1, p 3).

This suggests what will be worked on in more detail at a later stage when we discuss the education system, career paths and qualifications of managers and the considerably low status of industry in comparison to Germany, in the mother nation of industrialization, in England.

But there are quite a number of firms that have recognized this and try on their own initiative to take remedial measures using different methods and with different aims which are naturally determined by the general organization of the company. The works manager of a company in the food and luxury food industry emphasizes getting to know other cultures:

> In fact my company sends many of our managers to an offshoot of INSEAD which was funded by the participant companies. The important dimension it brought in was the European bit. We in Britain have always tended to be a little bit insular and so it was a vastly rewarding experience for the young managers that they went over to be doing syndicate work with a Dane, a Swede, a Spaniard, an Italian and a Frenchman (B13, p 3).

A German company manager mentioned another important point which in our experience applies to England too and is independent of all social and cultural differences:

> I think that for a time we were falsely led to believe that managers can quite quickly be created in some manager schools. ... But I think that what is necessary is to build up one's own managerial potential oneself. This is of course an arduous task ... . But we observe again and again that superiors have no interest at all in identifying in their own surroundings so-called managerial potentials, managerial talents within their own workers. This is a lack of sovereignty, a sign of weakness. A good manager must be interested in being surrounded by good people. This automatically leads to the situation where managerial talents are identified in one's own company and where they are looked for and systematically developed. And I think that if we do this then there will be no lack of managers in the Federal Republic of Germany (G101, p 1).

This means that there must be an inner willingness on the part of the managers to distance themselves away from their own fears of competition and to accept the new trainees.

In some cases some companies have not the courage to entrust young people with the appropriate responsibility because the young people can show no proof of them being top managers. It seems to be safer to employ 'experienced' managers than to risk giving young people a chance.

In a society where only success counts and where failure is in general punished at once, young people have no chances at all any more to really develop themselves as personalities. They are drilled by the companies to be 'avoiders of failure' rather than 'seekers of success'.

In this way the first step to lacking power of innovation is made.

Today young people are not given sufficient opportunity to really train to be an individual. I believe that the fact that today we try more and more to press people into a certain form leads to the fact that young people have less and less opportunity and also really the chance to develop themselves as 'an all-round person' (G87, p 10).

This applies to England in a similar way: indeed Sally Caird notes that the entrepreneurs are dissatisfied with the educational preconditions of their potential successors and their professional and technical flexibility but she doubts whether they really want employees who think and act in an entrepreneurial way (Caird: 1990, p 138).

This finding is also confirmed in Germany by a longitudinal study of 1,000 young academics who were observed firstly while looking for and finding employment during their last term of study and were observed within the space of a year for a second and third time of finding new employment (Rosenstiel et al.: 1989). Rosenstiel and colleagues show that university graduates (as potential managerial troops) with traditional perceptions of values are more readily employed by companies. Trainees who proved themselves by their personality but also by their specialized qualifications to be "broad thinkers" and "all-round people" and expressed changed opinions of values were exposed to a much stronger pressure on them to adapt. On the whole – according to the authors – their study gives the picture of companies who tend to cut themselves off from social processes of change as far as trainees are concerned.

The view of managers in Germany who judge managerial trainees critically, fits into this picture of preserving traditional value judgements because they feel also that the general belief in progress of the 1950s and 1960s is starting to falter to a great extent (this is particularly the feeling of those managers who completed their university training in the 1970s) and that this should be viewed negatively. Are these perhaps the late consequences of the highly-controversial 1968 movement in the Federal Republic of Germany (student revolts against the encrustations of the Adenauer era)? For the generation of the 30-40 year olds it is not necessarily an aim of their dreams to reach the very top of company hierarchy. Other norms push themselves into the foreground, norms that are connected to spare time, family, bringing up children etc..

A German manager of a mineral oil concern complains of the lacking spatial and mental mobility which is an expression of a safe way of thinking in the direction of hedonism:

Now, in contrast to many, what I see with regret when I meet young people is that I would hope or I would advise young people not to look into the future and emphasize the security of the future. Perhaps my own experience is not considerable nor applicable for the next 20, 30 years. But I must say that it saddens me to see that young people at the beginning of their professional career talk about pension claims and the end of the matter instead of looking for a job of which they are really convinced that they will enjoy it if they achieve what is to be achieved. You must identify yourself with this work and must rely on the fact that you will get on if you perform well. And you can only really perform well when you enjoy the work (G68, p 6).

Amongst other things this means that managerial trainees must also develop the ability to break away from the momentary hierarchical level in order to be able to try out something new. However the chances of the young managers to leave the formal career paths stand in a dialectic relationship to the willingness of the managing board to accept their individual professional concepts.

It is still open to question as to what extent the liberal understanding of the "older ones" and their objective detachment from their own role suffices to admit to the younger managers that they must not be "transferers of the members of the managing board" (a comment of the chief personnel officer of a large company, G80, p 11) but that they can certainly develop their own concepts that must be capable of withstanding conflicts.

We know from our interviews and the relevant literature that changes in social norms are nothing specifically German. In the Anglo-American sphere Bowey and White (Bowey: 1982; White: 1981) have noted the change in the modes of behaviour within society, the relationship to work, to organization and also to the concept of performance which took place between the 1950s and 1980s and which can be seen in Germany too. After the end of the second World War, in the first post-war decades, the economy expanded in England too. At that time managers could look relatively optimistically into their own professional future and could demand their share of the constantly increasing social welfare (Whyte: 1965; Gans: 1967). It was demanded of the managers, at all costs and without them asking too many questions, to be professionally and spatially mobile and to subordinate egoistic and familiar (private) interests this demand (Bell: 1968; Watson: 1964). As Bell continues, this was seen to be the price for a successful career. Managers belonged to an affluent and continually expanding middle class which was the expression of a "new" and "open" society in which more and more individually gained qualifications and proven performance pushed the widespread inherited class privileges precisely in English society out of place (Aron: 1967; Lipset, Bendix: 1959; Young: 1961). Some authors in the 1950s and 1960s connected this to a demise of capitalism. In our opinion the opposite had occurred. As a result of the enforcement of the social norm of competition and of the free development of the personality a process of defeudalization in society was connected to the final enforcement of the bourgeois society, moreover a process which had been implemented in Germany at a much earlier date and which – however macabre this may sound – had been strongly supported by the National Socialists.

Daniel Bell and Dahrendorf described this process of development of new social forms as "post-capitalism" (Bell: 1974; Dahrendorf: 1957) and as it primarily occurred after 1945 as a result of the increasing significance of large companies and of the State influence on the economy. Within this process the 'technostructure' produced modes of behaviour by managers which were stamped by values such as "the common good" (Galbraith: 1967). Such a post-war agreement – promoted in Germany particularly by the years of restoration – proceeded from a classless society, from an evened out middle class society (Schelsky: 1965, p 331) and demanded of the "organization man" (Whyte: 1965) a subordination of his personal and familiar interests in the face of "community" interests which were of course stamped by the economic interests of the company.

Such lifestyles, which deny one's own individuality and connections to the outside, in particular in the case of trainees, are more seldom to be found. There arises the question too whether such managers who are prepared to make sacrifices and who have the slight tendency towards martyr behaviour, are on the whole better company managers than those who discuss – with pleasure or unease – with the "whole" society and recognize this.

One current conclusion from the positive as well as negative answers of English and German managers could be that supporting trainees under the liberal motto "Give him/her a chance" is just as important as the direct, visible market success and that this should be recognized by a considerable number of managers.

2.2.3   Advice from top managers to young people

We wanted to approach the complex theme of 'manager trainees' from another perspective: therefore we asked our interview partners to give tips to young people wishing to reach the management level of a company so that they can organize their way of professional training accordingly.

To come straight to a result: the answers to this question were quite general, but were widely diverse and sometimes contradictory within themselves. We presume that here a certain basic pattern of managerial modes of behaviour and experience comes to light: apart from very few exceptions all our interview partners did not plan their managerial careers from the beginning in the sense of stringently working on their future career paths. We presume that this relative openness and unsureness regarding advice for young people is connected to the extensive lack of stereotypes as to what work in industry and in the economy generally means. But let us look first of all at the presentation of the individual results which show in part considerable differences between England and Germany:

Whilst in Germany almost 60% of the answers on this matter (sometimes answers to several questions) stated that academic training is a necessary requirement (only 2% considered such training to be unnecessary for later management careers), in England only half agreed with this. And to the east of the English channel almost a third of the managers saw the value of studying in achieving good basic professional training (only a fifth in the United Kingdom) and for all that approximately 12% saw academic training as a way of carrying out abstract thinking[6] – in England only 5%. These differences not only point to the fact that there is a difference in evaluating academic training for managers in both countries (we will go into this in more detail in the next chapter) but also show how managers cope themselves with their own, previously completed specialist training in a subjective way and thus how they project the advantages and disadvantages of their own situation in the form of demands on the younger generation. Again it is interesting to find something which the two countries have in common:

Those who see the function of studying in the imparting of basic professional and specialized knowledge preferred their own academic training in their advice: Business men recommended an apprenticeship in business administration or MBA course of study, engineers propagated their particular course of study etc..

An older examination of American Top Executives stated:

> The principal characteristics which the executives looked for in young men aspiring to top management positions were, in the main, similar to those previously mentioned as contributing to the executives' own advancement (Wald, Doty: 1954, p 50).

However scarcely one of our interview partners could explain exactly and rationally the reasons for the respective recommendations. By giving his own example, an owner-manager explained the fortuitousness and random choice of the subject of study regarding later management careers, that is if we disregard the subjective side or rather the specialized tendencies of those beginning their studies. He said:

> Well, I became a lawyer according to Spoerl's motto: medicine is too unappetizing, theology is too pious, philosophy is too laborious and what is left? Law. That is the profession that offered the greatest chances (G66, p 4).

---

6   In his empirical examination "Academics in the private economy", E. Lange (1981) describes some of the academics (economists, lawyers, sociologists and psychologists) in large industrial companies in Germany.

Here a small national difference is revealed: Whilst in Germany a legal training is still seen to be an essential academic way leading to top positions (although the lawyer monopoly within industrial companies has considerably been broken today), in England more emphasis was put on finance and accountancy:

> I believe that people with a financial training backed up by business studies are going to be in the best position in the future to take on senior positions within companies. An understanding of finance and the business is absolutely crucial as things become more technical and difficult to understand (B17, p 3).

As we will see, whilst technical training enjoys a high social and individual standing in Germany this is more often the case in England for the areas of finance, banking and accountancy. To this extent precisely in Germany it is remarkable and very seldom when future managers are asked to study sociology (a member of the managing board of a mineral oil concern did this) in order to combine a basic specialized form of training while studying with requirements of top management (this means human-resource-management which is seldom applicable to Germany). But there are managers in England too who overcome the prejudices found precisely in the economy about sociologists "who only cause unrest" and we hear from the chief personnel officer of a metal processing company:

> I think, young people ought today to be in the sociology territory and then to take IPM qualifications (Institute of Personnel Management), and then move into the personnel field (B4, p 5).

These argumentations show a direction which covered 12,5% of all German answers: Even during a course of study limited ways of thinking should be coped with as for example through a double course of study, MBA/engineer or a specific course for industrial engineers. In Germany the barriers between technicians/natural scientists on the one hand and businessmen/lawyers on the other hand are very great.

It was of even greater significance to note that there was criticism of higher institutions of education that impart too abstract knowledge which is not orientated towards practice and concentrates too little on the imparting of "personal and social competence" ("We need 3 years before a university graduate is creative at all so that we can really make use of him" [G105, p 9]). Even so 6% of those studying took on social-political functions and thus the responsibility with the aim of achieving social qualifications.

An English senior manager made a remarkable comment precisely with regard to moderating this very often unproductive tense and partly contradictory relationship between academic training and company practice or to organize productively the relationship between the adoption of an abstract capacity of thinking and specialist qualifications. He said:

> I think that the first degree doesn't really matter which subject you do as long as it is a subject that involves a reasonable amount of numerical analysis so you are looking at all the engineering sciences, some of the social sciences, economics, sociology, geography, they all have a much more analytical base than they did 30 years ago. The next stage I think is to get some work experience. By this stage you are into your mid-twenties. Without doubt then, I would advise anybody to do an MBA at the mid-late twenties stage. I think you would get more from an MBA after you have been working for 2 – 3 years, rather than go from your first degree into post-graduate work (B13, p 4).

The two following suggestions made by a great number of managers but with differing national emphasis aim in the direction of mixing training too:

1. 25% of the answers given in Germany recommended a stay abroad to young people – the length of time, whether during or after a course played no deciding role. In the case of a stay abroad it is not only perfection of the language which is of significance (knowledge of at least one, if not two languages is made a requirement – whereby the combination of languages is very different according to the company's relations and business) but above all it is important to come to terms with foreign cultural circles, to grasp and recognize other social norms. In an export-orientated country like the Federal Republic it is quite an understandable requirement qualification which is not necessarily part of a course of study in Germany. Contrary to this, in England not one manager mentioned a stay abroad as being a necessary component of qualifications. This may have two reasons:

a) Either stays abroad are for the English not worth mentioning as a result of the old Empire-past so that these are not considered to be special qualification requirements (especially since stays abroad in the old empire were not necessarily to be understood as getting to know foreign cultures but rather foreign cultures were adapted to the English one);

b) or – and this is more probable – the norm of "splendid isolation" still leaves its mark in the minds of English company managers in spite of looking towards the European Community in 1993.

2. Only 26% in Germany but 50% of the English managers are of the opinion that certain specialized qualifications can and should be achieved in practice in the company and not by studying. In Germany the commercial/craftman's apprenticeship was particularly mentioned (15%), in England emphasis was put on market experience and "getting on with people" as well as wide company training ("I think we should invest time and money in educating

those people in practical management techniques, not necessarily academic qualifications" [B1, p 6]).

The personnel manager of an English steel company made an interesting comment and we feel that it is the typical expression of a specific liberalness and individuality of English society in comparison to the German one. He said:

> When graduates first come to us they have their own views as to which part of management they would like to move in, when they actually come into industry and work they sometimes change their views in the light of what they have experienced whilst they have been with us. We will then move the graduates around as they wish until we can put square pegs into square holes. We find it works very, very well (B5, p 4).

It would be necessary to make note of an important aspect here: Politics regarding training and company recruitment do not only depend on the more subjective factors of the senior managers' attitudes but also depend on the more objective factors of the present economic situation and on the structural changes and within this framework also on the respective economic situation of every individual company. Company needs for managers arise from these factors. Thus there arises the comparison that in British companies regarding the need for managers and key specialist staff that in 1990 more general managers were sought after than in 1986 and that the big boom in the computer industry is over and that at the moment more emphasis is put on good managers in accounting and production (*Financial Times*, 25.1.1991).

At this point the question arises as to what extent the different emphasis of the significance of academic and company training as basis of a later career in top management finds its expression in the qualifications of top managers in Germany and England which represent – in their respective differences – again quite definite structures and philosophies of both national educational systems as well as the ways of dealing with employment and recruitment.

2.2.4   Practicians in England and academics in Germany? Regarding the professional training of managers

Finding the courses that mean business:

While the British economy may not be booming at the moment, one sector that is enjoying rapid growth is business and management courses. Poor management skills have frequently blamed for our commercial malaise and, at least, some remedies are being applied. More students are now opting for business related courses in further and higher education – not least because the resulting qualifications hold out the hope of finding a well-paid job.

This comment from the *Guardian* on 15th May 1990 could be dismissed as the usual complaint that the level of education in one's own country is very bad – a complaint which can be heard from time to time and again and again in Germany too. Apart from this a foreigner may at times gain the impression that the English have a strongly, pessimistic characteristic they call their own.

All this obliges the scientist all the more to look more closely behind the scenes of the educational system in general (this will be carried out at a later stage) and to look in particular at the educational level of the managers.

One of the essential sociological questions here is whether modern, social systems allow or even promote means that break open traditional class differences resulting from educational offers and whether in the place of the "born elites" such elites arise which are legitimized by their own individually gained abilities (Bell: 1974). Halsey (1990, p 89) states in his contribution that after long term observations (from the beginning of industrialization up to today) the modern systems of education and training can be thought of as State instruments to achieve equality of opportunities for all (condition is of course the theoretical assumption that opportunities in life are essentially determined by education). However critics object to this way of looking at things by saying that to change only one variable (that is to say the national education system) is not enough to bring this about. There is a whole list of other variables – as for example cultural and structural norms which are equally important for influencing social stratification.

But let us first of all look at managers' educations in Germany and then in England in order to be able to make a comparison:

Companies in the Federal Republic of Germany recruit fewer and fewer trainees directly after they have completed their "Abitur" or after having completed a 2 or 3-year apprenticeship. "Junior and middle managers may still come up from the ranks, but top and senior managers in large, but nowadays even in small firms are now predominantly graduates from either a university or a polytechnic" (Lane: 1989, p 92). Therefore after leaving school the potential management candidates mostly go on to university (final qualification: diploma or degree after 4.5 years of study, in most cases even longer)) or to polytechnic (Fachhochschule) (final qualification as e.g. business economist or engineer after 3.5 years of study) whereby there is between the two a strict division of work. The courses of study at polytechnics are much more practice-orientated than the courses at the universities although we must say that the admission requirement qualifications at polytechnics are somewhat lower. In German universities, but partly in some polytechnics there dominates a strong division between technical-scientific courses and the classical subjects (economics belongs to the latter). The course of study to become an engineer is very popular in Germany in particular because the "Techniker" are highly acknowledged in society and correspondingly they are financially well paid by the companies. In this case training, industry and high salary are closely interwoven. Behind this, there stands a certain entrepreneurial concept of leadership and management which will be dealt with in more detail at a later stage. But since the beginning of the 1980s the course of business economics in Germany (final qualification at university is "Diplomkaufmann" and at the polytechnics "Diplombetriebswirt") has gained great popularity. However these qualifications are quite abstract so that German companies quite often organize traineeships or introductory programmes for the university graduates. Such specific processes of selection in England often take place at Management Centres which are in connection with the universities to varying degrees. In Germany such centres lie outside the system of higher education, they do not award diplomas, teach only experienced participants (that is no university graduates coming directly from the university) and they impart very specialized knowledge (Sorge: 1978, p 92). The length of training is also a further point of criticism regarding potential management candidates. As a consequence of compulsory military service in Germany (momentarily 12 or 15 months) it is usual that "German managers are in their late twenties when they enter a firm and usually 30 before they begin to wield managerial authority" (Lane: 1989, p 95).

In his examination of West German managers Lawrence stated that the German system of education and higher education is an essential factor for the strength of German industry (Lawrence: 1980, pp 61-83). Unlike the English education system the German system knows no famous schools and has no Oxbridge. Lawrence goes further by saying that by emphasizing technical and scientific training (which can be traced back to the German mentality, the constant wish to know how something works) they are on the whole more pragmatically trained.

If we set aside the length of university study and consider the particular and sometimes embarrassing admiration of the German educational system by the English – although the seriousness of such compliments cannot be judged exactly since it is part of the typical British mentality to view their own institutions in particularly low esteem – it may be that precisely this German educational system – according to Handy et al. (1988, pp 161-162) could become a trap for the Germans in the concert of European competition:

> Could the West Germans become victims of their own success? Their reluctance to change a winning formula in the education, training and development of their managers is perfectly understandable in the view of their past record. But this same approach may be less well suited to radical shifts in markets or types of technology.

And Handy et al. conclude with the question, how West Germany can break the dominance of the Techniker tradition and begin to produce sufficient numbers of generalist managers with an international background.

However according to our own empirical examination in the Federal Republic there is a great misunderstanding in the statement which is often heard in the Anglo-American sphere and which expresses that German managers with their formal qualifications as Techniker are not generalists but specialists: German Techniker top managers think and act (at least they try to) as generalists and not as specialists. Apart from this it is scarcely possible to state that as a result of more theoretical considerations one can infer a certain specialization in the position as executive from a form of training as Techniker which was completed many years before the manager reached such a high position. According to this logic Diplomkaufleute or even MBAs would have to be specialists and this is mostly not the case.

However before we come to any further evaluation the English system of managerial training should be looked at a little more closely:

Let us firstly turn to the highly controversial thesis in England of the American Martin J. Wiener. He makes a connection between the low social image of industry in the United Kingdom and the abstinence of the British educational system regarding technical-scientific courses of study at the universities: "Elite educational institutions form the Victorian era on … reflected and propagated an antiindustrial bias" (Wiener: 1981, p 132). In spite of the fact that English politicians, animated by experiences made during the Second World War, gave much more attention to technical training and for example technical colleges were promoted first to advanced technical colleges, then to full universities, the new universities of the early and mid-sixties devoted most of their resources to the arts and social sciences (Wiener: 1981, p 133). The historian Cornelli Barnett, who teaches in Cambridge, judges the matter much harder and compares the educational system of Great Britain with that of the declining Venice of the 18th century (quoted from *Die Zeit* 4, 18.1.1991, p 23). David Granick states in his examinations of management careers in four different countries (France, Great Britain, USA and East Germany) that even in the 1950s and 1960s the better trained young men (mostly with a university qualification) did not go into industry as a result of the social scale of evaluation (Granick: 1976, p 552; Lane: 1989, p 91).

"British managers, like British gentlemen, were born rather than made" (Whitley et al.: 1981, p 31). If this sentence is really the expression of social self-understanding in England then it explains a certain amount in regard to the British educational system in general and about management training in particular. In comparison with Germany and France, Britain has the lowest percentage of graduates amongst top managers (24%) and even amongst all managers (Lane: 1989, p 91). However there is a relatively large range of statements about the exact percentages of graduates (Cox, Cooper: 1988, p 19; Whitley: 1974, p 70; Mansfield: 1980, p 16). Handy et al. (1988, pp 167-168) state a "numbers gap":

> Half of Britain's younger managers have left education before degree level, that half probably receive no significant formal training after starting work and that prolonged and serious study of business and management is reserved for a few. Britain in 1986 produced 2,000 MBAs or postgraduate students compared with 70,000 in America, and perhaps 10,000 equivalents to an undergraduate degree compared with 240,000 in America.

If we consider the background that

a) especially during Thatcherism much more was done for the training of and by managers than in the decades before (Caird: 1990);

b) as a result of the fact that in England in comparison to the Continent, school education plays a smaller role and MBA a greater role[7] (Lane: 1989, pp 91-92) there should be many more MBAs being trained is indeed the case.

On the one hand it is right that in England future managers prefer to go into professional life earlier than young people in Germany. This may of course be seen as an advantage (Bynner, Roberts: 1990, pp 200-201).

On the other hand however, the fundamental fact that in England specialized-formal training has much lower esteem generally than in comparative countries (Bynner, Roberts: 1990, p 202) leads to the situation that British society and British companies within it put too great an emphasis on personality-related qualities of young people instead of professional-formal qualifications and this is done even before the young people later become senior managers or top executives! This is the case although many entrepreneurs state that they would prefer to employ graduates best of all (*Financial Times*, 17.10.1990, "Career Choice", p 5).

Even on the job training occurs seldom. A more recent examination shows that only 8% of directors in Britain have had any training for their board appointment (Professional Development of and for the Board, IOD, 116 Pall Mall Street, London, cit. in *Financial Times*, 9.4.1991). The very low average per capita spending on training and development by British companies (in 1985 employers spent only 200 pounds per employee per annum on training, which represented 0.15 of company turnover; by contrast, it has been alleged that leading employers in West Germany, Japan and the USA spend up to 3%

---

7   See Whitley et al. (1984, pp 81-84) for the social structure of the MBA partici-
      pants.

of their turnover on training and development. Keep (1989, p 117) shows on the whole that the British educational system in schools and universities and the training system within companies in international comparison have a poor standing which is also confirmed by the OECD (*Financial Times*, 30.8.1991).

Practice in England is still orientated towards the old model of the view of management that management techniques cannot be taught and learnt at schools, but are gradually trained in the profession and is orientated also to conduct, and that an (inborn) talent is part of business and not formal knowledge.

Even in those cases where State administration is more intensively concerned with general professional training[8] this is done in the opinion of English critics at least partly in a highly insufficient way: The National Audit Office (NAO), a kind of watchdog, has criticized sharply the bad management of the Training and Vocational Education Initiative (TVEI) (*Financial Times*, 9.11.1991, p 7). The TVEI launched in 1983, is intended to help bridge the gap between school and work. Project grants are made direct to schools, with location education responsible for co-ordinating the initiative. According to the NAO, the employment department has failed to develop national performance targets against which to measure TVEI – this is possibly a further expression of the unsureness of the definintion of future potential job descriptions.

Nevertheless the significant changes of the recent time must be focussed upon:

1) In spite of the still relatively low number of MBAs, compared with the USA[9], this is also related to the number of the respective top executives, the number of Business Schools offering the MBA courses is rising constantly (Spring 1991: 113 institutions) as well as the number of course candidates (*Financial Times*, 9.4.1991, p 13), whereby on the part of the students there is an everincreasing emphasis being put on scientific training and on the

---

8   First there is the government's Unified Training Programme, announced in February 1988, which is to operate within a framework of mixed input from government, quasi-government (in the form of the Training Agencies), private industry and its associative bodies (e.g. Chamber of Commerce) and voluntary organizations (Lewis: 1991, p 204). In the 1990s the TECs (Training and Enterprise Councils) are to reconstruct Britain's approach to training and enterprise development. Employers, in partnership with the broader community, will be charged with reskilling the workforce and stimulating business growth (Lewis: 1991, pp 204-205).

9   The comparisons between American and British management in England were traditional (Stewart, Duncan-Jones: 1959, pp 61-62; carried out comparisons in the 1950s and 1960s; Holden, Pederson, Germane: 1968, pp 207-232) and were more popular than comparisons between Great Britain and EEC countries – this has its reasons in the particular relationship between England and the USA and in the obviously very painful process of European unification.

acquisition of new and improved managerial skills (an examination at the Ashridge Management College, Berhamsted, Herts gave the result that 62% of the students are sponsored by their companies and have work experience; see *Financial Times*, 4.1.1991). The wish for better income as a means of motivation for attending an MBA course only came in fifth place. According to the examination of Cranfield's MBA graduates, which was quoted in the *Financial Times*, students listed 6 merits of gaining a qualification as MBA of which two "hard" skills – long term planning and objective analysis – came first. Students are motivated by the relatively good prospects of employment for MBA graduates at a time of economic crisis in England (see *Financial Times* from 14.8.1991).

2) Under the pressure of foreign, in particular continental competition (see also the report of the OECD about the relatively poor English educational system in the EEC-comparison; quoted from the *Financial Times*, 30.8.1991, "Training remains an Achilles heel"), furthered by the present economic crisis and provoked by the election campaign, the large political parties put more emphasis in their statements on professional training of school-leavers and on the further education/re-training of the unemployed (see for example *Financial Times*, 17.12.1990, "Back at the top of the agenda"). This is even more remarkable because the Conservatives acknowledge that certain institutions – for example those of education – cannot solely be left to the powers of the market.

However, time after the general election of 1992 must show to what extent the old ways of the British State educational system can be changed and whether the intentions are really to be taken seriously.

3) But the market powers in Britain – in particular the entrepreneurs and their associations – have partly moved away from the long-standing and dominant procedure of not concerning themselves with the national education system.

Thus there is a Management Charter Initiative (MCI), founded in July 1988, which commits its members to a code of practice designed to boost the extent of leadership and management training across the country. More than 850 British companies and institutions have signed up, but – as Professor Leo Murray at Cranfield School of Management claims – it doesn't seem that MCI have much impact on British industry (*Financial Times*, 9.4.1991, on the "Management Charter Initiative").

More than 1,200 chief executives of British companies volunteered to sit on the board of 82 Tecs in England and Wales and take on responsibility for the country's industrial training (*Financial Times*, 3.12.1990, "Colleagues said if people like me did not get involved, who would?").

In autumn 1990 there was formed a Foundation for Education Business Partnership (FEBP) by 19 companies which are well-known for their educational giving (*Financial Times*, 22.10.1990, "Preaching to be unconverted"). The foundation's aim is to encourage more companies to establish some form of partnership with the educational world and to create links with all schools. The problem facing Sir Ian Vallence, chairman of British Telecom and chairman of the FEBP is how to persuade the bulk of British business not currently involved in educational projects that it is in their interest to be so (*Financial Times*, 22.10.1990).

And last but not least we must point to the electronic tutor system "helpline", which should play a substantial role with regard to the qualification offensive and which was prepared by British manager and entrepreneur associations for the managers of the country. The Council for Management Education and Development would like to design a curriculum with academic and practical content and a final certificate qualification (*Das Handelsblatt*, 25.3.1988, "Bald ein britisches Managerdiplom?"). The associations proceeded from the fact that company training would have to be quadrupled in regard to both quality and quantity if Britain wished to secure a good position upfront as an industrial nation. This aim has not been achieved two years later.

4) In 1988 a British-German School for Professional Training was founded by the German Chamber of Commerce in London and this was to train according to the German system of dual education. Young Britons learn here but so far not one English company has taken part (*Financial Times*, 20.10.1991).

To summarize the more recent efforts made to reform the British system of education and training, especially in relation to the training and further training of top executives, it may be said that Britain's development of managers is still a muddle, there is still no clear pattern of consistency (Silver: 1990).

Naturally the question arises here as to whether the German education system is so much more consistent than the English one – in an international comparison we must quite fundamentally state that there is more than one way of learning and training – even if the European process of unification and the common labour market within the European Community implemented in 1993 demand the necessity to adapt quite fundamentally the structures of the national educational systems.

Different and common factors in the English and German education and training system (and thus management training too) can often only be explained if we take a look back at the history: "Traditions in higher education which are non-economic in origins that, when the conditions of entrepreneurship changed during the second industrial revolution, became educational forms of greater or lesser use to an economy" (Locke: 1984, p 310). Thus the

German system of professional training arises from the social selfunderstand-
ing of Germany after the "breakthrough of large industry", essentially after
1870 (Warner: 1987, p 107). The fact that in 1987 120,000 worked in
registered accountancy in Britain whereas in Germany less than 4,000 worked
in registered accountancy (Handy et al. 1988, p 8) is an expression of which
norms in society in general play a role and which norms in economy in
particular. We may add to this that the percentage of academics amongst the
top managers is at 24% much lower in England than in Germany with 62%
(Handy et al.: 1988, p 9). This is not only because of the often quoted lower
social esteem of industry in England in comparison with Germany but it is also
because the formal education system in Germany brings other results than
those in England (in 1989 about 40% of young people in Germany gained the
"Abitur" and in England only 25-30% the "A" level qualifications [Bynner,
Roberts: 1990, p 206]).

Even the kinds of subjects to be studied in Germany and England are very
diverse: For example engineers in Continental-Europe and specifically in
Germany are trained at universities in a special respect with a closer
connection to practice (and thus to industry) whilst in England top managers,
as far as they have enjoyed an academic form of training are trained to be
generalists with little specialized knowledge (Fores, Glover: 1979). This stands
in a mutual process of management attitudes and the national education
system: German industrial top management is much more technology orientated than the English (Mansfield, Poole: 1981, p 45; Wagner: 1986).
However the statement which is often heard that these higher technical
qualifications in top positions lead to a decrease in the number of information
problems and save time by "personal" coordination and that on the whole
misinterpretations are avoided, is not quite right. Then top managers are
generalists and in the long run they must keep their heads free of detailed
knowledge. This difference in the filling of top management positions in
England and Germany owes itself to the respective different social self-
understandings: In Germany work in industry and specifically in top management is very much orientated towards technology and products and has a
different relationship to the staff which is less instrumental than in England. In
Germany the distance between the company directors and staff and works
council is much smaller than in England, management in Germany "appeared
to be more concerned about 'human relations' or 'people' issues than their UK
counterparts" (Millar: 1979, p 56). As we all know, this relatively great
distance in England between "the top and the bottom" is quite essentially
embossed by the strong and (at least in the view of the Continental Europeans)
rigid division of society into class levels. History was different in Germany:
Even the social legislation of the Bismarck era was expression of an attempt to
diminish the distance, the subsequent social breakdowns (1918: the abolition

of the empire, 1933-1945: Nazi era and final capitulation in 1945) brought with them a modernization in the direction of the "open society". And parallel to this there was also close ties of top management to the staff and this helped to settle social conflict.

But let us go back to the present and at the same time away from the responsibilities of the State for education: The companies themselves can do a lot (and bear the responsibility) to produce the 'right managers': This begins with the selection of management trainees for example in the companies' own assessment centres, this goes further with the willingness (in financial terms) of the companies regarding the organization of internal company qualification programmes for managers and ends provisionally with the participation in management programmes of further education which are offered by external sources as for example by company consultants and Business Schools.

In our opinion for a company it is much more successful to organize and use training and further education of managers within the company and not only from the viewpoint of qualification but with regard to the recruitment process and this in a much more intensive way than is done today. Apart from the general question, "what is the point of management training" (see *Financial Times*, 15. 11.1991, "Recruitment 1"), there is a particular problem in this framework, a problem of cost whether internal company organizations for management further education should be offered or whether external courses should be used. From 75% of those managers in Germany interviewed by us and in whose companies institutionalized training and further education for management is carried out, almost two thirds offer internal courses. In England it was also 75% of the respondents in whose companies training and further education was offered as a systematic policy for trainees. However here only about half of the managers go on internal company training programmes and the other half to the further education market. These differences between Germany and England have quite different reasons. One reason is surely the fact that in England there is a much broader external supply of management courses (for example at Business Schools) than in Germany. According to the information given by the English managers another reason may be that the "industry in the UK is less interested in promoting the juniors" (B16, p 6) or that "British industry wants training and education to show a result at once, they don't see it as a long term investment" (B10, p 11).

Nevertheless on the other hand there is a whole list of companies who make use of the wide range of external courses in England and they do this with certain strategic farsightedness and they try to interweave these in their long term company aims. A senior manager gave us a very graphic picture of such a strategy which is worth using as an example here:

What we do is that we have 1 or 2 courses which have become standard. We have a range of external courses and particularly distance learning we use. The standard courses internally are on management of people, we now call it managing people in times of change. The other one is about an intensive appraisal skill course, how to appraise your subordinates. … Recently we have adapted our internal management courses to give 2-day appreciation courses for people who are coming into the industry from outside and need to know something about how the industry is run. With regard to external courses there are one or two of those that we have used fairly consistently over the years. For example the … area is the only organization solely concerned with leadership issues rather than leadership plus other management things. We send almost all our senior managers there. It is a one weeek course and it is a very challenging and stimulating experience for them. … We also use places like Ashridge, Manchester, Cranfield, London Business School as appropriate. We have sent a number of people to Harvard and Oxford. … They would all say that the experience changed their outlook tremendously. We use that where it is relevant. We use well established courses for middle management but in the last few years we have used a lot of Open Business School programmes[10]. … They have now a three stage process with starting with a certificate, you study a numer of subjects like marketing, accountancy, production and so on. That would get you certificate status. Beyond that there is a diploma and for those that are interested an MBA. We wouldn't require people to go on to get an MBA but I am encouraging people to get certificates. … Because we have restructured and changed a lot of our ideas we wanted people who were going to act more like managers than foremen. So we had to give them a lot of help. We assessed them carefully and interviewed them carefully and they then underwent a distance learning programme on managing people. Most of them found that they actually enjoyed it. They started in a very difficult situation. We were under a lot of pressure from competitors so they were grappling with a new job and they had to cope with a new learning programme as well. They did well, two thirds of them completed the course which lasted about 4 or 5 months and they took the exam and passed. We are carrying out on using Open Business learning but what I now want to do is to key it into the corporate policy, the company strategy. In the past we have been a little bit indulgent because you have got to get people's confidence in something to get it off the ground. Now we must carry on what we started last year and say, in this particular job we really require you to do this particular programme. Last year we started this managing people programme because it is a big element in the shift management job. Now I think we have to carry on with that but really sharpen it with corporate objectives. There is another course called Implementing and Management Change and I think we have got to get used to the idea of change because it will happen whether we like it or not. We tend to have fairly low turnover. People tend to stay with us a long while so their careers develop within the company. When they get to a certain point we think then it would be relevant

---

10 The personnel manager of a big British steel company was also taken with these courses: "The fact that you can switch on to these short condensed open university courses are a very, very good tool to bolt onto your existing skills without having to leave the company on a full-time basis" (B 5, pp 2-3).

for them to do a particular course. People with MBAs tend to have somewhat inflated ideas of the salary they are worth. They don't fit in very easily (B11, pp 4-6).

It was worth bringing this long quote here because it shows in a rare clarity the connection between a long term company policy regarding personnel and recruitment, general aims of the company (for example aims of the company philosophy), short term profit demands and the further qualification of management related to this, which must also take into consideration the individual-subjective interests of those concerned (that is motivating the potential participants).

It appears to us that society and companies must stand in an obligation towards the young managerial trainees. By taking action they must ensure that responsible thinking dominates and indeed with respect to social values as well as internal company possibilities to solve problems. These are essential requirements for management courses being successful. But such a way of thinking cannot be achieved by talking about it, it can only take hold as a result of the example of others (young people). It is on this point that in England as well as in Germany the greatest deficiencies in managerial further education can be found. To overcome these, Anthony suggests that managers should also be politically trained in order to cope sufficiently with the social challenges at the companies (Anthony: 1986, pp 193-199). Weber emphasizes more the internationality of management training (Weber: 1990, pp 42-62), whilst Handy et al. proceed from the approach that every national culture has its own way to fortune, that is to say that by observing the experiences made by the Japanese and Germany, the English should be able to develop their own concept of recruitment and training and further education of management. The authors suggest the first way to be a "Charter of Good Practice", charged with setting the standards for management development and for advocating its course in society at large, with government and with the universities when needed (Handy et al.: 1988, p 183).

2.2.5   The academicisation of management – A necessary, but not sufficient requirement

In Germany both the careers of those managers we interviewed and their advice for young people pointed to the fact that the successful completion of a higher course of study may be seen as a matter of course for a later career (first step into a profession): 80% of German managers spoke of an academicising of company management. But 17% of these do not consider this tendency to be absolutely necessary; 18% give the reason for this academicising process as being the higher demands in the managerial occupation. A further 18% explain this academicisation of management to be the result of the fact that today – in contrast to former times – chances of education are much greater in Germany.

If we compare this with England we can confirm that the majority of our English interview partners spoke also of an increasing process of academicisation within English management but when we look at the specific level we see that the numbers of such qualified managers are much lower than in Germany (or America and Japan). Here are some figures: In the 1980s 24% of top managers in Britain had a degree, in West Germany 62%, in France 65% and in the USA and Japan 85% (Handy et al: 1988, Table 1.1, p 3).

> It seems that approximately half of Britain's younger managers have left education before degree level, that half probably receive no significant formal training after starting work and that prolonged and serious study of business and management is reserved for a few. Britain in 1986 produced 2000 MBAs or postgraduate students compared with 70000 in America, and perhaps 10000 equivalents to an undergraduate degree compared with 240000 in America. America is four times as large but these figures are twenty to thirty times higher (Handy et al.: 1988, pp 167-168).

However the weakness of a purely numerical comparison must be made obvious here: we must ask the question as to whether managers with an academic background are really better qualified than those without. This question may be justified especially when we consider the background of the British educational system: It has been the case in England so far (although we may speak of a decreasing tendency in the 1980s, Hannah: 1990, pp 7-8) that those leaving private schools and exclusive universities could be found in top managerial positions to a high proportion, whilst we know at the same time that the old social elite has drifted further and further apart from the business world. In addition to this, precisely this academicisation of top management[11] which could be observed in the 1980s, and is linked with the decline in the great significance of elite schools for the selection of future academics, can be interpreted as showing that the influence of rich families as a feudalistic feature has decreased in England and that in the economy there is a tendency for more importance to be attached to self-earned educational merits (Hannah: 1990, p 18).

Furthermore in the case of international comparisons we must take into consideration that for example to the British (different from in Germany or in the United States) management "has always been a more practical art than an applied science" (Handy et al.: 1988, p 7).

One manager from the food and luxury food industry is of this opinion and warns of an over-evaluation of academic training:

---

11 In 1979 there were 19 chairmen of top companies in Britain without university education, 10 years later there were only 14 (Hannah: 1990, Table 10.2, p 20).

> People seem to be more interested in the academic qualification than in the talent. We've lost the art of talent spotting. It's formalized but we ourselves take on graduates in production(B1, p 5).

But on the other hand many of our interview partners stated that

> there is a need to improve the levels of attainment in British managers, educationally. It is very neglected, I believe (B10, p 9).

However such a statement can be understood as criticism of the usefulness of knowledge gained at universities for actually carrying out the managerial occupation:

> All you can try to do is to get some basic raw material like a degree but then once you are in that door it is down to the non-academic things really. The academic stuff tends to be taken for granted – this comment was made by the works director of a factory in the food and luxury food industry (B13, p 5).

It can also be understood as a call to the companies to prepare young academics practically and for the specific purpose of their new task. We found in England much more often than in Germany that there was a certain amount of scepticism regarding the belief that academic training should be a basic requirement for the fulfilment of management tasks. Let us look at the following quote:

> Graduates seem to be the flavour of the month. We have a difference of opinion in this company that there is a senior school of thought who believe that the future captains of industry within this company … have to come through the graduate intake. I don't share that view. … It's the blend of talent. At the moment I think it's lob-sided, it's one-sided. Graduates yes, a graduate, if they've got a degree, it doesn't matter what it's in, and they can be idiots these people. But if they've got a degree they must be OK we'll take them in.And we find at least half the graduates we get not very good, particularly in what I call some of the strange subjects, what I call fringe subjects, English literature, history, geography, lovely! but we want people in this business with vision and drive and enthusiasm (B1, p 6).

One first and careful conclusion could be that in Germany in the self-understanding of society in general and in the specific system of norms of managers there are no or only few inconsistencies between intellectual abilities (which can be both a requirement and product of academic training) and work in industry. In English society it is a different matter for management work in industry has very little social status and there are different traditions of the evaluation of academic training for later management work than in Germany.

In both England and Germany the majority of managers are required to have a professional specific qualification (this consists to a high degree in Germany of technical-scientific elements) and to be able to think in an abstract way. However whilst German managers saw a course of study, complemented of course by certain company traineeships, as a suitable medium, the English put more emphasis on company practice, that is to say on more "on-the-job-training".

However it is remarkable to find the following common features in spite of the different way of looking at academic training regarding the later demands on a top executive in England and Germany. Let us look at these points:

-   lack of a (rigid) concept of management careers[12] (this is substantiated by the relatively unplanned nature of the respective careers of our respondents),
-   the openness regarding the value of training for a later career.

This leads us to other quite essential observations and conclusions:

a) The great significance of practical experience in the profession was emphasized again and again as being an essential foundation for the later career; in England this is to be achieved by an early start to the profession directly after leaving school; in Germany by completing an apprenticeship (here the cult of the German system of dual professional training was preserved) or/and by practices during a course of study but also by an early start to the profession directly after studying;

b) Professional performance and physical[13] endurance in the case of doubt play a greater role in the evaluation scale of managers than those skills gained as a result of training and professional qualifications.

Performance means here the successful overcoming of obstacles of different kinds[14] and the solving of different problems. As Pross/Boetticher show (1971) this view can lead to the belief that "in the existing society every competent worker has his chance" and this possibly produces a conservative attitude (p 112);

c) In this respect the differences of status and qualification gained by a course of study are recognized as being quite normal (this is because they do not have

---

12 In this respect the thesis of Peter Lawrence (1980) can neither be verified or falsified by us. The thesis states that German managers are less career and more performance-orientated than their Anglo-American colleagues.

13 A good physical constitution as an essential requirement for a successful managerial occupation has been a matter of reflection for some time; see here the results of the questionnaire carried out by Wald/Doty at the beginning of the 1950s on American top managers (1954, p 51).

14 In his well-known examination *The General Managers* (1982) John Kotter comes to the conclusion that the work requirements lead to the consequence for the General Manager ("GM") that "the typical GM faced significant obstacles in both figuring out what to do and in getting things done" (p 122).

crucial significance, if we disregard starting out in the profession) and seldom arouse feelings of envy. Contrary to this we see that it leads to top managers with poorer formal qualifications being acknowledged by their (formally better qualified) colleagues – the main thing is that they perform well (we have here the example of a member of the board of directors of an internationally-orientated concern in Germany, who 'only' completed a commercial apprenticeship and not a course of study [G68]).

2.2.6   The recruitment of top managers: Internally or externally?

The advancement of young trainees and the judgement of academic grades are closely and partly very directly connected to the philosophy of every company regarding in which way and with which means top positions may be filled. In company practice as well as in scientific discussion there is often the question as to whether managerial positions should be filled from outside or from within the company.

In answer to this question German managers (52%) preferred a flexible strategy (according to the applicants situation, top management positions are filled from external and internal sources, however in second place 41% supported fundamentally internal sources).

In England the emphasis was similar, approximately half of the managers preferred the two strategies of recruitment which we have already mentioned (the small difference between the two countries is not worth mentioning).

At the beginning of the 1990s an examination carried out by the Cranfield Management School and Price Waterhouse found out that in an international comparison internal way of recruitment was in second place in the UK (*Financial Times* from 29.6.1990, "Recruitment I") but that an examination carried out in the first half of the 1980s in 23 companies put a much more definite emphasis on internal recruitment of managers (Goldsmith, Clutterbuck: 1984, p 77)[15]. Three reasons for this are given by industry leaders (Goldsmith, Clutterbuck: 1984, pp 77-78), because

–   "these companies often see themselves as the harbour of best practice anyway; therefore the talent that they need is most likely to be found within";

---

15   A study of management policies and practices of fifteen leading industrial corporations which was carried out in the United States in the 1960s made clear that there was quite a definite preference of the internal way of recruitment. See Holden, Pederson, Germane (1968, p 213).

- "outsiders do not easily adapt to their culture when plugged in at senior level";
- "they see promotion from within as a means of keeping the people they want, of extending the 'family' concept".

According to our realizations there are neither in England nor in Germany any fully developed or laid out rules for the way of internal recruitment. The rule of procedure known as "moving up instead of moving in" cannot be seen as applicable in every case. In addition to this a disclosing of this philosophy of recruitment can only seldom be found. There are often only informal agreements of those who make the decisions and which depend on internal as well as external conditions and can only be realized slowly.

Recruiting from external sources is often justified as a way of breaking from old established procedures:

> The beauty of going for external management is that they bring in new ideas. They open existing managers' eyes to new concepts and that can't be a bad thing – this was quoted from the personnel director of a metal processing company (B5, p 6).

The danger that someone who had moved up within a company would not have sufficient authority over his subordinates (who were once his colleagues) was also mentioned.

So far we haven't said anything about the way of external management, which can vary quite considerably: newspaper advertisements, individual applications, suggestions by banks and/or other familiar companies or the way which has been used more frequently in recent times is the employment of company consultants regarding recruitment.

The examination we have already quoted by the Cranfield Management School even speaks of the fact that recruitment agencies are the runners up in Germany (*Financial Times* from 29.6.1990, "Recruitment I"). However this method has become suspect as the often negatively used concept "Headhunter" goes to show[16]. Apart from this by emphasizing external recruitment too strongly there is the danger "that would be a demotivating factor for your existing staff" (B3, p 12).

On the other hand internal recruitment is often connected to a certain kind of internal company officialdom, bureaucracy etc.:

> You have got to guard against that sort of philosophy where people feel that they have got an automatic right to be promoted to the next position. That really is in-breeding (B3, p 12).

---

16   See here J. Priewe, D. Weber, D. Lamparter (1988, pp 82-104).

But in the case of internal management the familiarity of the candidate regarding the company and the existence of the right 'company aroma' is often valued in a very positive sense. In the following chapter we will deal with this tense relation in more detail in connection with the professional and career paths of managers.

Perhaps we could alleviate this tense relationship through a limited public process of selection – a process of selection that is practised for example by an English company from the vehicle construction industry:

> The basic philosophy is that we advertise all vacancies so that employees can apply and the employees would be given the first opportunity if their qualifications were equal. Of the present senior management team most of them have come in from outside (B4, p 6).

One advantage of this procedure would be to filter out the most professionally qualified applicant and to provide him from the very beginning with an objectively viewed professional authority.

The filling of managerial positions also presents a market process within whose framework the companies not only stand faced with internal or external selection. But they must also offer the potential managers something before they are at all interested in the managerial positions on offer. More than half of those we interviewed in Germany as well as in England[17] were of the opinion that indirect and direct remuneration were not necessarily at the foreground of managers' motivation but that they were essential conditions.

In second place in Germany there were approximately 40 managers who mentioned the "task to be fulfilled" and "the position to be filled" as motivation for managers. "Promotion possibilities of the position" were less important but in England the situation was completely opposite.

Let us make two comments to this:

1. The relative indifference at the mention of financial reasons as a source of motivation for managerial work, which seems at first strange to the outsider, proves to be only make-believe. Outwardly top managers in general are very unsure to what extent a (socially) open declaration for the "income gap" in comparison with other professional groups would considerably offend against social rules, because

---

17   There is quite a difference between England and Germany regarding fringe benefits given by companies to top management in order to attract top managers: In England companies allow their top executives many more gratifications regardless of their salaries to a much higher degree than in Germany as e.g. purchase of company shares, financial support for medical treatment, private telephone etc. (*Financial Times* from 17.8.1990, Recruitment, p 10).

- in Germany (more than in England) social norms proceed from a certain social fairness of distribution and therefore they have the effect of easing conflicts;
- in England in the face of the economic crisis and of the real losses of income for the majority of the working population it does not seem favourable to talk about the very considerable growth of salaries for top executives which have occurred over recent years beyond the framework of the legal duty of publication. Such social norms and expectations of behaviour beat down on widespread political slogans in Germany such as "performance must be financially worthwhile" and in England as a result of the favoured individualism (egoism) of the Thatcher era and in general in comparison with the 1960s and 1970s beat down on a strong neglect of the social principle of the common good. This contradiction produces an individual behaviour which hides the financial function of motivation for external purposes but that secretly acknowledges this.

In our interviews managers spoke quite openly about money, career success and the material advantages bound up with this:

> You spend over 50% of your waking hours at work and if you are not going to move into an enjoyable position then it is like giving yourself a life sentence in prison, that you are just going and enduring it and getting nothing out of it (B5, p 7).

With a wink in the direction of the sociologist interviewer an executive of a textile company in England said:

> I mean a lot of sociologists believe a person gets esteem and job satisfaction. I think money is vital as well as that (B14, p 3).

But Monks Partnership, the company remuneration advisers, demand that such internal admissions as a disclosure and explanation of the salaries of top managers would have to be written down for the wider public: "Those companies which make full and informative disclosure of their directors'earnings generally receive a better hearing, for the simple reason that they are taking the trouble to explain actions which, in most cases, are reasonable and defensible. ... But full disclosure in itself is no guarantee of escaping the headline", Monks' annual report says (quoted from *Financial Times* from 14.2.1992, p 9).

Monks' report suggests guidelines for good disclosure practice designed to give shareholders and other annual report readers a clear picture of how and why directors' emoluments have changed. In the *Financial Times* (8.4.1992, p 14) companies are made the three following suggestions as a way of avoiding the regular spring open season of attacks on top pay:

- First they should start to abandon the normal system of free stock options in favour of a long-term incentive programme which fosters a real sense of ownership;
- Second, companies should make a reality of their claims to share "visions and values" with their employees, they should extend many of the incentives lower down;
- Finally they should keep packages relatively simple.

In Germany public companies are obliged to give information about their directors' salaries in their annual reports. However many income and salary shares in other positions in the balance-sheet are hidden so that the wider public reacts with mistrust at these figures.

In England the legally prescribed publication of top managers' salaries is often only formal:

> At present, only about a 10th of British companies even mention in their annual reports whether any performance-related incentive is included in the scanty remuneration figures which they report. A mere handful say whether this is an annual bonus, a three year bonus, or a longer-term scheme such as stock options. Fewer still show how the package breaks down. Yet many companies pay all three year – and other perks beside (*Financial Times* from 8.4.1992, p 14).

Nevertheless even with a total disclosure of the salaries the fundamental problem of the legitimation of the managers' income is not yet solved.

2. The difference between England and Germany regarding this question appears interesting. The question is asked as to whether the professional interests of managers can really be defined as strongly directed towards career success, including financial gratifications, or whether there are other orientations, perhaps regarding the work content. As a result of our interviews we agree with Lawrence (1980) that German managers on the whole are more interested in keeping a deadline and are proud of technology and of the products of their own company. Together with the relatively high prestige of industry within society in Germany (compared with England) the company manager enjoys a high status within and outside the company and this contributes to the system integration of the staff. According to Lawrence, German managers are more performance and less career orientated than their English colleagues.

The personnel manager of an electronic company, when comparing German modes of behaviour with English modes of behaviour, complains of less emphasis on the "task" as motivation for managers:

> You spend more time negotiating the salary than you do negotiating opportunity. Very few British managers ask about opportunity. They spend a lot of time arguing about salary (B10, p 12).

The American psychoanalyst O'Thoole (1979) describes how from William H. Whyte's *Organization Man* (1965) as characteristic feature of the American manager at the beginning of the 1970s the "Corporate Gamesman" has arisen. The American top managers of today are, according to this, inflexible, bureaucratic, resistent towards innovations, insensitive towards the needs of the employees and their social concerns. He only thinks of his own career and it doesn't matter to him in which company he works and with which content problems he deals with. The "Heartless Gamesman" is the complete opposite of Weber's "Professional Worker" and corresponds completely with the European clichee of an American top manager. The question arises here as to whether elements of this clichee can be found in the modes of behaviour of English and German managers.

On the basis of our examinations we found out that precisely in German industrial companies top managers are proud of the product and high level of technology. Combined with an active sense of punctuality – which is partly felt to be rather harrowing but which is considered to be an expression of reliability, "good character" discipline etc. – all this appears for the managers to be a good capacity of the German economy in the European process of unification.

German managers are approved by the English in their discussion about taking on the "German model".

But it is precisely this smug self-satisfaction on the part of the Germans in comparison with their European competitors, and the old-fashioned form of work organization in comparison to Japan (let us think of the studies of Harvard/USA in the car industry, key word: lean production) which allow doubts about the industrial location Germany to arise; these are doubts which also include the qualification and role understanding of top managers.

But do the professional and career paths of 'our' top managers confirm the orientation of the English towards career and income and the relatedness of the Germans towards work content?

2.2.7   The professional and career paths of industrial company managers

Since the mid 1970s there has been a whole series of examinations in Germany which have dealt with professional biographies/professional developments of different professional groups (Brose: 1987). But works about the professional biographies of industrial company managers have scarcely played a part in this research boom. The few examinations which exist regarding this theme were mostly completed at the beginning of the 1970s.

But the literature situation in Great Britain and in the USA[18] is quite different. With respect to this theme there were in the 1950s examinations (e.g. Clements: 1958; Lewis, Stewart: 1961) which have been continued up to today with more theoretical discussions as well as with empirical examinations (e.g. Mansfield: 1973; Fores, Glover: 1978; Child, Kieser 1975; Pahl, Pahl: 1971).

But let us first of all look at a few of the national peculiarities, independent features of professional and career paths of top managers. Companies produce certain orientations of promotion and rivalry for competition which are central elements of the management career:

> The professional interests of managers regarding promotion, together with the promotion criteria of success produce rivalry within company dealings for promotion in the top positions of company management. ... Competition regarding promotion within the organization is a crucial feature of the career patterns for managers if we follow the perceptions of W.H. Whyte jr. about the 'Organization Man'. According to this a career pattern is more or less typical where young college graduates are recruited by the company, mostly and first of all for company training so that they are then able to take on staff positions in lower and middle management. They are promoted after a probationary period although the criteria of this 'probation' often remains unclear. It is uncertain whether a relevant move is a matter of promotion or demotion. ... In addition to this there is the fact that career success for the individual manager is often the only indication of the success of his organizational action so failure in getting on signalizes to him that he is making professional mistakes (Beck, Brater, Daheim: 1980, p 123).

In the 1960s Zapf tried to sketch out the typical professional route for the German top manager:

> The German (top) managers ... are between 55 and 60 years old. They were born in West Germany or South Germany, they are Protestant, they come from the upper bourgeois class. Often their fathers were doctors, lawyers, top government officials or factory manufacturers, leading employees or self-employed businessmen. They studied and in fact either law, economic sciences or even more often engineering science. After studying most of them went to a big concern where after 6 years they became head of department, after 15 years executive or works manager, after 20 years managing director. 25 years after completing their studies they belong to the board of directors. At the age of 65 they retire and devote themselves completely to their numerous honorary functions (Zapf: 1965, p 136).

David Granick, one of the best authorities in this field, tried almost at the same time to type the career pattern of English top managers (Granick: 1962, pp 144-149): Type 1 is the former student of Oxford or Cambridge who has

---

18   We will not go into more detail about the career paths and professional biographies of American top managers here: Cf. Holden et al.: (1968); Wald, Doty (1954); Stewart, Duncan-Jones (1959); Newcomer (1955); Warner, Abegglen (1957).

graduated in the arts. "The emphasis on the professional is for him one of the worst social sins". He doesn't feel like an expert because his training stresses the amateur nature and the general view which he is proud of.

Type 2 has reached the top from the production. Approximately 50% of this kind went straight into industry after the high school, completed an apprenticeship and by attending evening classes gained their engineering diploma. "In a society in which the amateur is celebrated the qualified engineer is a professional. As such he begins with a feeling of inferiority".

Type 3 is the chartered accountant. This managerial group is unique to Great Britain.

Type 4 is the heir who is of course at home in all economic forms of free enterprise and is not specifically British.

It is interesting that examinations which were carried out 20 years after those we have quoted state that managing directors enter their careers from a wide variety of backgrounds and educational levels. But two main routes into top management in England become clear (see Cox, Cooper (1988, pp 45-46):

> Accountancy, or working one's way up through a large corporation. ... A few succeeded without any formal qualifications, but this is probably changing. As more of the professions require a degree as an entry qualification, and in an age when it is easier for a bright youngster to enter university, it will become less common to find senior managers who are not graduates. ... In terms of career, managing directors have wide experience within a range of different companies and across several functions. Early responsibility, often in a strange environment (e.g. overseas) is an important factor. This develops self-reliance and leadership qualities at an early stage. ... Chance probably plays a part, but our respondents were adept at creating 'good luck' and at capitalizing on opportunities. They had not usually planned their careers, and their skills were developed mainly from job experience and short courses on specific topics, taken as the need arose.

Career paths and qualifications cannot be sufficiently explained without referring briefly to social origin. From the empirical examination by Poole, Mansfield, Blyton, and Frost at the end of the 1970s and which also dealt with top management in England, it is possible to see that with reference to the origin of the managers there is quite a closed society in which the upper and upper/middle class is over-represented and the working class clearly under-represented. It becomes even clearer if we look at the examination of British company chairmen by Stanworth/Giddens in which only 5 from 460 came from the working class, but 66% from the upper class and 10% from the middle class (there were details for 23%: Stanworth, Giddens: 1974, pp 83-84).

If we differentiate the branches, banking, which is highly esteemed by the English society, even 74% of company chairmen came from the upper class whilst in industry 14% came from working class households. This tallies with the central theses from the examinations by Glover and others that the complete education system in England still strongly prefers the upper class. In spite of opinions which are often heard and which contradict this, the decade of Thatcherism has done little to change this: From 79,000 students who had gained a place to study at a British university in 1989, 69,9% had parents in professional, managerial or senior administrative occupations. That compared with 23% with parents in skilled occupations and 6% in partly-skilled. Only 1% of entrants came from homes where parents were unskilled (*Financial Times* from 1/2.12.1990).

In England on the whole vertical mobility is still lower than in other comparable European nations: "Our analysis shows that Britain lacks a modern system for ensuring that a good proportion of her most able people reach top positions in manufacturing industry" (Glover: 1978, p 176).

Comparisons are often made with (West)Germany where according to relevant literature, there is considerably greater vertical mobility regarding the filling of top positions in the economy. There is one reason which is presumed for this that precisely the national-socialist period in Germany destroyed traditional structures in a very specific way which was also intensified by events of the war. In our opinion there is additionally the fact that the formal qualifications necessary for reaching top positions in German industry – specifically technical and scientific – are more readily available for children from the lower social levels of German society as a result of their mentality. And a third point is: the specific German expression "Leistung" is of great significance as criteria for selection for top management and is first of all independent of the social origin of the candidates. The above quoted tendency of the low social mobility in England is put into doubt by Granick in his studies of European managers where he confirms that at the beginning of the 1960s top management in England and in the economy was composed of non-elite groups. Thus a successful career in industry is possible to such men(!) who haven't got the "right" origin and training (Granick: 1962, p 107). Granick uses here the criteria of the social background and the attendance of "good" schools and universities.

Such a contradiction is not cancelled out in its tendency by the fact that the samples of different empirical examinations regarding the social origin of British top managers as well as the expressions used are partially very different from each other.

In this discussion of literature we would like to refer to the more recent findings by Cox and Cooper who as a result of their examinations could observe that there are two main streams in terms of social background and education among managing directors (1988, p 21): "There is one group from professional backgrounds with public-schools and Oxbridge educations. There is a somewhat larger from predominantly lower socio-economic backgrounds, who have attended grammar schools and provincial universities, or taken up articles or apprenticeships leading to professional qualifications". By the way this second group is covered by the results of the study by Crocket, Elias (1984) that approximately half of the examined manager group has no special formal qualifications in comparison with the whole population but that the specific group of general managers has university grades to a more than average degree. However these very general observations must be differentiated further as Cox, Cooper explain (1988, p 21):

> There is a distinct bias among the Oxbridge men towards the larger, London-based companies, and among the others towards smaller, Northern-based companies. In fact, there is, for this generation of Oxbridge men, a bias completely away from industry. Several mentioned during the interviews that they had taken up industrial jobs only after failing to gain entry to the diplomatic or senior civil service. There were a number of individuals who stood out against all these trends, including a significant minority who had no formal qualifications. In general, there is some evidence that the social base of Britain's top executives is widening.

This last observation led the *Financial Times* at the end of 1990 to speak of a "social revolution in the boardroom":

> The decline in the importance of a public school education to industrial leaders is reflected in a lessening of the importance of Oxford and Cambridge. While both are still the most dominant universities – they now account for 32% of chairmen against 38% in 1979 – the share of company chairmen from "other", most red-brick universities has more than doubled" (*Financial Times* from 3/4.11.1990, p 11).

If we look at the formal qualifications of Britain's top 20 company chief's (*Financial Times* from 28.11.1990) this statement is only strengthened.

The question which is often asked by the public whether such a change in trends has been brought about by the decade of Thatcherism or – as a consequence of the stormy economic and social development – has germinated for a long time as a seed in the bosom of British society, this question cannot be definitively answered by us. Nevertheless we think that changes have always developed over a longer period and partly independently of government decisions. Laws and regulations have only codified what was already slumbering in society and which was also partly practised. This becomes clear through the observations by Giddens regarding the change of the elites in British society (1974, pp 1-21). According to these observations a former dominating class in Great Britain was split into elite groups as a result of many influences. This class was described for the capitalist class by Marx in a very fragmentary and much too homogenous way. The most important influences were the rising worker's movement and the institutions which were differentiated by modernization. The former compromise of power between the nobility and the bourgeoisie has been pulled apart particularly by the separation of property and control. Giddens continues that this brought about a certain de-professionalization of the elite which helped the trade unions to establish themselves as opposing powers and finally caused the disintegration of the economic elite. With this differentiation of new institutions or rather their tendentially increasing significance (e.g. media, trade unions, above all education system) centres of power and thus also their elites are unravelled. Every institution develops its own practices of recruitment and management and the personnel of their management committees is relatively heterogenous in a historical comparison. Nevertheless Giddens rightly points out to the fact that not all institutions are equally important and so offer the respective elite groups different patterns of recruitment and careers. Since British society still gives the banking and financial sector greater significance than industry, the economic elite in banking and finance is very much more elitist and feudalistic.

This is sufficient about literature. To follow we will examine our own empirical material – English and German – with reference to the different patterns of managerial professional paths. Here we wish to develop a harmonious system of organization and at the same time wish to consider the factors of time and planning. It is often the case that in literature the time factor is neglected as one of the central dimensions for a career. This is similarly true for the question of a conscious planning of career and profession.

Basically – according to the sociological approach regarding the "manager's profession" – our material allows us to divide the professional careers of company managers into 3 types:

- owner-manager;
- side-stepper ("Seiteneinsteiger");
- trained managers.

The owner-manager: Not only because of the historical development (see the chapter on owner-managers) but also under the aspect of managerial professional careers may we say that the owner-manager presents a 'dying' picture. In Germany only 2 from 111 managers we interviewed can be put in this group. This is also the case in other examinantions (Zapf: 1965, p 144; Kruk: 1972, pp 220-223). Similar is true for Great Britain even if 3 of the 16 interviewees can be put in this category which is more the result of our specific sample than otherwise.

It is true for both countries that in large industrial concerns this type of manager is practically no longer to be found – with the exceptions of conglomerates (according to Hanson). On the other hand this type is found in small and middle-sized companies and particularly in the tertiary sector although we must say that it is the heirs in comparison to the founders who dominate here.

It is our thesis that – although of course the rise of the heir into top management of the company is pre-determined – education, knowledge and the capacity to think analytically etc. also play a considerable role and this is similar to the case of employed top executives.

But let us turn for a moment to a German heir amongst the owner-managers i.e. a company manager, who gained his position and function primarily through birth. A typical pattern of his professional career may look like this:

"O" level qualifications (Mittlere Reife) – a commercial apprenticeship in his parents' company – Some "years of experience and learning" in different companies (in different regions) in the commercial sector – return to the parents' company – then rising from the bottom of the ladder, doing everything in the company – manager of the commercial side – managing partner (G65).

Let us look at the career of a founder in England who started his career as a technician (apparently this is quite untypical for England):

Apprenticeship as a fitter in the brewing business – head of department in a building firm – development engineer of a delivery firm for the brewing industry – in the same company the responsibility for a department – in between the completion of his engineering diploma at night school – as a result of the collaboration with another firm now responsible as manager of a technical project – later change to a big company in the food and luxury food industry as works engineer (assistant of the works director) – with the subjective feeling of lacking knowledge in the field of industrial relations change to a similar function to another company – for 2 years the junior-owner and managing director of a small firm of the delivery industry for the brewing trade (B2).

This founder changed his company relatively often with the view primarily to qualify himself. His formal training as a fitter and engineer is also typical in England for this type of top executive since it is precisely the manual workers who have a great chance to find their way into industry and then to found of course smaller companies.

In principle there are, of course, several variants to the career patterns as for example the practician versus the academic, the fast mover who moves up to the top of the ladder within a relatively short time or someone who works his way slowly through the company etc..

But now if we look at the heirs amongst the owner-managers we can see that in spite of the varying career patterns there are also common features which justify being summarized as a specific pattern of a professional career:

– one common feature of heirs is the special occupation and company-related process of socialization in preparation for the later take over of management functions within the parents' company;

– furthermore heirs have not gained their position in competition with other applicants but their professional path has been predetermined for them through birth. This does not mean that they are naturally the 'poorer' company managers because for them the principles of competition and selection do not apply and because it is not necessary for them to justify their position by some kind of standard of performance.

At this point we must look at British society with special interest: since vertical mobility of top executives is much lower than for example in Germany the professional group of top managers moves easily into the category of a "closed society" – independent of the fact whether top executives are owners (heirs) or employed managers. Only in this respect does the difference between type 1 and the two other types (side steppers and qualified managers) play a lesser role in England. The question arises here as to whether there is a general tendency amongst British top executives which approaches the more feudalistic structures of an owner-manager class – in spite of the change confirmed by Giddens from a dominating class to differentiated elitist groups. Of course there is one general view which opposes this. It is the view that structural conditions of the economic process like (international) competition with other bidders and a dependence on the market force the owner-managers to carry out their function rationally and efficiently, otherwise there may be the threat of economic decline.

However, with regard to the career pattern there is a central difference between the heir and the 'property-less' managers and this can be stated to a greater degree for the German society than for the English: There are no gained or freely gainable qualifications and requirements which determine the career of the owner-manager. Such qualifications and the proof of qualifications brought about by good performance are however the crucial catalytic factors of the professional and career path of the employed manager (in our classification the side-stepper and the trained manager).

The side-stepper – a second career: Under the heading of the side-stepper we refer to those members of top industrial management who after many years of professional occupation in another area come from 'outside' to a position and function within company management and indeed directly into the first or second management level.

In Germany we found a total of 10 (9%) side steppers within our examination group. But we may differentiate within this group between those who moved from an occupation within an association (6) and those who moved from a professional occupation (3) and those from an academic-scientific domain (1) and came into industrial management. There was a group of higher administrative officials and politicians who were missing in the German group and who had played a much greater role in earlier examinations (Zapf: 1965; Kruk: 1972).

The low number or almost complete absence of senior officials and politicians in top industrial management is the expression of the poor (compared with the USA and England) exchange between the social areas of politics and the economy – although in our British sample only 1 respondent can be described as a side stepper. Sir Ralf Dahrendorf describes the English situation very aptly (1977, p 288): "That someone becomes Professor of Classical Philology, Brigade-General, Member of Parliament, Director of an Investment Trust and Minister for Health during his lifetime is certainly an exception even in England" but, and we must continue this is, in principle, possible whilst in Germany it remains unthinkable.

In spite of the differences between Germany and England regarding the number and social acceptance of side-steppers there are certain basic common features with regard to career:

As we have already mentioned, the side-steppers have not completed a professional training within industrial management but the occupation in company management is a second career for them. Correspondingly therefore side-steppers begin their managerial career at a relatively advanced age. For example a German academic at the age of 50 moved from being a senior official in education to top management of a large concern (G78); an English teacher and organizer of youth schemes became head of department at a building company at the age of 44 (B4).

Since the side-stepper's processes of promotion take place in their 'pre-industrial' time, their second career progresses very rapidly: they move in at the top of the company which is often to the great regret of old 'company bureaucrats' with decades of professional experience.

For the companies there is a whole list of reasons for employing side-steppers. It is often very important that by bringing in the new man from outside they are bringing in a distinct expert or specialist into the company, who possesses a qualification that is not available within the company. Side-steppers are frequently occupied in their specialist domain after changing to the industrial company – even if as general manager.

Apart from this there are also politically-compelling reasons for a company to employ a side-stepper. By calling on certain persons the trust of the banks for example should either be gained or increased. Or by employing certain people it is possible to get special political connections into the company.

For the side-steppers themselves there is a whole variety of motives for moving into the management level of an industrial company. However it is our opinion that it is basically decisive that the change for those concerned brings in an objective and subjective way a clear improvement of their professional position and situation. And this is not only in a financial respect but also with regard to influence and power, which can be exercised through the new function and with respect of social status (although in England this is relative).

For these improvements former self-employed give up their (supposed) independence and step in next to 'trained' managers, who present the majority of industrial management in the companies.

The trained manager – professionalization or bureaucraticization of industrial company management: According to our definition trained top executives are those who have neither come into managerial functions of industrial companies through ownership (as a founder or heir) nor as a side-stepper from a different professional occupation. On the contrary this group has systematically and purposefully learnt the occupation and profession through training and further training as well as practical experience.

In Germany 99 of our selected group (89%) fall in this category, although we can identify 2 structurally different career patterns within this group. There is the group of industrial bureaucrats with 53% and the group of changers with 36%.

In England the tendency is similar: 12 of our 16 respondents can be ascribed to the group of trained managers, 7 of those as industrial bureaucrats and 5 as changers.

Let us look at the industrial bureaucrats: According to Reinhard Bendix (1956, p 302) the careers of such industrial bureaucrats are quite generally "usually from a series of employee positions which lead to a managerial position"[19]. And Pross/Boetticher continue (1971; pp 72-73):

---

19   In his *Organization Man* (1965) W.M. Whyte describes very impressively the different aspects of the industrial bureaucrat.

> The professional history of managing employees in large companies today resembles that of officials in public administration rather than the history of entrepreneurs from the time of industrialization. ... The moves which characterize the existence of the classical entrepreneur, as well as the risks and leaps up the ladder are strange to him.

Zapf describes such a career pattern for Germany (1965, p 142):

> The rise of German managers succeeds ... within 'industrial bureaucracy' according to quasi-bureaucratic patterns. There are fixed steps in promotion (Assistant or scientific worker, head of department or head of development, managing clerk or works manager, director, member of the board of directors). There are established rules of seniority. However flexibility within industry is greater than in government bureaucracy and therefore leaps and fast career are seldom but possible.

Clements described the top managers for English industry as a result of his examinations in the second half of the 1950s as men "who have not marked experience outside industry, outside their own firm, or outside their own line of work" (Clements: 1958, p 151). And Granick adds to this statement as a result of his own observations (1962, pp 142-143).

All this is confirmed by a look at the length of time (here: British) managers have been at a company: Clements (1958, p 151) writes that almost half of all those top managers he asked had spent the whole of their working life so far in only one company. And Poole et al. noted as a result of their interviews of 1058 managers (half of these were top managers) from private and State British economy at the end of the 1970s that as a rule managers were often occupied in the same company long before they reached their present status; the average length of service at a company was 11.45 years (this included middle management whose members are usually younger and cannot prove as many years service as people in top management) (Poole, Mansfield, Blyton, Frost: 1981, pp 48-52).

We used the career pattern of the industrial bureaucrat as follows in order to evaluate our empirical findings: All those are classed as industrial bureaucrats who are members of industrial company management and who worked/work as a trained manager after their professional training in 2 companies at the most and who have completed their way up the top of the ladder into top management in one company (or in the case of employment in 2 companies in the second one).

A typical German professional career would look like this:

Attainment of "A" levels (Abitur) – study of economics – entry into a big industrial company as assistant of a managing director – head of department – head of main department – manager of a larger field – managing executive – commercial management of a company as member of the second management and hierarchy level (G64).

The manager concerned considers this to be quite a normal career path; he has never been particularly ambitious and has "just slipped into" every position.

A typical English industrial bureaucrat has – almost – the same professional career path:

Apprenticeship as a fitter – 2 years in the army – entry into a company in the car industry, a little later personnel officer – later university, diploma as personnel manager – later entry into a big company in the food and luxury food department, still there after 20 years – today Group industrial relations manager (B1).

The real difference between the German and English industrial bureaucrat becomes clear when we look at these examples: Whilst academics are highly represented in Germany (78% of the German bureaucrats are academics) the practicians dominate in England. In our example our English bureaucrat (although he could be classed as an academic) came to his university diploma via practice. He wanted to have a qualitative qualification. The different significance of further education in England to that in Germany also becomes clear in our comparison.

Although we see in our examples that the rise of the managers progressed relatively quickly from one level to the next, the way to the top of the company lasted quite a long time, as a rule between 20 and 35 years. By the way this slow but constant rise is not only true for the practicians amongst the industrial bureaucrats but in the same way for the academics. The latter solely go into the company at a higher level.

This is confirmed by the examination by Stanworth/Giddens of the demographic profile of English company chairmen (1974, p 87): Only 2% became company chairmen within 10 years of starting their career whilst 60% needed 30 years or more for this[20].

Indeed this points to a career which is long-term, continual and which progresses over a few or more stages. This is not dissimilar to a career within the civil service (at least) in German public administration.

This corresponds to the recruitment strategy of the companies: As we have seen in chapter 2.2.6, British as well as German company managers prefer

---

20   Older German examinations also make clear that the the type industrial bureaucrat dominated; see Kruk (1972, pp 132-133); Pross, Boetticher (1971, p 74); Zapf (1965, p 143).

internal filling of company management positions and in this way further the career paths of industrial bureaucrats.

By the way this structural similarity does not say something a priori about the quality of those top managers classed as industrial bureaucrats but is solely the expression of a specific pattern of career and professional progress.

However we cannot go as far as Kruk who says that the progress of a manager in his career does not depend on obtaining a position by sheer length of service but by merit (Kruk: 1972, pp 132-133).

In our opinion such merit by performance is not exclusively based on professional-objective criteria, as Kruk's observations suggest. Good professional performance must

a) be traced back to the respective individual. However in a highly labour-divided organization like that of a company, individual performance is often only presented as part of collective performance; to go on further we may say that individual performance is only possible at all within a team so that there are problems of assessing an individual's performance;

b) attract the attention of those who decide about promotion in top management. There are quite different things which play a role as objective criteria for performance, as for example the ability of those interested in promotion to present themselves. The very interesting study by K.Underwood shows that it is precisely the situation of top managers which is characterized by much dramaturgy. The top executive

> is quite aware that he is involved in an often elaborate and subtle performance in the conduct of business. Much of his time and energy goes into the dramatic composition and theatrical representation of his position on problems of the company, and his office is in great part to be understood as a setting for his performance, his colleagues themselves cued almost by habit and instinct to keep the show going (Underwood: 1964, pp 197-198).

Furthermore certain political-tactical motives play a role in the promotion into top management. Internal company considerations receive additional emphasis for promotions: For example the strength of a certain main department where the candidate comes from or tactical manoeuvring of different working constellations by the preference/discrimination of certain representatives of these constellations or simply personal sympathy/antipathy.

As we have already emphasized, the bureaucratic career patterns of top managers do not say anything about their quality. We know of course that in public there is an indifferentiated refusal and dismissal of 'bureaucracy'. This dull prejudice of politics and public administration and the 'grey average' of the civil service, especially in Germany cannot be reconciled with certain conceptions of an economic elite at the top of companies. This is a thought which has already been made by Max Weber and in particular by Josef Schumpeter: "Rationalized and bureaucraticized office work will drive out the personality, the calculable result the 'vision' in the end. The manager will become more and more an office worker who will not be difficult to replace" (Schumpeter: 1980, p 216).

But for us the career of an industrial bureaucrat has in no way a negative taste. With the growing sizes of companies and the differentiation of the managerial function this manager type is unavoidable and with regard to the economic success of companies can in no way be evaluated as being better or worse than other professional careers of industrial company managers[21].

At least in large companies industrial company management is organized in the necessary way for the company and always in a bureaucratic way. The majority of top managers we interviewed agreed with this and the tendency is similar in Germany as well as in England. In reply to our question as to whether a company manager can still be an innovator or is more an administrator (as was already mentioned by Schumpeter) the answers were:

–   the company manager has a plentitude of administrative tasks but innovation is very important nevertheless and is possible in some fields: B: 37%, G: 48%;
–   innovation is still the primary task of company management: B: 31%, G: 39%;
–   The company manager is primarily an administrator: B: 32%, G: 13%.

Apart from the factors which we have already mentioned, there are also other things like luck and chance which play a considerable role in the progress of a career. Our interview partners often reported that they had only moved up one crucial step in the hierarchy because their boss had been suddenly promoted or had left. Since a successor for this vacant position could not be found so quickly they had filled the gap and had only confirmed their somewhat fortunate leap ahead by respective performance at a later stage.

After the 'industrial bureaucrats' let us look at the 'movers' amongst the trained managers: In Germany and England the movers present the second most frequent pattern of career. With regard to the numbers of academics and practicians similar to the industrial bureaucrats, there is here also an essential difference between the two countries: Whilst in our English sample there are no academics amongst the movers, in Germany there are 4 practicians and 36 academics.

---

21   One glance at Japan makes it clear that there the industrial bureaucrat dominates much more strongly than in Western Europe, cf. *Der Spiegel* 46, 1989, pp 172-173.

Here are some distinctive examples to illustrate this career pattern:

"A" levels – study of business administration – entry into an international large company in the field of marketing/sales management – here 2 promotions, parallel to this obtaining of a doctorate – change as sales director to a company in the food industry – managing director of another company in the food industry, after 1 year here chairman of the board – chairman of the board in a significant manufacturer of office supplies – member of the board of directors at an international food and luxury food concern (G7).

The professional career of this German manager is enlightening in many respects: So far the career path has led him to 5 companies and if we think that the man concerned is in the age group 40-49 years, we may see that his career is not completely finished yet. In this respect he may be classed as a 'job-hopper'. He is a model example of a strategically progressing career planner, who are in the minority in Germany (but also in England). His company moves have been organized consciously and systematically whether it be in order to perfect himself professionally in functions considered to be essential or in order to prove his worth in a new position and so to be prepared and recommend himself for further promotion. Correspondingly the time of advancement of this manager is considerably shorter than that of the industrial bureaucrat: He needed only 15 years from the start of his professional career to his position as chairman of the board at a large limited company.

The career pattern of a British mover is presented as follows:

Left school at the earliest possible point in time (at the age of 17) – apprenticeship as a professional footballer at a famous English club; this apprenticeship proved to be lacking in professional chances and so soon left it – took on a job in industry and at the same time attended a college and night school for 5 years (works studies) – qualified as textile engineer – apart from working attended courses at the Institute of Works Management in the field of management (3 years) – later worked in different textile factories in factory management – later for a shorter time director of a small textile factory – has been executive director at a famous English textile factory for 5 years (B14).

Here the determination of the career becomes clear; in addition to this it is clear that in comparison to the industrial bureaucrat the length of time between starting the profession (for German circumstances it is most unusual to think of a football apprentice) and his present position as top executive is much shorter; the difference between the academic in Germany (from the very beginning of the career) and the practician (with later academic education) in England is obvious here too.

On the whole and this applies to both countries to the same extent these two managers represent the prototype of the mover, possibly of the public widespread picture of the top manager. But our examples are in this clear form even amongst those movers that we classified more the exception than the rule, but they represent the structural features of this pattern in a particularly distinct way.

We assume that in the case of the movers their chances of moving up are better than those of the industrial bureaucrats because they can be determined more strongly by individual career planning. In comparison, the career planning of industrial bureaucrats always orientates itself by the framework of internal company procedures of recruitment and position filling where limits for an individual's promotion may be set.

Although the career path of the mover is considerably shorter than that of the industrial bureaucrat there is no direct connection with 'manager quality'. The mover, although he corresponds with the picture of the active individual constitutive for bourgeois society, is not naturally a better manager than the industrial bureaucrat. The same can be concluded of the industrial bureaucrat with his greater knowledge of the company and the 'smell of the stable'.

Planned or unplanned careers – a conclusion: One conclusion of our considerations regarding the professional careers of English and German top managers is that the professional path of members of top management in industry can fundamentally neither be viewed as a fixed career nor as free creation of an individual. It presents itself rather as a contradictory unit of the accumulation of knowledge and ability and of the gaining of functions and positions. As a rule in Germany scientific training and a practical apprenticeship form a part of the basis but in Great Britain it is more company practice and the additional formal qualifications which are gained during work (e.g. through institutions such as the "Open University"). Certain processes of learning form a basis in both countries. These processes were either put upon the individual or he undertook them himself (e.g. a change of company or stays abroad).

Therefore in the self-understanding of top managers there is a developed personality behind the fulfilling of tasks and the managerial position. This personality has at his disposal in principle an economically strong concept of solving different problems and resources to overcome different obstacles in the company and in his environment.

In Germany it is essentially unimportant where one has studied whilst in Great Britain the social selection function of Oxbridge has continued to function in the last decade in spite of many changes. However it is the case for England that the range of this rather feudal academic selection process is limited by the fact that relatively few top managers have academic training anyway. On the other hand this phenomenon is justified by the low social status of industry in comparison with other societies. This means that it is more worthwhile for young academics to go into the free professions, into politics or into the world of finance. On the whole this means that on the one hand in England's industry certain feudalistic criteria for the entry into the manager's profession do not have as much significance as in other professions and branches of the economy but that this is rewarded with an indifference of society that determines the destinies of British industrial companies and therefore also a very important part of the English economy and society.

But let us go back to the other features of the professional and career paths of managers:

It is interesting that the majority of our interview partners had not planned their careers from the very beginning. This stands in stark contrast to the picture of the career of top managers that is widely thought of by the public. We assume that this is connected with the extensive lack of stereotypes as to what managerial work in industry and in the economy really means. Our assumption is even intensified by the fact that in answer to our question about which advice managers could give young people who wish to move into similar top positions, the comments were either very general or widespread and even contradictory within themselves. The examination of a company consultant in Germany appears to confirm our results: According to this examination 80% of 117 interviewed managers in industry, trade and the services had begun their career without any career planning (Mülder and Partner: 1982). Cox, Cooper confirm this trend for England with their examinations of top management: "While most of the sample were ambitious men, they did not admit to an early desire to become a managing director or claim to have mapped out, in any detail, their future career paths. Success was more a matter of attending to the job in hand and doing it well" (Cox, Cooper: 1988, p 33).

Indeed as a result of our own examinations we could differentiate essential typical career patterns of top managers; but these appear as such neither in the consciousness of the managers themselves nor do they provide a formalizable model for a general binding career path for industrial company managers.

In general, managers' careers proceed with breaks and depend essentially on

– the selection processes of the companies, e.g. in and with traineeship and further education courses for managers;
– the individual initiatives of managers to reach a certain position;
– the applicants' own qualifications.

The non-planning of their careers which the managers mentioned themselves must be relativized in a certain way. Most of the career paths only appear to be completely unplanned if they are measured according to a strictly systematic search process which functions on the condition of full information. As

Granovetter has already shown, looking for a job and a career are always a part and result of a social process and not necessarily of a rationally fixed and purposeful search strategy: "Job finding behavior is more than a rational economic process, it is heavily embedded in other social processes that closely constrain and determine its course and results" (Granovetter: 1974, p 39)[22].

Thus every career path – in England and in Germany – inevitably shows elements of chance. But if we ignore these we may say that strategic career planners amongst top executives are far more seldom than is believed by the public. On the other hand the extensive lack of a formalized career pattern also means chances for the trainee who must then qualify and indeed can qualify by

- "Leistung" in Germany, a very specific – sometimes mystically used – concept of work which enjoys a high value in this society;
- and by "doing an excellent job" in the United Kingdom. This is linked to more pragmatism and is directed to the place of work.

As we have seen, professional and career paths are not only determined by the more subjective side, by the individual wishes and interests but they occur in organizations whose norms present the objective side of professional and career paths. This creates a field of tension which produces social forces, which will tend either to change the organizational system or to maintain the status quo. As Mansfield (1973, pp 128-129) describes

> In highly stable social systems such as the village communities … the passage of individuals through positions in the social system (is) typically highly predictable and timetabled. … In social systems where positional changes are less regularized and where the impact of other systems is both greater and more immediate, then it is to be expected that the values and abilities of those in particular grades in the system will change over time.

Of course, work organizations like companies belong to the second type. On the one hand they ensure a necessary amount of stability with their bureaucratic regulations but on the other hand – if we follow the model of bureaucracy by Max Weber – they can lead to rigidity. This would mean that any changes for the necessary further development and flexibility of companies would have to come primarily from individuals (here: from the very important group of company managers) and their subjective career interests.

> This would suggest that the conflict inherent in the position of the individual in a work organization may be functional for the organization in that it will cause the system to change and develop as long as the organizational forces are not so strong as to swamp the effects of individual development (Mansfield: 1973, p 129).

---

22   This thought is also strongly emphasized by R. Jackall (1988). He finds out in particular that manager careers are built or broken in a web of relationships, which are primarily personal and whose objective examination is hardly possible.

Therefore the more subjective side of the professional and career paths, that is the top managers' own conceptions of management, understanding their role and their opinion of management rather than Weber's idea of "Beruf", are of considerable significance for the further development of companies.

2.3   Have German managers got a "Beruf" and their English colleagues only a "job"? Regarding the managerial understanding and qualifications of top managers

The work of the managers and its quality is quite essentially determined by the managers' subjectively founded understanding of management and leadership as well as by the managerial qualifications demanded by the company and society.

2.3.1   The managerial understanding of company managers

When asked the question ("What does management control really mean? Are there typical examples?") both our German and English interview partners had a surprise in store for all those outsiders who had believed up till now that management meant taking decisions.

Only 23% (England 19%) of the replies were related to this and thus put the matter of "taking decisions" in third place behind "motivating" (65% in Germany, in England only 22%) and integration (26% in Germany, in England 16%). In fourth place in Germany there followed "communication" (in England only 6%) and "bringing all resources to one aim" with 20% (16% in England).

We may conclude with care for both countries that the kind of management of former times with simple models of procedure (with almost exclusive emphasis on decisions) and which were often not well thought out, has disappeared. Today management is approaching more and more complex and very provisional managerial definitions (like motivating or integration) which are often much more related to reality than the old formal formulas found in text books. Nowadays managers have a conception of a company which must not only function according to technical-economic rationalities but which above all must present a social coherence – even if there are different kinds of emphasis in Britain and Germany.

These are the common features in England and Germany regarding the basic change in management and leadership. However there are considerable differences in how far these basic changes may be realized within the company. Motivating is not as important for the English as for the Germans. Communication – that is a fundamental domain of industrial relations – plays a more subordinate role in England than in Germany. It may be the case here that in spite of the breaking away from old company (trade union) methods which was achieved during the Thatcher era in England, the importance of involving the staff in the company's affairs is not high as it is in Germany[23]. Thus the answer of a personnel manager of a national service company in Britain is only an exception:

> There is also a very heavy emphasis on industrial relations and employee relations (B8, p 9).

Of course in Germany as well as in England there is a certain range of answers.

A member of management of a medium-sized mechanical construction company in Germany links the necessity to take decisions for management with the fact that people are involved:

> But I would also want to differentiate between management and leadership. Basically management means that you have certain aims to achieve. (These aims) must be controllable. We can forget every aim that is not controllable (G18, pp 2-4).

And his "English equivalent of the same opinion", the personnel manager from the car accessories branch says here:

> The main thing that I want from it is regular feedback of information. … Too many decisions have been made in my own life in the stomach and not on the basis of good information (B10, p 12).

However his German colleague adds:

> When we talk about management this does not only mean it is about a thing. It involves guiding employees to make use of their abilities with regard to their aims (G18, pp 3-4).

To summarize this point we may hear the voice of a member of the English building industry:

> I tend to think of management as someone who is actually managing people (B11, p 12).

---

23   See here our observations regarding corporate culture and Human Resource Management in chapter 3.1.

Thus the answers vary between the main poles of the view of what management really is:

– on the one hand it may be seen as an activity which is directed more towards motivating the staff;
– on the other hand it may be seen as an activity which is concerned with formulating future aims for the company and with ensuring that these aims are carried out in the most efficient way possible in the company (focussing on resources).

Of course we must remember here that the style of management depends on whether the company is financially-orientated, production or marketing. A manager from the food and luxury food industry gave his own concrete example:

> We're marketing. There is a lot of new product development. So everything is geared to high volume, low cost. It's a very risky business. It's fiercely competitive. So our major management problem is trying to respond to massive fluctuations in business whether you try to keep a constant labour force but our production dips. In the summer some things dip down (B1, pp 8-9).

This leads our considerations to the situative concepts of management which have been frequently discussed in recent times and which are determined by two essential factors:

– Firstly there is the point which was expressed in the quote above that every branch has its particularity, and to a lesser extent there is the (cultural, geographical etc.) specific nature of the appropriate region;
– secondly there are the technical, economic and above all social components of the inner constitution of the respective company:

> I think that you should not force your management style on your employees but you should take your employees as they are (G88, p 8) – this was the opinion of a member of management from Germany.

In Ireland for example the Amdahl Corporation (manufacturer of high-performance mainframe computers) practice this. In this company managerial success means:

> Promotional opportunities depend on managers' abilities at participating in cross-functional teams, not their ability to build empires within functions. Furthermore the progress management has made in training Amdahl's workforce is such that the company has set the objective of turning the 300 or so workers engaged in manufacturing and testing its computers into 'self-management' teams. ... Self-management is the antithesis of the so-called scientific management with Frederick Taylor and still so widespread in industry today (quoted from *Financial Times*, 12.4.1991, "Management").

The range of the evaluations and answers we received in England and Germany regarding what is understood by management reflects the variety of theoretically based and empirically founded definitions which can be considered to be normative and found in current literature. Therefore we would like to mention these approaches in order to be able to discuss later the common and different features of management styles in English and German industrial management.

A summary made by Neuberger (1985, p 2) will make the range of these approaches quite clear:

> Management is every aim-related, interpersonal source of behavioural influence with the aid of processes of communication (Baumgarten: 1977, p 9).

> … organizational management consists of a reduction of insecurity (Bavelas: 1960, p 492).

> Management is pointing and steering the behaviour of other people in order to achieve a certain aim which includes the use of material means. An essential feature of successful management is its dynamic (Deutsche Bundeswehr: Military regulations 100/200, No. 101).

Management is considered to be

> the influencing of the attitudes and behaviour of individuals as well as the interaction in and between groups with the purpose of achieving common and definite aims. Management as a function is a role which is perceived by different members of the organization on a different scale and to varying degrees (Staehle: 1980a, p 338).

> Management is … the enforcement of leadership on the way to motivation (Stöber, Binding, and Derschika: 1974, p 9).

Peter Drucker puts these very abstract definitions in concrete form by naming the 6 tasks of top management (1974, pp 50-52):

1.   Laying down company aims;
2.   Coping with the big gap between plan and reality;
3.   Taking on the responsibility for the building up and upholding of the human organization;
4.   Cultivating main relationships which only top staff brings about;
5.   Fulfilling 'ceremonial' functions (dinners, public engagements etc.);
6.   Emergency measures for bigger crises.

It is interesting that more modern definitions of management proceed from a conception of management which takes no account of one-sided 'personnel management concepts' and sees company organization and company work

politics, the interaction relations within a company and firm as politically defined points of reference for top management. Thus: the micro level of the company is also viewed as the level on which social orientations and values play a big role.

Hans Ulrich (1981, pp 12-16) refers to the American theory of management in his attempt to systematize this. In the American theory there is a difference made between operative management (task: the organization and steering of the current activities of the company) and strategic management (task: defining the aims and performance potentials of the company). He adds a third level to these two: "normative management" should lay down management philosophy, the attitudes, convictions, evaluations according to which a company should be managed.

On the one hand this approach opens the view to individual, quite different processes of socialization of the managers which for their part produce certain pictures of management. On the other hand the fading out of social norms and institutions (e.g. property, market and contract relations) as main sources of motivation and influence means that there is

a theoretically and empirically unavoidable omission.

Neuberger picks this point up and defines management as social action which is defined by

–   ideological (here: personalizing);
–   political (here: social-dynamic); and
–   structural (here: anonymous-structural)

dimensions which complement each other (Neuberger: 1985, pp 4-6). Neuberger continues that management is not only social action but it also demands action of a personnel and technically-objective nature.

Such an understanding of management as social action goes back to Max Weber who differentiates between authority and the legitimacy of authority. According to this we must systematically differentiate between the sources of authority on the one hand and its legitimacy on the other hand. In his typification of legitimate authority Weber unites both concepts of authority and legitimacy. There are three kinds of authority – legal-rational, traditional and charismatic:

> In the case of legal authority, obedience is owed to the legally established impersonal order. It extends to the persons exercising the authority of office under it only by virtue of the formal legality of their commands and only within the scope of authority of the office. In the case of traditional authority, obedience is owed to the person of the chief who occupies the traditionally sanctioned position of authority and who is (within its sphere) bound by tradition. But here the obligation

of obedience is not based on the impersonal order, but is a matter of personal loyalty within the area of accustomed obligations. In the case of charismatic authority, it is the charismatically qualified leader as such who is obeyed by virtue of personal trust in him and his revelation, his heroism or his exemplary qualities so far as they fall within the scope of the individual's belief in charisma (M. Weber, "The theory of social and economic organisation", in Pugh: 1990, pp 3-4).

If we bring to mind the answers of our English and German managers when asked for the definition of management it is quite striking that – remaining in Weberian categories – the impersonal authority which is legitimized by institutions is presupposed by our managers. Managerial definitions and qualifications which arise from traditional and charismatic authority are more important for top managers. Thus it is not the official or positional authority which plays a role in the understanding of management for managers because this is presupposed. But it is the charismatic/personal authority, based on personal qualities and qualifications which is more important. There is also management resulting from professional qualifications and competence but this does not play a crucial role for top management level.

But this means that the social institutions which form the base of official authority (property, market and contract relations) no longer appear to be in need of legitimization. This is the general view and it is not necessary to have a public discussion about this.

To summarize we may say that the legitimacy of company action as a result of legal authority has become a matter of course. This is not only because it corresponds to the subjective opinion of the managers but above all because in its significance for top management, capital property in industrial companies has been considerably deemotionalized if not relativized by the development of a no longer property concentrated 'professional' and 'scientific' kind of management. Within this there lies hidden a kind of generalization of the management situation.

That is enough of the short mention of the theory whose practical-empirical arrangement is supplemented, covered up and corrected by cultural and other norms as they have arisen historically in Germany and England. In her splendid presentation of individual empirical examinations of German and English management style[24] Christel Lane (1989, pp 96-104) takes the criteria "Employee vs. Job-centred style" as the first point of departure of her presentation. She quotes the examination carried out by Budde et al. (1982) in the late 1970s regarding the aims of German and British top managers. These

---

24 Smith and Peterson (1988) give a more exemplary view of leadership in its cultural and organizational context (leadership as the management of conflicting demands, as situated action, as the management of meaning, as negotiation etc.).

authors hypothesize and display greater concern for the well-being of subordinates and their personal development than German ones, whereas the latter make greater use of procedures to minimize control loss than do their British emphasis to task-related sources of satisfaction. Cox, Cooper maintain in their examination regarding the British "High Flyers" that "the motivation of successful managing directors springs from their being ambitious and determined people with a reasonably high need of achievement, who find managing a major company an interesting, enjoyable and worthwhile activity. ... Their pleasure (is) in developing the business and its products" (Cox, Cooper: 1988, p 68).

Thus this is a somewhat different opinion of the popular picture of the difference between German and English managers. If we take into consideration the background of other observations – for example of the developed system of works councils in Germany and its acceptance by German top managers – we find that the firmly established views of managerial styles (the staff-orientated style of English managers and the German managers' activities regarding the development of a product) begin to falter.

Lane criticizes in particular the thesis of Budde et al., "these authors can be said to perpetuate rather uncritically the popular stereotypes 'British management is good at handling people' and 'German management is authoritarian', ignoring any evidence which might contradict these claims, such as the relatively poor British record in handling industrial relations" (Lane: 1989, p 98). According to Lane the more fundamental opinion which can often be heard that German standards of performance can only be reached at the price of authoritarianism whereas the relatively poor British performance may be the price paying for democratic management is wrong insofar as "the production-orientated German style has an inbuilt integrating focus which provides a common basis for relationships and encourages cooperative attitudes" (Lane: 1989, p 103).

It is possible that such attitudes stem from the information that in comparison to English companies German firms have a greater degree of centralization regarding operational decision (see here the examination of Child, Kieser: 1975, p 19) and therefore it appears quite natural to equate such centralization with certain (authoritarian) managerial styles.

Lane suggests that both criteria (production-centred style and concern for employees welfare) should not be used as solely contradictory but as complementing standards of judgement. Lawrence (1980 and 1984) proceeds in the same way and one result of his Anglo-German comparison is that in comparison to Britain there is much emphasis put on production in Germany but that this cannot be put on a level with authoritarianism.

As we have already mentioned Lawrence sees such a product relatedness of German management as being justified by education and training on all levels of the company. A strong task-orientation generates a sense of common purpose and of shared responsibility for production. It thus evokes a deep loyalty to the firm.

However, in our opinion it remains open as to whether general changes of social norms – e.g. individualization – undermine such loyalties and respectively such styles of management.

Bessant, Grunt (1985) come to a similar result but they have different reasons for this in their Anglo-German comparative study regarding the role of Technik in industrial management. They proceed from the view that it is the individual company manager within his sector and on the strength of the position of his company who shapes the organization rather than the different cultural-social patterns. Indeed

> in West Germany Technik is part ... of the national culture and this may explain why the general context in which German managers operate is more suited to innovation. But Technik-like approaches can be developed in the UK – as our firms have shown; it is essentially the product of management activity which places getting the job done above other considerations (Bessant, Grunt: 1985, p 329).

But such a product-orientation of German top managers does not rule out the occupation with social questions of staff including the development of company work politics. Thus the corporate identity in German companies is not only related to "the product or the range of products, but at the same time it is also related to a somewhat diffuse description of the company as a family" (Bessant, Grunt: 1985, p 322). The partly different orientations of German and British managers are expressed in the respective professional and career paths we have already discussed. This is also the case for the respective opinions which will be discussed in another later chapter whether top managers see themselves more as generalists (according to popular belief this is what the English do) or as specialists in certain fields (German variant of top management?).

The position of industry in both societies plays an essential role in explaining the different professional opinions of English and German managers. This refers also to industry's public reputation and the objective demands for action on top managers which arise from this: as we will explain later, British managers are much more obliged than their German counterparts to maximize short-term profits than to make their company competitive (also internationally) on a long term basis. Together with the stronger Technik orientation of German top managers this produces significant – subjective – differences in behaviour which are intensified by the philosophy of filling managerial positions: Whilst in Germany top management positions ("Vorstand") are mainly filled on the basis of Leistung

> British boardrooms are, in contrast, ... still populated by a significant proportion of members of a social elite who owe their positions to the social skills they are believed to possess and the status they lend. Their ideas of leadership, acquired in the elite schools, have not only had a significant impact on management-employee relations, they have also influenced the priorities adopted in the larger British enterprises (Lane: 1989, p 101).

However in the smaller English companies where a more shop-floor mentality prevails as a result of the history of their origin, the management style corresponds more to German patterns – if on a lower professional level and characterized by "learning by doing" (Bessant, Grunt: 1985).

We may point to a common feature of British and German managerial understanding as we have confirmed by our examination, by a quote from an English firm for company consultancy:

> British manufacturing suffers from too many tuners and not enough shakers among managing directors of operating companies within large industrial groups. Shakers are people who are not satisfied merely with tinkering when they believe their organization needs to undergo fundamental change. By contrast, tuners are happy to stick with incremental improvements (quoted from the *Financial Times*, 20.11.1991, p 12).

Thus we may say that independent of different social norms and historical experience there is a perhaps anthropological recognition of human ease and convenience which is enriched by the inflexibility of large (industrial) bureaucracies that through the works of Max Weber stimulate public discussion.

2.3.2   Professional qualifications or personality-related qualities? Specialist or generalist?

In Germany as well as in England we asked about qualifications (professional-formal qualifications or/and personality-related qualities) within the context "management".

Thus we entered into a discussion under the key word "The top manager: generalist or specialist?" which has been going on for a longer period in the Anglo-American sphere but which is just being carried out now in Germany.

1) In Germany two thirds of those we interviewed said that personality-related qualities are more important for company management than formal-professional qualifications:

> It is quite clear that personality-related managerial qualities are dominant. The specific formal qualification is pushed further into the background, the higher you climb. I have a laboratory here and there are specialists in all areas. I know that I can rely on them (G103, p 5).

This comment was made by a leading manager in an automobile company. Indeed it could even be harmful if too much special knowledge would hinder the "knowledge and way of thinking of the system" which is necessary for management.

2) An English owner-manager supplements this view by saying:

> The top executive must select the right people to do the real work (B2, p 13).

In England we have a similar tendency to Germany (the majority of our respondents agree with the principle of the general manager) but with a clearly lower percentage (50%). Nevertheless 14% of managers we asked in the United Kingdom think that formal-professional qualifications are more important – in comparison to 9% in Germany.

At first glance these differences are astounding: England is widely seen as the country of the generalists, and in Germany it is supposedly the specialists – especially those with a technical background – who feel particularly at home. Without examining this common opinion in any more detail at this point, this reversal of opinions – as we found out from the answers of the managers – presents a kind of psychological projection and is highly interesting at the same time regarding future evaluations: German managers want to get rid of their repuation internationally that they are only interested in the products and neglect real management – they wish so much to be seen as general managers. And in England the discussion about the system of vocational and professional education has led to the tendency, as a result of pointing the finger at Germany, to pay more attention to special professional qualifications.

In spite of these more psychologically explainable differences there remains the fact that personality-related qualifications in both countries are seen by top managers to be the most important requirement for a top manager to fulfil his tasks.

This thesis has had validity for the Anglo-American sphere for a long time: Approximately 55 years ago the American Ch. Barnard (1938) assessed the value of formal training for management action as being lower than other qualifications; about 20 years later Burns, Stalker (1961, p 211) confirmed that personal qualities for the general manager are the most important; and today this conviction is more than ever the keynote at Business Schools and other educational institutions. This opinion is supported by the more recent examination by Cox, Cooper (1988, p 124): "British managing directors perceive themselves as person oriented, in the sense that they see themselves achieving results through their leadership of people". For the Manchester Business School, as one of the most well-known on the island, the need "for general management with a wide portfolio of skills" is an essential consequence of the growing significance of information technology whereby Prof. Canon from the Manchester Business School emphasizes the change in significance of personality-related qualities: "One of the most quoted definitions of management is 'getting things done through people'. I think in future that this will change to 'getting things done with people'" (*Financial Times*, 9.4.1991). This collaboration between staff and top management can occur at two levels:

a) At the personal level: The personnel manager of a large company from the food and luxury food industry gives us an example here:

> It is the way you can project yourself, the way that you can direct others, the way that you can organize and the way you can motivate and even the way you can enthuse and give people the enthusiasm for the job that they are doing. You must also give them some pride in achieving the end result (B3, p 14).

So it is being proud to be a producer, with the emphasis on "Beruflichkeit" of the direct producers;

b) At the level of industrial relations: As we read from an examination by Marginson et al. in British companies, "industrial relations appear to be of importance in the process of strategic decision-making for decisions with employment implications in many, but not all, large organizations" (Marginson et al.: 1988, p 235)[25].

But even in Germany about 20 years ago 62% of top managers gave the answer to the question about the requirements for securing authority by managers that this authority is the "authority of the persons" (this can be equated with our concept of personality-related qualifications) (Pross, Boetticher: 1971, p 85).

The question arises here as to which type of personality-related managerial qualities are meant here. One first abstract approximation can be that there is an extensive concept of professional authority, coupled with the specific managerial understanding of performance which can be understood. However many circumstances of their own professional situation have remained unclear to the managers themselves and this is documented in the examination by Clements (1958, p 159) which was carried out in the 1950s. But this phenomenon cannot only be seen as the consequence of lacking reflection of

---

25 We will give more details of the opinions of top managers on industrial relations a little later.

company managers but is justified by the matter itself – the complexity of the managerial and performance situation.

In ranking order of those answers given, our interview partners mentioned the following personal qualities:

the ability to motivate, the ability to communicate, the ability to integrate. In England and in Germany almost the identical percentage, in total about two thirds, decided on these "soft" cognitively immeasurable and untouchable criteria. Much further behind were the ability to analyse, flexibility, charisma, ability to assert oneself as well as imagination/creativity. The older examination by Wald, Doty lists the following as essential personality related qualities "the ability to get along with people, social poise, consideration of others, and tact in personal dealings" (1954, p 50). In Copeman's comparative examination of management methods in the USA, Great Britain and Germany 44% of those interviewed explained that the most important ability of top managers is the talent to treat and motivate people in the right way. After this point analytic and creative abilities were mentioned with 27% and personal drive, strength and vitality with 13%. Knowledge of the business came in with 9% (Copeman: 1972, p 332)[26]. How do professional-formal qualifications relate to the personality-related qualities asked for on all sides? Fürstenberg spoke of a double-tracked manager role, about the discrepancy between the awareness of promotion and the reality of promotion with regard to criteria of selection (Fürstenberg: 1969, pp 142-144). At the beginning of the professional and organization related career it was the professional qualifications above all that could be assessed in the formalized system of appraisal and it was these that were crucial for the career:

> The formal qualification is one thing. It is a passport. Once you have got, it it is your personality that actually determines how you succeed or you don't (quoted from the factory director from the English food and luxury food industry) (B13, p 8).

Now, when you are "at the top" the tasks have indeed changed but the very strong emphasis of personality-related qualities as the real important qualifications can be an expression of the delimitation of top managers "downwards" that is to say in the face of their younger colleagues at a lower hierarchical level. Younger colleagues often have better, more modern formal-professional qualifications; thus top managers could escape from pressure of competition from below with reference to immeasurable personal qualities rather than those

---

26 We will do without a further presentation of empirical results focused on the Anglo-American sphere and will do without a theoretical literary discussion about personality-related qualities. In this connection we will point to the essay by Johnson (1990).

which are crucial for manager work. On the other hand lacking or insuffi-
ciently trained personality-related qualifications for a top manager cannot be
hidden in the long run, as a Brtish manager reports as a result of his rich
experience:

> If you haven't got the personal qualities then I think formal education can help to
> prevent you making some bad mistakes but I don't think it will ever make you a
> good manager (B11, p 13).

Arising from the fact that the company is not only a technical-economic, but
also a social coherence (whereby this fact was perceived by German managers
at a later date than English managers – although the consequences of this in
the Anglo-American sphere were perhaps not the right ones) there are on the
one hand considerable implications for the managerial occupation, qualification and subjective work through top executives. On the other hand these are
clear in a rough outline but have not (yet) been adopted to a sufficient degree
on the political-practical level of action and concrete understanding. This
unclarity, but also the range of perceptions can be seen for example in the
information given by German and English managers. Some of the answers
emphasize more intensively the economic-organizational field of top managers
(companies must be led to success etc.), others refer more to the "social
coherence of the company" and to the modes of the behaviour arising from this
(individual reactions must be calculable for others; managers must influence
the behaviour of the staff by their politics, managers must show an optimism – even as far as personal and physical charisma – which can influence
others).

One member of the managing board of a German energy supply company gave
a summarizing and precise answer in this respect;

> I think there are three fields: professional knowledge is of course necessary. ...
> The second is, that he must have the ability to recognize the development
> tendencies of his industry and society ..., also to have visions. ... The third is, ...
> that he must have the human ability to convince his employees, the staff, carefully
> of the right way and not only to give orders from above (G22, p 3).

And a personnel manager from the Automobile supply industry summarizes
this tendency in a typically English objective way:

> I see people ... who are extremely high qualified but don't know how to use it, it is
> a waste. I believe you really and truly need a mixture of the two (B10, p 13).

For this kind of mixture between the formal-professional qualifications and
personality-related qualities as essential requirements for the occupation of an
industrial top manager the concept of the "adaptive manager" by Ronnie
Lessem seems to be particularly appropriate:

While analytical managers are specialists in financial marketing, operations or personnel management, adaptive managers are not generalists in the normal sense of the word. They are adapters. They are either able to switch transactions vertically within a function or, if they attain managerial mastery, able to switch horizontally between functions. In summary, compared with their analytical counterparts, what adaptive managers lose in depth, they gain in height and breadth (Lessem: 1990, pp 176-177).

Our own examinations in Germany and England show that there are no fundamental differences regarding the views of top managers about the essential requirements to fulfil the tasks. As we have already mentioned, there are of course differences in both countries regarding education and the objective job description. In Continental Europe the universities are educating practice-oriented (and industry-oriented) the necessary engineers and (since 1945 ever increasing numbers of) economists for marketing, sales and finance. In contrast top managers in Great Britain are educated as generalists with little professional knowledge and who work together with specialists (Fores, Glover: 1979). This is one reason why we agree fundamentally with the statement by Lawrence (1980) that German managers are much more product-related and technology-oriented than the English or American for example. It is precisely this orientation towards the product or technology that is described in a more recent English study as "technology narrow-mindedness". In comparison to English, US-American, Japanese and French circumstances the question may be asked as to whether the successful German managers of the last decades have not become "victims of their own success". The authors demand the breakdown of the technical dominance and ask for the education of trainees as "general managers with an international background" (Handy et al.: 1988, pp 125-162). It seems to us that a false understanding of the orientation towards technology and product lies at the bottom of these statements. Because precisely in our examination the orientation of the German managers towards technology and their identification with the product and company prove to be assets in export and in competition with foreign companies. Engineers as top managers think especially in a commercial and not only in a technical way (see chapter 3.2 for more details). Besides the British principle of generalists has to fight with other difficulties than only with German specialism if we follow the rough classifications which we do not consider to be adequate here as a result of our examinations. In the British generalist system there are difficulties especially when specialists should take over a general task (Sorge: 1978, pp 102-103).

We can say from literature and from our own results that the great range of views about manager qualification and the unclarity of the expressions and regulations are common to top managers in both countries. For the outsider this could give the impression (perhaps a little hastily) that a German owner stated:

> I have made so many decisions where I have said that they were made intuitively and above all were lucky. ... At the army people preferred to go to the 'lucky officer' and not to the one who could do the most (G66, pp 25-26).

The company manager – a lucky officer?

This can hardly be the case because such a concept in the long run would never stand up to the complexity of demands of the managerial occupation. But it is the complexity of the position and the situation of company managers that brings John Kotter to the conclusion in his empirical examination of the General manager that "at least some of these jobs are constructed in such a way that no talented or experienced manager could fulfil them. And you can imagine a time when the differences between the individual jobs outweigh their similarities" (Kotter: 1982a, p 124). In this respect we may continue that every effort to generalize manager action and qualification which would be of benefit for training would be in vain.

But we do not agree to the thesis of the manager as a lucky officer nor are we willing to interrupt our study at this point because of the hopelessness reach more general statements. For us it is much more important for an objective, demystifying discussion about managerial qualification to consider the point made by a member of management in the German air and space industry that in order for a company to function, the ability of a top manager is a prerequisite to develop a specific understanding of his role and profession (G105, p 5) and thus to determine the requirements of qualification.

2.3.3   Management as a "Beruf"?

We were curious whether top managers have an exact conception of their own "Berufsstand" as a social group with their own identity. Here we proceed from the consideration that the relationship that a manager has to his work like any other worker at a given moment and at a certain level of his professional and social development is surely very complex and dependent on many factors. On the one hand it is social destiny and on the other hand the result of his own activity that the respective work really represents for him. There are long-term attitudes developed to do the work as well as relatively short-term and changing assessments of work. Some things about the work may seem quite self-evident for him and other things are at the foreground of his work awareness because the complex of concepts that are brought to the work in social connections, draws attention to it. However we may assume that every experienced worker has a sufficient concept or theory of his own work.

With our question about the professional self-understanding of top managers we presupposed a cultural-historical significance of the concept "Beruf" which primarily proceeds from the considerations of Max Weber (1972, 1979) and which is deeply embodied in this form especially in Germany. There is for example no adequate translation of the word "Beruf" in English – neither profession nor vocation nor occupation will suffice. For this reason there have been some contradictions between German and English research results regarding this complex theme which we would like to look at here in more detail.

Although the concept of "Beruf" has been used in Germany partly in a mystic sense and has been strongly criticized for this in recent times, we agree with Brater's thesis that the concept "'Beruf' ... in its everyday version points to social structures and units in the field of social work which can neither be adequtely portrayed in its dimension nor in its system or characteristic processes of constitution of scientific concepts – especially qualification or occupation" (Brater:1983, p 43). Instead of the usual (and in Germany even official) definintion of "Berufe" as a bundle of occupations Brater suggests one definition of "Beruf" according to which "Berufe" are seen as

> socially normed and institutionalized combinations and limitations of the abilities of people to work for business purposes; as institutionalized structures these 'Berufe' appear to be predetermined stereotypes of individuals according to which their working capacity is bundled together, specialized, defined and handed down from one generation to the next; the concept 'Beruf' refers to the fact that productive skills and occupations of people are fixed in our society, specialized and are put into categories of workers (Brater: 1983, p 59).

We would like to go one step further and try to make a conceptual connection between occupation – "Beruf" – profession which, we hope, will allow us to make an adequate interpretaion of the empirical material as well as a bridge between the German concept "Beruf" and the process of the professionalization of management which is often described as such in England. Here we follow the thought of Hartmann who describes a process of development which includes work (occupation) and "Beruf" up to profession as the highest stadium (Hartmann: 1972, pp 38-39). On the other hand "Verberuflichung" and professionalization mark the steps of development from work to "Beruf" and finally to profession (Hartmann: 1972, p 40):

"Verberuflichung" describes the process of the transition from work tasks (individual occupations) to "Beruf", whilst "professionalization means the change from a somewhat marked to a very strong systematic structure of knowledge and the spread of social orientation from a moderate degree to an exclusive orientation of collectivity" (Hartmann: 1972, pp 40-41).

Concrete fixed points		
1. Work	2. "Beruf"	3. Profession
	"Verberuflichung"	Professionalization

We have already spoken about the specifically German tradition of the "Beruf"; there is also a tradition of the concepts in Anglo-American countries:

– "Profession": often used as a professional description for free professions as for example: doctors, lawyers etc. – we must include all legal professions here;
– "Professionalism": the process of acquistion of certain skills is described here which emphasizes a "professional" in contrast to an "amateur".

It is precisely this process of professionalism that is often discussed in the Anglo-American sphere in connection with management.

> Professionalism, as it has developed in Britain and the United States, is character-
> ized by an isolation of separable tasks and jobs to be claimed as the specialists
> domain of members of each profession. ... Specialists in industry, especially if
> they belong to the 'staff' rather than to the 'line', are likely to understand a
> professional approach to doing their jobs in term of instituing what are accepted as
> good procedures within their occupation. For the personnel manager this may
> include records and procedures for manpower planning, selection and training
> (Child et al.: 1983, p 66).

Proceeding from the Anglo-American understanding of professionalism, Child et al. as representatives of this historical-cultural determined concept, describe the difference between England and Germany – and in a similar way to us and by quoting Weber, Brater etc. they interpreted the difference from the German understanding and said:

> There is no distinct word for 'profession' in German. It is usually rendered by the
> word 'Beruf'; but 'Beruf' is also the standard word for occupation or employment
> of the kind where some preparatory off-the-job education or training is required. It
> is reasonable to argue that a society which has not bothered to label a phenomenon
> probably does not attach much importance to it. ... The word 'Beruf' has
> secondary connotations of 'good respectable' jobs, in the primary sense of
> profession in the English language. However the interesting thing from a British
> standpoint is that the 'good' jobs are not necessarily professional jobs in the British
> sense. In terms of this secondary connotation of the word 'Beruf' the design
> engineer is a good candidate for inclusion as the doctor, the sales manager as the
> clergyman (Child et al.: 1983, p 67).

Child now makes an historical excursion and says that in the England before 1918 industrial management was perceived indeed as a "distinct profession" and had been discussed in literature correspondingly (Child: 1969, pp 51-53); in the 1920s the discussion about professionalism was conducted at a much more intensive level (Child: 1969, pp 72-75). In the 1950s Lewis, Stewart judge the process of professionalism of management in England, compared with that in the USA, (see Newcomer: 1955, pp 151-153) with much more scepticism: "In America, management is accepted as a profession; the business schools have laid enormous stress on this. In Britain, there is much more scepticism about either the possibility or the desirability of making management a profession" (Lewis, Stewart: 1961, p 66). These authors also link the process of professionalism of top management with the fact whether good management can really be learnt by experience on the job (this would support the amateur thesis) or whether it can be learnt systematically – starting with business schools and going up to a systematized form of further education. John Child leads on from this and describes a debate that was carried out in England in the 1950s (Child: 1969, p 139): At this time there appeared in England a monography with the title *Is Management a Profession?*. The author L. Urwick was

> concerned to promote the idea of professionalism for different and more technically-oriented reasons. In Urwick's eyes, professionalism was no longer valuable so much for providing an ethical basis on which to secure social legitimation, but rather as a means of stressing the technical importance of the existing body of management principles and techniques which he felt must be taught to managers and management trainees. He bitterly attacked those business men whose argument, that successful management could only derive from 'learning by experience', cast doubt upon the value of management studies. For Urwick, professionalism now meant primarily that management should turn its back on this 'amateur' approach, which he thought in many cases merely represented social prejudice against trained managers on the part of company directors, and devote far more attention to systematic study (Child: 1969, p 139).

John Child points to the deeper core of this debate described by Urwick: "It is at this point that Urwick touched upon one of the principal debates which persisted throughout the development of British management thought – the extent to which good management depended upon art or science, upon experience and personal flair or upon systematic training and careful investigation" (Child: 1969, p 139). Child touches on two complexes here and both play a significant role in our examination:

1. The very topical question about which types of qualification a good top manager should have. This question is asked to the same extent today in England as well as in Germany, even if with different points of emphasis;

2. To what extent does the so drastically described picture (that is typical[?] for English society and was described by Wiener: 1981) of the amateurish

relationship to industrial society touch the self-understanding of industrial managers?

The personnel manager of a company from the automobile industry gave a very clear opinion regarding the last point:

> I think the professional is not recognized in British society as much as the social structure placement of a person. ... Professionalism whilst it exists in Britain is not looked upon the same way as it is in Germany. ... People still get jobs in this country on the basis of their social status against their professional qualification. There are people moving into extremely important jobs, on boards, who are generally incapable of doing it from a professional point of view (B10, p 14).

And the company director of a luxury food factory made this even clearer with reference to the popular self-understanding of a "profession" in British society:

> I think it is very much more conservative in this country in that a profession is considered a lawyer, a chartered accountant, a teacher, a university lecturer. Those are conceived as professions. I actually would believe that the pursuit of management is actually a profession, depending on one's definition of the word – but British society wouldn't (B13, p 8).

We tried to to find out about these concepts in front of a background of those management qualifications we have already mentioned by asking the following question[27]:

"In Germany the concept 'Beruf' (profession) plays an important role, (possibly a more important role than in Great Britain) and is linked to relatively definite conceptions. We can say, for example that a medical doctor or a lawyer or a skilled craftsman has a 'Beruf'. Would you define your managerial function also in the sense of a 'Beruf'/(profession)? If so, what are the 'beruflichen'/(professional) interests of a managing director?".

The answers to this question reflect almost exactly the different conceptual definitions of "Beruf" in German and "profession/professionalism" in the UK which makes it almost impossible to make a typification of the answers to the national-cultural particularities:

About half of the German top managers (exactly: 54%) answered that company management is not a "Beruf" but a function or task and avoided the equation of company management with "Beruf". Furthermore those who said "No" claimed the professional definition of the long-running formal training, although at least at the top level of company management the managers are occupied as generalists and hardly any more as specialists. In England it was only one (of 16) top executives who answered this question similarly.

---

27   The question was put almost exactly to German and English top managers except for the addition of the half sentence in brackets for the English respondents.

The situation is completely the opposite with the tendency in the category: "Yes, company management is a 'Beruf'/profession": Only 36% of the Germans gave us this type of answer whilst it was the overwhelming majority of British managers (13 from 16 answers) who gave this answer.

With reference to the German top managers we were surprised by the fact that only a minority was convinced of the "Beruflichkeit" of the managerial occupation. For previously a majority of company managers had said that personality-related qualities were much more important as managerial qualifi-cations than formal-professional qualifications. Thus the German top managers appeared to have said goodbye to a traditional picture of "Beruf"[28], which was related to a learnt "Beruf" (formal-professional qualifications). They had stated that company management had another picture of "Beruf" at its foundation (hinted at by the dominance of personality-related qualities). Do these results and contradictions amongst the answers of top German managers point to the fact that they do not really have a proper concept of their own position and situation?

One could almost be inclined to agree to this hypothesis if we look at the amazingly high percentage of those who reacted to this question in bewilder-ment (10%). Our interview partners were scarcely more unprepared for any other of our themes than this one – this was in complete contrast to their English colleagues who answered this question with a matter of course.

We would not go quite as far with our own doubts about the concept of "Beruf" of (German) top managers. For the answers confirm the working hypothesis formulated at the beginning of the examination that the transition from intuitive managerial action to professional behaviour of the entrepreneur who is no longer an owner but an employed manager (in Marx's sense) is indeed unmistakable. But precisely at this level of professional qualifications relatively independent, personality-related qualities (like the ability to assert one's authority or the power of deduction) are still decisive for the move into or stay in such positions. But if, in spite of all the different cultural and social traditions, we make a comparison between German and English top managers with the inclusion of the dynamic course by Hartmann (from the "Verberuf-lichung" to professionalism) we may even dare to make the thesis under the aspect of the self-consciousness and the subjectively based legitimation of their own position as top managers that the English managers are one step further than the Germans in this respect. Nevertheless this statement must immediately be modified by referring to the different meanings of the concepts "Beruf" and profession which are only the expressions of the different status of

---

28   In the Anglo-American sphere it is precisely this picture of "Beruf" which is seen to
     be more typical than for Germany.

top managers in both countries which are difficult to compare and which are quite special to both societies.

The absence of a certain formalized career pattern of top managers is seen as the expression of a not fully-developed conception of management action.

The findings are also similar for both societies when we talk about the "beruflich"/professional interest of those managers who answered the question of whether company management is a "Beruf"/profession with a yes:

1. One part of those we interviewed defined the interests from the demands of the company, its organization and the self-understanding of management (also partly ideological) which are linked to it;

2. Others derived "Beruf"/profession and "berufliche"/professional interests from their own individual claims and (also political) interests as employees, independent of the respective companies/concrete domains of occupation.

To 1) It is first of all the organization and the hierarchy within the company, which makes quite definite demands on "Beruflichkeit"/professionalism. Two things must be differentiated from each other here:

The bigger a company is, the more it is involved in the (world) market, and the more the unspecific side of the managerial occupation becomes "Beruf"/Profession. And the higher you move up in the company hierarchy the more leadership becomes "Beruf"/profession. It is these special managerial qualifications which are of great significance in order to understand those special workers working under you in their argumentations and actions without the top manager falling into the trap of presenting a sometimes too special and often 'company blind' form of argumentation. This means that a top manager must develop the ability to remove himself from his learnt qualifications and special knowledge which was needed at the lower and middle level without losing sight of the needs and demands of those who work as specialists under him.

The reference of an owner-manager to the definition power of the social function of company management is remarkable. According to his comments the professional interests of a company manager is to be found in

> the way he arranges the company under his management, a company that has a social function on the market and therefore makes profit. Whereby I say these things especially in this order … Primary striving for profit could also lead to the view that you can achieve profit by negative means (G66, p 9).

Is perhaps an intrinsic, that is coming from inside, form of motivation of company management clearly evident? Or are we talking about an analytical differentiation between the "Berufs" worker and the wage-earner which is usual in sociology and which has been systematized by Max Weber. It is a differentiation which assumes that every worker, even the top manager has not only material interests (earning one's living etc.), but also "berufliche"/professional interests regarding the content oriented towards the work.

To 2) One manager from the German synthetic and textile processing industry gives a reason which appears exotic at first glance because in the course of the separation between ownership and control it has disappeared from the social awareness. This manager defines company management for himself as being

> a vocation, which has developed from a learnt process of our family business over the last four decades (G65, p 4).

Indeed this attitude is not surprising when we are thinking about an owner-manager because in the ideal form of family capitalism the problem of succession plays a central role. Succession, care of the children and payment/-compensation for brothers and sisters influence the economic calculation of the company – the children and future company managers are correspondingly socialized. But apart from this very narrow sector of owner-managers, who impress the concept of "Beruf"/profession on their successors according to their situation, there is, as we have already seen above, a view held by company managers of their "Beruf"/profession which is predetermined by the social origin of (employed) company managers. This view is very much oriented towards social norms like "satisfaction through and at work" and towards work content (like e.g. taking on responsibility). A personnel manager from the English food and luxury food industry specified this by linking the social aspect of the greatest possible care (care for the employees) with the aspect of his personal qualification achievement:

> It is a profession in the sense like a doctor because you have to look at a doctor who is highly regarded as being a very professional individual with a wealth of knowledge behind him. The manager in industry is the same sort of animal because he needs to have had that basic education in this profession. He needs to be able to diagnose a problem and he needs to be able to indicate the remedy to that problem. ... You may have to find out what the problem is, before you can even start to address yourself to that problem (B3, p 15).

A German personnel director of a middle-sized company from the "High-Tech" industry gives a similar reason but takes into consideration the ethical viewpoints. His primary "berufliches" interest is in the desire to take on responsibility – a desire, which according to the manager can only be productive if self-doubt may be institutionalized at the side of this desire, as its twin (G82, pp 6-7).

Let us summarize briefly:

On the one hand top managers from both countries state that the previously achieved professional qualifications are no longer dominant for today's company management. On the other hand German top managers are frightened by the thought that in their definition of "Beruf" they will leave the so sure terrain of the learnt profession officially. As a result of such a logical consequence they feel robbed of their roots although in their majority they carry out management work as "Berufs" work. To say it in simpler terms: The majority of German top executives fulfil the occupation of company manager as a "Beruf" but they do not know it, that is to say that the level of self-reflection has not reached this last stadium yet.

But we must admit that the "Beruf"/profession of the company manager is so complex that a fixed professional field and corresponding definition to the extent of a structural steel engineer or a surgeon can never be reached. This is the case for the UK too whilst there the fight of the professionals against the amateurs in company management still reigns.

But on the other hand the partial absence of the managerial picture of "Beruf" in the managers' consciousness with the extensive absence of a specific career pattern also means chances for trainees who must then qualify themselves for the job by their performance.

Finally, in spite of all cultural differences, which are reflected in the subjective understanding of our respondents as well as in the more objective social norm definition, we can state that company management

– is a "Beruf"/profession, with regard to an independently organized field of knowledge as well as in its cultural significance (Drucker: 1974, vol. 2, pp 13-15);
– is subject to a permanent process of professionalization.

2.4   The daily run of work, job satisfaction and the private sphere of the top managers

How are all the demands, criticism and self-understanding and even insecurity of company managers reflected in their actual work, and what does the relationship of working time to free time and family really look like, how are the pressures of work and job satisfaction experienced? All these questions have been discussed for many years but with the aim of filtering out 'recipes' for successful management. In spite of numerous works on this theme the work of Herry Mintzberg 20 years ago still applies today. At the end of his examination *The Nature of Managerial Work* (1973) he asked with a somewhat ironical tone: "What do managers really do?".

2.4.1   Job satisfaction

Traditionally questions regarding job satisfaction play a big role in sociology. In the analysis of motivation the answers are used as empirical material and are often seen to be indications of the extent the managers identify with and in their work. When differentiated accordingly they are also indications of which conditions of work are felt to be particularly satisfying and which are especially a burden for the managers. Our request of the top managers also had this double function. We asked them to say what was the most stressful in their occupation and which experiences were particularly satisfying.

In the case of the German top managers we experienced a surprise: 13% of those we interviewed considered their occupation not to be stressful at all (in England this was only one from 16). A managing director of a larger German shipyard makes the difference between modern demands and stress:

> In my work I do not know of any strain, in my profession I do not know of any stress. I have stress symptoms when I am sitting in my car, on my way to the airport and I am stuck in a traffic jam, then I feel that I have stress because those are situations that I cannot change myself. But situations in my profession – it is my task to solve them, and therefore I have no stress because I must simply try to solve them as well as I can. And if I work 16 hours then I am tired but I do not call this stress (G112, p 10).

But in contrast to this very optimistic statement, which may be interpreted as repression of strain, there are the results of a questionnaire regarding the life style of European Chief Executives from the largest companies (Cooper: 1990):

– Over 1 in 4 CEOs feel that they are above average risk from heart disease and job burnout – with nearly twice as many of the younger CEOs perceiving this risk than the older CEOs;
– Stress is likely to get worse in the 1990s, because almost half of the CEOs are anticipating shortages among middle and senior management in 1992.

Such contradictions are surely founded in the fact that there are different interpretations of stress.

The columnist and satirist Gabriel Laub quoted results of American medical research over 15 years ago (Laub: 1974):

> Dr. Henry Johnson, director of the medical department of the Life Extension Institute examined 27 000 managers and concluded that there is no illness that is more dangerous for managers than for the average worker. Dr. Lawrence E. Hinkle from Cornel University studied 270 000 male employees from the Telephone Society Bell for 5 years and found more heart disease and more coronary disorders amongst workers, skilled workers and employees than amongst managers. It

became clear that stomach ulcers and nervous complaints amongst managers do not appear more frequently than amongst others.

The result of the article: "Managers are healthier than others".

Laub justifies this three-fold:

– Managers have a good bill of health, otherwise they would not be able to box themselves through to the top; weaker ones do not manage to reach top positions – is Laub showing us signs of Darwin's principle here?
– The feeling of responsibility which often opens out into stress is not dependent on social position; as a personal quality it may cause more stress amongst nurses and pointsmen.
– The intensity of stress does not depend on how expensive its cause was. "A street trader who finds 300 DM loss at the end of a month can be much more frustrated than an industrial boss who has sold off a complete factory; a father who cannot buy his child new shoes buys himself much more stress for the missing twenty Marks than the bank manager for twenty million."

In the edited collection on *Managerial Stress* (Gowler, Legge: 1975) different approaches towards stress research are presented and these make it clear why contradictory results may be observed in questionnaires. The editors themselves prefer an approach which proceeds from connections between the individual, his roles and organizational success criteria. This model emphasizes the importance of the influence of organizational success criteria in that they both define and evaluate roles. Gowler and Legge make the general point that individuals are likely to become anxious if, on the one hand, they feel they must achieve while, on the other, the success criteria which define and evaluate their achievement are either ambiguous or non-existent. Furthermore those individuals in these circumstances find great difficulty in establishing legitimate organizational roles, which may also be a source of stress and frustration. The approach of Gowler and Legge are those criteria like uncertainty and avoidance, of course related to the organization and the roles therein. The whole domain of environment in general as well as the family in particular as significant stress factors are left to one side.

But let us go back to our empirical results: We can divide those under stress into three groups. These are different amongst the German and English managers:

1. Those who see the decision regarding personal measures not only as a consequence of the company but also as a decision affecting personal fates and thus quarrel with these. 22% of the German managers were burdened by personal measures (this was the highest amount of strain amongst the German managers):

A managing director from an internationally trading company said:

> It is relatively easy to make a decision, to make a certain investment and to make an investment in a social plan. But it is terribly difficult to live with the effects of this investment on the individual, ... because it follows you in all situations of life. You can't just shake it off (G68, p 12).

The English answers irritated at the beginning: Not one manager described personal measures as being particularly stressful for himself. But by looking more closely there was a slightly different picture. It became apparent that for English managers pressures as a result of personal measures were felt to be those produced by misunderstandings and/or desired quarrels with the unions. We often heard such opinions as that of a manager from a food and luxury food concern:

> Dealing with people is the heaviest demand too. I feel I am logical in what I do. A lot of my junior management make quite a lot of mistakes which I have to rectify and try and smooth over because we do deal with unions. There are still a lot of views in Britain where the labour force should be treated in a close way, under your thumb. That is not the way life is now and I am forever trying to rectify local management's errors and try to train them in the correct way to deal with them (B14, p 6).

It is precisely these differences in the perceptions of German and English top executives that make clear in an exemplary way the different reference points of the social discussion in the two countries: In Germany the theme of company collective bargaining (here works council, there management) proceeds in an orderly manner (see here the following chapter 4.2) but the role of the individual socially as well as within the framework of collective bargaining is controversial and therefore a burden and becomes a problem for top managers. It is almost the opposite situation in England; in principle the free independent Englishman is unquestioned but in the era of Thatcherism it is the role of the unions and shop stewards that causes controversy. The rules of collective bargaining lie on the special attentiveness of British top executives which in this point is marked by insecurity.

2. A second group complained of a time factor and the restrictiveness of a tight appointment calendar which no longer allows any individual scope (17% in Germany, 2 English respondents).

A general manager of an English textile company stated:

> The job used to make terrific demands on my time in the sense that I worked long hours. I don't now but I did. My daughter as a small child, I only ever saw her awake at weekends. That caused quite some dispute between my wife and myself. It caused a strain. If I went out tonight with someone I worked with and had a drink, within 10 minutes we would talk about this place. So I make a conscious effort not to socialize with the people from work. Every morning I give people lifts to the

factory but I wouldn't see them any other time. I leave home at 6.30 a.m. in the morning. I never have lunch and I work these days until about 4.30 p.m.. I used to work here about 16 or 17 hours a day. As you get older and I am 60 years old but a couple of years ago when we were terribly busy I was getting here at 6.30 and getting home at 10.00 at night. You can't turn off. It wasn't for the money so I made a decision a couple of years ago that I would stop it (B16, pp 8-9).

Is this an expression of bad time management, lacking organization of one's own occupation or simply 'only' a bad conscience towards the family, other private obligations and finally towards oneself?

3. A third group of company managers sees the pressure primarily in their dissatisfaction with people inside and outside the companies (incompetence, a lack of openness, competitive behaviour etc.); a total of 25% in Germany and a very high number in England: 7 from 16 answers. A personnel manager of a German company, that depends very much on State orders, complains about the nearness to politics, whose representatives he fundamentally sees as irrational:

We are strongly politically dependent and are influenced. I can live with that. But the dominance of politics gives me less pleasure because I am strongly economically defined and act according to results. There are many grey areas which are improved or put into question by politics and where this in my opinion would not be necessary. Although on the other hand it would be sometimes quite good to view things from the political side (G82, p 9).

Apart from these external factors of distraction and pressure and stress there are also internal company factors.

–   Those factors related to groups and group interests. An English industrial relations manager of a food and luxury food concern had a surprise for us here. Instead of making the trade union representation of interests responsible for pressure he mentioned the management:

The heaviest demand on me are from management. 99% of the problems for the areas which I am involved in are caused by management. Very few of them are caused by the workforce in general. Each year they submit a wage claim and we spend some time negotiating with it but that's not a problem. That's a function. Most of my problems arise from management, bad management in many respects. Careless, thoughtless, selfish, arrogant. If there's an argument it's lack of communication. It's generally by management. Many of whom are not as good at their job as they should be or they think they are better than they are or they don't understand the situation. They don't understand what the policy is and they go off and they act in an unreasonable independent manner and you lose control of the situation. ... I've often said that if we got rid of the trade unions it wouldn't make any difference to my job at all (B1, pp 10-11).

–   Secondly there are factors on the individual level in the company:

> The biggest demand on my time is caused by people not paying attention to detail (B5, pp 10-11).

Relatively few complained about the pressure of success (in Germany 5%, in England 1 of 16 respondents), lacking organization within the company and of their own work (a total of 8% in Germany, 2 answers in England).

Only 1% of the German managers and not a single English manager felt particularly under pressure by the fact that company managers must take risks – is this an indication that all company managers are innovators in Schumpeter's sense of the word and are not bureaucrats? Like all other comments regarding job satisfaction these assumptions must be seen with the greatest care because it is our experience that precisely in these questions the interviewees answer very subjectively and of course these answers depend on many other factors, like for example their own fears, hopes, disappointments etc.. At this point we would like to briefly look at the results of a non-representative study about the attitudes of British senior executives where the result is: "Top bosses find changes as good as a pest". In 1990 475 top and senior executives in 364 large British organizations, in both the private and public sectors, were asked by the consultancy "People in Business" about managing change. 91% of the sample consisted of directors; the result regarding resistance among senior managers stemmed entirely from the private sector:

> In Britain, resistance to change among senior executives is soaring to such an extent that top managers now claim it is becoming almost as serious a barrier. Not only that, but top managers say that resistance from their own board colleagues, albeit less intense from middle or senior managers, has become a greater problem than opposition from junior managers or even from trade unions. Some organizations are now suffering from a 'siege' mentality among their managers (*Financial Times*, 10.6.1992, p 10).

Without wishing to over-evaluate the answers we may proceed from the fact that the three great moments of stress of top managers are caused by the difficulties with and in the work with the interaction with other people – this may be dismissing or changing the members of staff, difficulties in daily collaboration with other people, difficulties in the private sphere because of long working hours and high work pressure or it may be in working with collective bargaining.

We can in no way agree with the opinion of Hofstetter that the "sufferings of the managers" are primarily to be blamed on their double situation between capital and work (Hofstetter: 1980). Apart from the fact that this examination refers to the perception of managers from skilled workers to main department managers (first hierarchy level is not regarded) there are many other concepts that remain unclear. "Our" top managers however have no difficulties in defining themselves as company managers – even as employed managers.

With his very original thesis of "The end of management" Fletcher makes known another managerial complaint:

> I hold that the current generation of managers cannot survive their employment conditions, that no future generations of managers are being trained, and that the alternatives exercised by managers indicate their knowledge of these facts. ... They have known the contradictions of their jobs. Now they are being exposed. Management is neither art nor science nor skill. At base there is nothing to do. A manager is hired for what he knows other firms do; what he can find to do, and what he can be told to do (Fletcher: 1973, p 136).

Apart from the fact that Fletcher's conclusions refer primarily to middle management, his thesis is neither verified by our results nor can we say that his more theoretical reasons are tenable. But they give us some stimulus so that we can think about the peculiarities of the "professional" picture of management.

On the whole the dominance of those stress factors mentioned by our interviewees could be an indication that the managers see their action in connection with other people, that they have recognized that a base of resonance (from staff, employees, colleagues, society) is necessary for the management of a company. In this way the fairy tale that "great managers" act only from themselves – that "(only) men make history" – could be dismissed for good. But as we have already said there is only an indication of a possible tendency whose empirical relevance could only be proven by a connection with other variables (e.g. the relationship to team work, to the works council etc.).

We are left to ask whether the fact of the unsureness to define management, of the complexity, dynamism and external influences of the managerial situation stand behind these stress factors. At a time when there is a boom of ready-made procedures of action (see the discussion about corporate culture) which are marked by the non-controllability of many social and internal company processes, the myth of the all-powerful, omniscient, but lonely and isolated top manager at the top of the company is particularly oppressive. The many complaints about lacking contacts, communication and discussions free of dominance and competition may be explained as follows[29]:

> It is very difficult to find someone who you can really talk to trustingly. ... It is not a level of friendship that you are moving on in business (G35, p 10).

With this we touch upon the social isolation of the general manager within the managerial group of the company, their life within an "unreal world" (Burns,

---

29   See the examination by Jürgen Mülder and Partner (1982).

Stalker: 1961, p 212). The situation of competition within the managerial group is enormous and objectively stands in a contradiction to the demand of team work within top management. This individual competition is very often suppressed and only appears in confidential self-reflections of their own situation (as we prompted by our interviews).

This great willingness on the part of many top managers to give us information so openly may perhaps be explained by the fact that they see us as neutral, objective scientists who cannot above all endanger or become dangerous for their own position.

But which things are not stressful for the company managers, which experiences do they find most satisfying in their working and professional life (this was our question) and are these factors motivating? Let us first of all quote classical authors, namely Maslow and Herzberg.

The "Maslow Need Hierarchy" contains 5 need categories (Maslow: 1954):

1. Self-actualization;
2. Self-esteem;
3. Love and belongingness;
4. Safety and security;
5. Physiological needs.

The needs higher up in the hierarchy only play a significant role in the individual's behaviour when the needs lower down are met. For example the needs like job security or safe working conditions must be met before the subjective attentiveness of those concerned can be steered towards self-actualization. For top executives this would mean that first of all their own contract conditions including payment, the organizational structure of the company and responsibilities would have to be settled to the satisfaction of all those concerned before any thoughts and conceptions regarding the role definition of top managers could be used as they have been expressed in all the clever essays and thoughts on corporate identity.

Herzberg's "Hygiene-Motivator Theory" (Herzberg, Mausner, Snyderman: 1959) includes the attempt to connect professional roles with needs. Herzberg's "Two-Factor Theory" proceeds from two different factors, which produce satisfaction and stress in the working situation: Factors associated with good feelings about the job (motivators) are mostly derived from the job itself. The second set of factors (hygiene factors) are mostly external to the job and involve aspects of the physical or psychological environment. Herzberg comments that an improvement of the hygiene factors (like e.g. working conditions) may indeed lower the stress but could in no way improve the work motivation. The right motivation arises only from factors that are directly connected to the work, e.g. sufficient offers for the career, recognition and clearly drawn up responsibility. Here the approach by Herzberg differs from Maslow's and it emphasizes to a greater degree the necessity to work out a real understanding of "Beruf" (if we use Weber's terminology here) of top managers.

But how do top managers see themselves? The examination of American top managers by Wald, Doty in the early 1950s found out that the interviewees

> felt that they had always been more interested in their work than had most of the other individuals with whom they were associated in business. And given a free choice 85% of them would have selected positions similar to their current ones. Asked why they worked so hard when they did not have to in order to earn a decent living, the executives usually answered either that they derived a sense of accomplishment from their efforts or that they enjoyed their work more than anything else they did. ... The participants derived much of their job satisfaction from the growth and development of their companies. ... What aspects of the executive position did the group members like best? Almost half of the members were very much interested in day-to-day dealings with people – in human relations (Wald, Doty: 1954, p 49).

Thus the authors stated a high intrinsic motivation to work and therefore incline more towards Herzberg's theory. A comparative examination of American, English and German top managers at the beginning of the 1970s found out – the results were not differentiated according to nationality – that

> approximately 15% of top managers ... appeared to be mainly motivated by the pleasure of their profession and work. This was followed by the desire to prove to oneself that they could achieve something new or solve a problem in the best possible way. Together these opinions made up about half of the means of motivation put in first place by the interviewed top managers. It was only later that there arose the desire to have more money (Copeman: 1972, pp 331-332).

Fifteen years later Cox, Cooper confirmed this trend in their examination about the anatomy of the success of British top managers:

> The motivation of successful managing directors springs from being ambitious and determined people with a reasonable high need of achievement, who find managing a major company an interesting, enjoyable and worthwhile activity. They have a restlessness and feeling discontent with their current situation, which is expressed, not in complaints about the situation, but in a drive to do something about it; hence their pleasure in developing the business and its products. They also enjoy working with people, have some need of power, and also require some degree of independence (Cox, Cooper: 1988, p 68).

We asked English and German managers for the most satisfying moments of their work. According to their answers we can define three strands of the managerial professional and working life which are defined by managers as being particularly satisfying – of course, with different German and English emphasis:

1. Success, including the fulfilling of long-term aims of the company as well as the short and middle-term solution of arising problems. This also includes the producer's pride, the achievement of certain economic results and organizational performance ("smooth functioning").

In Germany almost 50% of all comments concentrated on this block. In particular the technicians amongst the managing directors, whether in the car, air or space industry, or in the ship-building industry, develop a special kind of producer's pride:

> It is particularly satisfying to watch the product grow, to follow this (G112, p 10).

Non-technicians would admit to a different opinion:

> This is not always shared by people who are perhaps not as technically involved as me (G107, p 9).

In England 13 from 16 answers were fixed on the criterium success as being a particularly satisfying moment at work:

> The most satisfying thing with me is actually doing a job professionally and knowing that you have done it professionally (B9, p 20) – this was a comment made by the personnel manager of an English textile company.

However the criterium "success" is interpreted in different ways by German and English top managers: The Germans are more inclined to mean pride in production as success whereas the British primarily mean commercial success, measurable in money terms.

We could not confirm a difference in job satisfaction between the German and English managers as it was seen at the beginning of the 1970s (Child, Kieser: 1975, p 22). However it appears to us that the reasons given by Child and Kieser[30] at that time are historically out of date.

The second block of comments give other facts than those that could be confirmed almost 20 years ago:

2. The autonomy of the scope of decision-making and the possibility to make use of their own creativity and imagination: In Germany a third of the interviewees found these points to be especially satisfying whilst only one

---

30   "The higher job satisfaction of German managers therefore suggests that the limited authority and variety which tends to characterize their jobs is expected and accepted as legitimate. Such acceptance would almost certainly be a product of social culture, and may go back to the dominant role of the German father in the childhood" (Child, Kieser: 1975, p 22).

English manager mentioned this. A managing director of a German middle-sized steel company commented on this freedom very clearly:

> I must simply say that the best thing of all is the freedom to decide. That is to say that as far as possible (we are all part in a social system and we cannot just simply do what we want) we can try to put through our own ideas and own opinions to a relatively high degree and it is good to have the possibility to do this (G83, p 12).

3. To make people (employees) feel satisfied in their work (almost a fifth of all answers in Germany, in England 2 from 16). This constitutes a situation for top managers in which their subordinates develop trust which is expressed by situations in which "everyone can speak openly with the company manager" (G79, p 12). This was quoted from the works manager of an international company. To reach this situation it is necessary for the manager to make every effort to motivate his workers:

> It is the way that you can direct others, the way that you can organize and the way that you can motivate and even the way that you can enthuse and give people the enthusiasm for the job that they are doing. You must also give them some pride in achieving the end result (B3, p 14).

A further requirement for this is team work. A managing director from Germany spoke of the most satisfying experiences in answer to our question:

> The shareholder would expect me to tell you that it is making profits. That is not the case at all. But that you are terribly dissatisfied when you don't make any profits is also clear. It is quite simply because you get into constraints that you cannot avoid but of course this must be. But what gives me the most pleasure is the functioning of the team. Really working together openly and honestly. I take pleasure in my work from this every time and it is this fun that you need to make you come to work cheerily in the morning (G68, p 13).

And – amazingly enough – an English personnel director of a famous steel-producing concern included industrial relations as well as his individual opinion:

> I think one of the greatest compliments that I've ever been paid came from the trade unions. They said that even though you work for the management you are the only person who tells us the truth whether it be good, bad or indifferent. We know that if we come to you, you will not flannel us. You will tell us the truth whether we like it or not. Very often I have to tell my managerial colleagues the same sort of thing. If you once start to deviate from the truth in dealing with people, if people find out that you have been less than honest with them, then they remember that for a long, long time. It then takes you to climb a very big hill to resolve the problem (B5, p 11).

The first two types of answers – success on the one hand and autonomy on the other – were almost pre-programmed in our expectations as scientists. By taking into consideration what was mentioned in the question: "What attracts good managers?" as a reflection of the managers' own wishes it was clear that the managers give preference to their work content and success. Autonomy and the realization of imagination and creativity are almost immanent to the self-understanding and general picture of the top manager[31]. But we were surprised by the relatively high number of managers who "suck the nectar out of the social coherence of the company", that is to say those mangers who pay particular attention to the interests of those employees/workers entrusted onto them. A comment typical of this comes from the personnel director of a famous English metal processing company:

> It is difficult handling dismissals and terminations but yet I believe it can always be done without stripping the individual of dignity. If I can do it without the other individual feeling demeaned or diminished then I find that satisfying (B4, p 9).

Can such a high feeling of responsibility be assigned to the general change of paradigm in the West (a stronger emphasis of the individual in his personality)? Or is a particularly clever calculation being expressed here which makes use of people for their own purposes? Or is all this simply a relict of the patriarchal style of management which forcibly includes the welfare for the subordinates? We will only receive a (preliminary) final answer when the questions of the relationship to staff, works council but also corporate culture are explained in more detail below.

It seems remarkable to us that only one interview partner remarked that satisfaction in and by the working situation can also be achieved by the exercising of power and authority – within the company as well as within the society, graduated according to the economic significance of every company[32]. An explanation for this not being mentioned could be that the exercising of power and authority in its function as stimulant in our societies is a taboo. For example the managing director of the Deutsche Bank, Mr Herrhausen, who was later murdered, explained, in all comments, that in his position he did not exercise social power but only influence[33].

It appears to us that it is time for society and top managers to break through this taboo and to discuss quite openly that in every society and also in ours, power and authority is exercised and must be exercised within certain borders and with certain content. As a result of this public recognition of power and

---

31 An examination by EMNID in 1985 brought similar results. The examination dealt with work motivation of managers in the German economy, cf. Bertelsmann-Stiftung, Institut für Wirtschafts- und Gesellschaftspolitik (IWG) (1985, p 25).

32 The popular English TV series "Yes, Minister" and "Yes, Prime Minister" as well as the political thriller "The House of Cards" give a wonderful presentation of the fascination to exercise power and authority on people.

33 His final comment was made in an interview with Gero von Böhm in a radio programme from Südwestfunk Baden-Baden, transmitted on 20.10.1989.

authority, even the discussion of this can limit the exercising of authority to its proper necessity and can thus adapt to a democratic common good and can legitimize democratically – a necessary process of modernization which makes every society superior to the other less open society (see here the events in Eastern Europe). There is a certain social recognition connected to the conscious and public exercising of power, which does not only restrict itself to the company but which is always mediated politically and thus has an effect in society. This can have a negative or positive effect. If this social recognition is positive then it could be an additional satisfying moment in the job satisfaction of company managers[34].

The EMNID study also confirmed for German top managers that recognition by the society is not a dominating factor for the interest in the profession (Bertelsmann-Stiftung, IWG: 1985, p 25). Is such a perception a result of managers' distance from politics or of their high identification with work? Basically this should not be the case because company management is unavoidably political and therefore more than other professions must prove itself in a social context (we will come back a little later to the relationship of the managers to society).

There is a similar abstinence with respect to material incentives: here we can record that there is not one manager who mentioned this. Either material wealth is presupposed by managers or is outwardly hidden so as not to injure social taboos.

The concealing of certain factors seen as social taboos applies to a career in their function of satisfying or motivating the managers. But it is by no means the case that we wish to presuppose that the professional career in its intrinsic value is dominant in the action of individuals. But on the other hand it is strange that professional progress does not play a role in the 'job satisfaction scale'.

One interviewee made a remark which was otherwise not mentioned by anyone:

> What gives me pleasure is that I get to know lots of people and I can learn from them all. You can meet interesting people and they always have something to tell you (G64, p 6).

The consideration behind this is the general striving for a developed, extensively educated personality who is considerably influenced by his profession and work but who does not see his aim as directly being employed in the company. This almost completely lacking desire in the consciousness of top managers to be a 'worldly citizen' in Goethe's sense of the word and which

---

34   Only one (German) interviewee mentioned such a motive (G 35, p 12).

derives from a humanistic ideal, has of course many reasons. They can extend from a high degree of identification with one's own work (which hardly allows any other thoughts) to the very long working hours which leave only little time for free time and family.

2.4.2   The top manager and his family

An essential step forward made by the bourgeois society in comparison with the feudalistic society is the division between work and the private sphere. In the feudalistically defined society the prince, feudal lord, workshop owner, the master etc. could not only determine all conditions of work of his employed/dependent worker but at the same time he could decide over his private life (living conditions, family affairs, political commitment, permission to marry and "ius primae noctis"). This changed fundamentally with the establishment of the industrial-capitalist way of work and economy within the framework of the bourgeois society. In principle work and private life are strictly separated and it is the decision of every individual to keep his private/family sphere away from society or to approach the public eye to a greater extent. Even a so-called tabooing of the private sphere has arisen. And indeed this is above all the case for those social groups who can afford this financially and comfortably (detached houses etc.) and who, parallel to this stand in their professional life in the public and media eye and whose family and private sphere needs certain protection. Company managers – next to the English Royal family – certainly belong to this group.

Work and the subjective carrying out of work stand in a mutually arising relationship of influence to the family/private sphere. In our examination we were concerned with at least touching on this relationship and in entering into taboo zones, without actually making the family situations of the top executives a real concern of our examination.

We asked for the managers' compromise between their private and professional life, in relation to the working time and we asked managers to choose between the following positions:

1.   No compromise, private life must submit to professional life;
2.   No problems in coordination, family bears the professional role;
3.   No problems because working time is not considered to be a particular burden;
4.   Free time (evenings, weekends, holiday) belongs to the family;
5.   In certain times of the career the family was neglected;
6.   The family is the stabilizing influence but tends to be neglected.

We can interpret the distribution of the answers on these positions by consideration of different criteria, e.g. with respect to

a) *The managers' perception of the role of husband and wife and the stress put on the family as a result of the husband's work:* It may be confirmed that the top manager has a perception of the relationship between his professional and family situation that proceeds from a submission of the children and his wife to the requirements of his work: if we add up the positions 1, 2, 5 and 6 then there are 70% of all German and 11 from 16 English top managers who prefer this very traditional role definition and who must submit to this mode of behaviour which is expected of the companies and of their professional position.

It is amazing that in comparison (if we add up positions 5 and 6) only 14% of all Germans and only 1 from 16 English managers state that their own professional situation is not good for their family or rather that the family is neglected. This means that a greater number of top managers who proceed from a traditional understanding of the role of the family and especially of the wife feels that the priority list we have mentioned is not a burden for the wife;

b) *With respect to the managers' general perception of free time and identification with work and career:* If we consider the long working hours which we will look at later in detail, then the answers to the question we asked at the beginning allow us to make the conclusion that company managers (cannot) or haven't any marked hobbies. The main occupation that they have during their free time is with their family. The concept "family-centredness", with a specific perception of the different roles, applies to the understanding of the top managers under the aspect of free-time behaviour.

Other examinations confirm this thesis: the older study by Wald, Doty about American top executives states that

> although business kept them from spending a great deal of time with their families, the group members were vitally interested in and close to their wives and children. Less than 15% had ever been separated from their wives or had previously been divorced. Without exception, their homes and families constituted a great source of satisfaction to them. Many said they were looking forward to retirement primarily so that they could enter more into family activities (Wald, Doty: 1954, p 51).

In spite of social changes more modern studies confirm the continuation of the patterns of stable marriage and family background. At the end of the 1980s there was the tendency amongst British managing directors that

> the wives had been prepared to cope with the family and household problems, leaving their husbands free to concentrate on work and their careers. These wives in general did not have careers of their own. ... Marriages were ... very stable. ... Much of this pattern is ... a function of the age of this group. It is likely that the

next generation of MDs will have to find a way of coping with dual-career families (Cox, Cooper: 1988, p 65).

In all these examinations it is striking to find the very high degree of managers' identification with their work and their great loyalty towards their company.

K. Underwood comes to similar conclusions in his examination regarding the personal and moral situation of American "Chief Executives". Indeed these company managers do not devote their whole life in its totality to the company but they give their whole personality with all their possibilities, at least during work (Underwood: 1964). A department manager of an internationally and highly acclaimed service/transport company in Germany told us:

> I live with this firm. And I am internally completely involved with this. I cannot differentiate between private life and company because I identify with it so much (G57, p 13).

And an English owner-manager confirmed this whereby in his statement we see that the aspect of enjoying life is not neglected but that everything revolves around work:

> I went to see Pavarotti the other Saturday night. I like art and I like music, I like all the things in life. I like good wine and eating out but all of those at the end of the day probably revolve slightly around my work because there is not a segregation between social life and work life. It's all the same (B2, p 16).

If this aspect does not apply in every case to all our interviewees these statements apply fundamentally to the general mode of behaviour on top management level. Not even the "workaholic", who as a result of his personality structure or individual isolation with his environment knows nothing but work, fits this type description of the work-centred manager[35].

But there are very often requirements that arise out of the complexity of the management situation, which determine this work concentration. Burns, Stalker stated too that the position of the general manager demands extreme identification of the individual with his work which automatically leads to a distancing away from the family (Burns, Stalker: 1961, p 234).

---

35   The works manager of an English food and luxury food concern: "I like work. I like things associated with my work. I like the people I work with. So I do spend some time socially with those people. When I look back I have probably not spent as much time with my family as I should have done. But I cannot honestly say that if I had had that spare time that I would have spent it with my family. Knowing me I would have probably spent it on a rugby field or on a cricket field" (B 13, p 9).

At the same time the role of representation, that we see as "social commitments", forces the top managers to bring their private sphere into their work organization, and thus this reinforces the traditional roles within the family:

> My private life and business life is a completely fused mixture. … It gives me and my wife pleasure to have important business guests or shareholders and then we make a meal at home and I invite my colleagues so that business and private life can no longer be separated (G68, p 14).

On the whole we can say that – in the course of a career the carrying out of hobbies can become more and more difficult

("I have set myself priorities. I know only work and family. I have dispensed with any hobbies" – this was the comment made by the member of the board of directors of a large German chemical company [G61, p 14]) or that not doing any social activities is not considered to be a loss ("Unfortunately I worry very little about social activities" – quoted from the personnel director of a world-wide operating British chemical concern [B17, p 6]).

But such a loss in the understanding of the managers is offset by recognition of their own performance with the recognition which is associated with career progress and is offset also by the scopes of autonomy of top managers and this means that their own creative wishes can be extensively realized.

To add to this, there is very often the time argument that is presented as a reason for stress:

> I often feel that some senior colleagues perhaps spend the amount of time at work that they do because they are not happy at home (B9, p 21).

The question, that we will discuss later with the example of political commitment, is whether this is a typical structural feature for top executives or whether it is a particular problem for the older generation with their traditional perceptions of the family and its role.

But there are often other reasons why managers do not pursue hobbies, e.g. because it is more convenient for them or simply as a result of bad time management.

On the whole we may agree with the experiences of the Kienbaum company consultancy agency who stated that there is a certain inability on the first level of company management for the managers to really enjoy their very limited free time as such (Sachse: 1988) – this means not to think about their profession all the time and to do private things, that feed on quite different ideas to those that are otherwise dominant at work and in the company. One manager from the German air and space industry expresses this re-orientation as being a challenge to the manager himself and to others:

For me it is important that private life should be regulated to a certain extent, whether it is as a set-off, whether you make music, whatever kind it may be, or the manager can read, but not only professional literature but a broader scope of subjects, that he can afford to go to the theatre, I mean afford in terms of time, that he can go to a concert, that he knows that he has not only read about Mozart but that he has actually heard him, and that he even has a family who can give him the support he needs, because without any support he will not be able to take the pressure. Perhaps he will take the pressure for the first 5 years but not over 20 years (G72, p 6).

But this is only one exception to the rule. Our findings regarding the extent to which top managers identify with their work and their neglect of hobbies and spare time activities (although they concentrate on traditional family structures), refer to the levels of senior management according to our topic of research.

We were forced to a different way of thinking about this apparently iron rule for managerial behaviour, especially for every manager who wanted to make his career and wanted to keep up in senior management against hard competition, by the comment made by an English industrial relations manager. He said:

This company buys my skill, my knowledge, my talent. It does not buy my soul. I am prepared and I think it is reciprocal my loyalty to this company is reciprocal to their commitment to me. It's what they pay me, it's the way they treat me. I see it quite frankly as an economic relationship and I don't disguise this fact. I know that this company if they didn't want to employ me after tomorrow would not employ me. Equally if I was offered a much better job tomorrow I would accept it and leave. So that is my relationship with this company. Anybody else who says something else are very often fooling themselves (B1, p 12).

But above all in middle management (it is on average the case that the managers are 10 years younger than top management) have quite different orientations.

The Britons Scase and Goffee found out in their empirical examination about work and "lifestyles" of middle management that many managers make a compromise between their work and their free time so that their free time activities do not suffer (see Scase, Goffee: 1989, pp 179-183). Thus they are "reluctant" managers. The middle managers, aged between 35 and 50, do not strive for career success with all their energy if this only occurred at the exclusive expense of their personal, family relations. Therefore they are less willing to submit their personal interests to the demands of work and their career. On the whole they tend to resist the potentially overwhelming demands of the company. Therefore they cultivate strategies in order to uphold the autonomy which they can maintain in their non-work domain.

This change in values can be justified by the greater social changes in society in the last decades. In particular the 'psychological' contract between them and their company has 'intensified' because the pressure of costs in the companies has put a considerable pressure of performance on young managers. Many younger managers think that they have to work harder under greater control. But their companies do not offer them any more job security or promotion in return.

So why should the managers really make such an effort?

There is a certain counterstrategy that feelings of psychological well-being can be maintained by limiting the extent of their professional and personal ties and identification with the company.

The middle-class life style (a higher degree of consumption etc.) has increased the significance of the non-working lifestyles and free time behaviour. Scase and Goffee continue that the identity of (middle) management is not exclusively influenced by work but also by other factors. On the contrary those who identify themselves to a very high degree with work are often called "workaholics".

Such a sharp division between work and private life has also the advantage that threats by the company can be worked on more easily.

On the other hand these "reluctant" managers find themselves in a conflict of roles: the company demands the complete identification of the managers with their work; but the young managers are reserved. This means that the "reluctant" managers must appear compliant to the top level. But this has quite considerable negative consequences for the tense relationship between middle and top management. On the whole it damages the strength of performance of every company.

However there are also exceptions: According to Scase and Goffee, a minority of younger managers try as hard as they can to make a career (often with MBAs and renounced as Yuppies).

And there is one ray of hope, that a reservoir of trainee managers, which has not yet been touched, can compensate for the free time orientations of young (male) managers: According to Scase and Goffee, there is an increasing number of young women who are coming into junior and middle management and who are achieving great economic success in that they motivate those below them by an innovative management style.

As we have said, these results refer to Great Britain but corresponding examinations and statements show that the thesis of a change in values at middle management level and with young trainees can be transferred to German circumstances.

Dietmar Gottschalch (1982) carried out a questionnaire of personnel experts in West Germany and found out that the desire amongst younger managers not to reach the first level in a company is on the increase: The thoughts of security and material possessions continue to increase and private life has become just as important as work. As a result of this, there arises a negative selection process because those managers that would be needed at the top are content with a position in middle management. Ulrich, Probst (1982) also state that in their examination of Swiss managers' values there is less identification with the company amongst younger managers than amongst older ones and a stronger emphasis on free time. This tendency intensifies amongst younger managers who only work in middle management and not in senior management. The Bertelsmann, IWGstudy also shows us (1985, p 25) that there is a turning away from those values that can still be found amongst older managers by younger managers in the West German economy. The older managers are characterized by the fact that "considerations regarding free time or the compatibility of profession with private interests and concerns are seen to be particularly unimportant". The transferrability of the English results to German structures regarding the change in values amongst young managers is also confirmed by the experiences of company consultants. A leading employee of a large German company consultancy firm said that as a result of his experience this trend has continued up to today and that a return to a more career-oriented way of behaviour cannot be found amongst today's 30-45 year old managers:

> Indeed today's generation is just as willing to be self-reliant as before. However social values like free time, hobby, family are taking up much more emphasis amongst young people. They no longer want to make a top career and are satisfied with a certain income and with certain company status. In contrast there is a small, continually growing group (the Yuppies) that only knows professional career and nothing else. To a certain extent they are wild about their professional career (G50, p 1).

Thus the "reluctant" manager is a cultural phenomenon in all Western industrial and consumption/free time societies who is embedded in the individualization process in general and who is determined by its generation.

Let us remember: There is family-centredness amongst the (mostly older) managers of top management as well as amongst (mostly younger) managers in middle management. However the two groups take different consequences from this:

1) The younger managers who have not reached such a high level in their career take their wives' wishes into consideration in order to live their own individuality – whether it be the recognition that their wives can also realize their own professional wishes or whether it be a high degree of time allowance

or the consideration of certain regional wishes. The circumstances for the children also play a greater role for this group, beginning with the willingness of the middle managers to devote more time to the children up to the recognition that the children cannot be burdened with too frequent change of location.

However the question must be asked whether such new orientations are to blame for a general social change in paradigm (so that a new definition of the roles of the sexes is produced) or whether they are specific according to age. The middle managers mostly find themselves in a phase in their life where they are concerned with founding a family up to the point where the children become teenagers. This means that here a biographically determined period in life defines the specific family-centredness of the 30-45 year old managers or we may say: What is generally understood as "family life" is concentrated in this period of the managers' life. Therefore the husbands/fathers are simply forced to take more consideration of their family than at a later time in life when the children have left home and when family life runs a different course and is presented differently.

We think that there are two reasons – the paradigm change in society as well as the biographically determined components – which play a role so that younger managers have a different view about profession and family than older managers.

2) The relationship to the family of older, more established company managers as our actual examination group proceeds from a clear submission of the family to the professional demands of the main wage-earner:

> My profession is my life. I don't want to say that my family come to terms with it but they accept it (G107, p 10).

This was a comment made by a member of management of a very innovative German air and space company. The management examination by Mülder and Partner (1982) also states that most of the company managers have come to an arrangement with their families in the sense that the majority of wives do without their own professional occupation.

The working situation of managers structurizes the family (Pahl, Pahl: 1971, pp 104-107), whereby a new examination of top managers showed that almost 50% of them find that the demands of work on family life is a major source of stress; but their spouses tend to underestimate this as a pressure for their partners (Cooper: 1990).

With this not only are the traditional family structures and division of the role of the sexes between man and woman created. In addition they are intensified because the top manager is a man and he finds himself in a specific working situation which according to objective as well as subjective interpretations appears to demand an almost total submission of the family to the demands of precisely this working situation.

As we have already mentioned, many managers attach great importance to an intact family life which should act as a support and a processing reservoir (by the way top managers expect the same view from young trainee managers). But at the same time this means that in most cases the family must submit to the professional requirements which are expected of top managers. This submission can have three consequences:

1) The top manager tries to involve the family as far as possible in his professional affairs and the family, especially the wife, has not only come to terms with this but also identifies herself with this in a positive way:

> I have tried to involve my family by a) not being too tired when I come home. I must still have resilience when I come home. And b) I try to involve my family, but especially my wife, in my problems and thoughts about work ... At the same time I try to take my wife with me to external activities, and they occur quite regularly in our company, press events, business trips. Of course I try to do this according to the age and independence of our children. ... All this is binding (G77, p 10).

2) The high level of professional strain of managers is not suppressed. It is experienced by the family as well as by the top manager as being a strain:

> The demands of the job make tremendous incursions on private life and sometimes what was regarded as private life was some sort of social activity that you had to undertake because of the job (B3, p 16).

This can lead to constant dissatisfaction in the family sphere. The wife in particular feels that she is being neglected and cannot come to terms with this role but she remains in her situation:

> I have trouble at home as long as I am in higher positions at work. ... In the last 10 years my wife has always managed to phone me up at a certain time to ask me when are you coming home? Come now, and I have always said, I haven't quite finished, I have got people here, or I have got to do some correspondence and it will take an hour, so that I have constant trouble with my wife. I understand this that she has been sitting at home all day and would like me to come home – although my wife can occupy herself, that is no problem. ... But the expectations of my wife have not yet really been satisfied (G102, pp 11-12).

3) This dissatisfaction culminates to such an extent that the manager and his wife separate. There are some top managers whose marriages have broken up as a result of psychic and physical strain, if we put this into blunt terms.

In our examination we have no statistics about the rate of divorce but it happened more than once that our interviewees spoke of a separation from their partner in answer to our question about the compromise between profession and family. But for reasons of discretion the pressure resulting from unhappiness which managers suffer – especially when there are children involved – cannot and should not be presented here.

The comment of a manager from a middle-sized chemical firm in Germany is interesting that on the one hand it is a personal decision to carry out a managerial profession. But on the other hand the demands which arise from this work and which often force such a decision, cannot be personally influenced:

> Yes, and regarding the family, you have to make compromises, and you know, that many families suffer as a result of the time managers must put in. It is mostly the wives and children, who suffer, and you know that many families break down because of this. And then it is a personal decision, whether you take the risk or not. I think that you can't make so many compromises then whatever position you are in, there is a minimum demand set and if this cannot be brought into harmony with what your family expects of you, then there are problems (G7, p 10).

However it is often the case that at least at the beginning of the professional career there is no awareness that professional strain in a long-term process can lead to serious and then mostly painful consequences for the family situation. A much-occupied member of management of a successful shipyard reflects about a possible correction:

> It is very difficult to recognize this, it is mostly recognized when it is too late. But if you decide on the second step, on the career, then you must do it completely. To do this only to 70% or 90% would not suffice (G113, pp 11-12).

But a manager from the second level of an international mineral oil company contradicts this view quite vehemently. He puts other values than those associated with work into the centre of his life:

> And I am attached to my family and I think it is very, very important, and I have a house with a garden and everything with it. And then you must constantly make compromises with your time, because of course in a managerial position you can spend an awful lot of time. You can do everything better and more perfectly and you can make a greater commitment and put everything into it but somewhere you must say, with regard to time, you must do something different now (G75, p 9).

Thus: Managers too should live their life as a whole and should not simply see it as a career ladder with family connections.

Linked with this we may quote one of our German interviewees from the automobile industry who sees total concentration on the career and working situation as being counterproductive in the sense of the companies, who demand good performance:

There are many managers who achieve professional fulfilment and a career at the expense of their family. In my opinion these are bad managers. They are bad managers because they cannot decide between their obligations. They decide on one thing and that is bad management. … I have the ability to drop everything quite suddenly and to bother about nothing and to work in the garden or do something else because I know from experience, that what I do as a break, a creative break, can be put into what I do afterwards to a high degree. I sometimes see that someone who fights through some long stretches of work, then that is uneconomical and not clever. Life consists of breathing in and out and of rhythms that you cannot always adapt to but where you can do something (G78, p 10).

However such opinions are rather the exception to the rule as we have already seen.

A typical example in this respect are the "nice boys from Detroit" as Yates (1983) calls the top managers from General Motors. By examining the recruitment, internal company career paths and lifestyles of this group, organized as a caste, the author comes to the conclusion that the families of top managers are also indirectly employees of the concern. "It is as if one is a priest" says Yates (1983):

The young people leave college and find a way into the system at regional level. From then on the concern does everything for them. The company sells their house when they have to move, gives them a new car after so many thousand kilometres and takes them to the right clubs and so on. They even retire together in General Motors colonies in the South and South-West of America. It is one welfare state from the cradle to the grave. The further they move up, the more they live like monks. They simply no longer know what happens in the outside world (*Der Spiegel* 35: 1983, pp 126-136).

And it is here that the intention of company politics to bring up a sworn (top manager) community with the aim of the highest possible efficiency, turns into the opposite: The "Spirit of Detroit" is one mode of thought that is partly responsible for the difficult situation of the American automobile industry in the face of international competition: One study has found out that from 6,000 top managerial General Motors employees two thirds of whom have never been occupied elsewhere – less than 1% gave up their positions or were dismissed. The spirit of Detroit insists upon conformism in questions of taste. For Yates this is one of the explanations why the American automobile industry cannot really assert itself on the clear domain of design in the face of the Germans and the Japanese.

Although this example does not occur very often and originates from the USA we can conclude in general that 'company blindness' promoted by the company itself, has a counter-productive effect on company management. Greater distance, which of course presupposes more free time, and the ability which must be learnt to cope with criticism from others (this takes a lot of time), are still better conditions for fulfilling the requirements of the company than a total orientation towards the job which is promoted in a socially closed space.

On the whole we can maintain for Germany and England that the top managers (mostly over 45 years old) use their family as a possibility to retreat and to "fill up" and that a traditional family picture dominates: The family must submit to the demands of the father's/husband's profession but as compensation the family receives considerable, mostly material advantages in return. At the same time the reason for conflict, which arises from the traditional family picture and which is obvious in some manager families, cannot simply be solved by the fact that the consequences are taken note of and then become part of the order of the day.

We think that in order to reach a solution of the conflict for the future, and in the face of the trend towards more free time and more occupation with the family, the private/family domain, which is extremely important for the effect it has on the managers' level of performance, must take on a new form, and in two ways:

1. "Work, free time and family should be understood more and more as a feedback system which needs a mutual enrichment of all domains of life as its basis. Isolated observations are often bought at the expense of increased conflict matters in one of the neglected spheres" (Streich: 1987, p 224).

2. We have observed since the 1960s that there has been a process of individualization amongst women in general as it was amongst men 100 years before during the process of industrialization (Beck-Gernsheim: 1983 and 1986). This means too that we may observe an increasing number of professional wishes amongst women – whether they can be realized at the moment or not. And we were also able to confirm this tendency amongst younger managers and their wives.

However there are now two individual professional interests within a marital partnership which must be harmonized and this is very often not at all easy. And it is important in this statement that it is not always and mainly the fault of the men as individuals. Society with its norms, that are designed for male employment biography, often makes a change in the roles of the sexes impossible, regardless of the strong will of those involved, and limits the striving for individualization of the women e.g. a striving for their own profession as a worldly form of identity. This brings partly unsolvable conflicts within the families. It should be possible that the labour market for managers and the performance demanded of managers by the companies should proceed from a model of employment that gives wives enough space for individual (professional) arrangement and that this should be in the interest of the strength and willingness of performance of the managers and thus of the companies.

But it will be a long time before this utopia becomes reality as a glance at the working time of managers will show.

2.4.3   Working hard – less celebrating: working time and weekend

"Managers work more" – "Managers do not know a home" – "Whoever wants to get to the top must decide at an early stage between private life and work".

Many opinions, which are widespread in society are similar to these when we talk about the managers' working time and we know from our examination that they are not only prejudices. We asked about the top managers' weekly working time:

The minimum working time of top managers amounted to 43 hours. But only 26% of those we asked in Germany and only 12% in England work 43-50 hours per week. The majority, namely 74% in Germany and 88% in England work according to their own statements more than 51 hours. One third of these (in Germany) work more than 61 hours a week and 13% (in Britain) stated the same.

A comparison with the average working time in both countries should make the dimensions of these numbers clear: The average working time of all employed people in Germany in 1988 was 39 hours per week, only 14.2% of all German employees spent 42 hours and more weekly at their place of work (Statistisches Bundesamt: 1989, p 135); in Britain the average weekly working time for all employed people in 1986 was 38.7 hours (Jowell et al.: 1989, p 34). This means that those top managers we interviewed in England and Germany by no means come close to the average working time a week.

Of course we must ask whether extremely long working time (in individual cases over 70 hours per week)

– has a counter-productive effect on the managers' performance;
– can be traced back to false time management and with this the inability to concentrate. An English industrial relations manager said:

> And I find a lot of people here and in a lot of other companies I've worked for, spend 14 hours a day in the place, 6 days a week and do about 30 hours work in a week. Most of the time they are sat drinking coffee, smoking, reading the paper, telephoning the friends. They are inefficient, they are not doing anything. It's concentration (B1, p 12);

– is based on a false concept of management. In this connection one interview partner spoke about the art of delegating:

> You must have the courage to gap. And that is also a philosophy that you must learn. … The Germans are inclined towards a certain perfectionism. And you must free yourself from this perfectionism, … because you can't do everything yourself. So you must delegate. … And you have other priorities than to check in every minute detail what you have delegated to see that everything is OK. And that is the 'courage to a gap'. You must simply be prepared to take the risk that something may go wrong (G75, p 10).

– is based in the individual's psyche: Either there is a workaholic working here, as for example the younger company director of a luxury food concern ("I need the spiritual satisfaction of working long hours" [B13, p 9]) or the job satisfaction is so high that extra long working hours are not experienced as being a strain ("If you get job satisfaction then it doesn't matter if it is 35 hours or 45" [B4, p 10]).

Detlev Müller-Böling confirmed in his examination of managers' daily work that the average working week's hours for German managers amount to 59 hours. Only a small minority work fewer than 50 hours, and in contrast 15% work 70 hours and more (Müller-Böling et al.: 1989, pp 105-106).

The examination of the Bertelsmann-Stiftung also came to the conclusion that two thirds of those interviewed work more than 50 hours (Bertelsmann-Stiftung, IWG: 1985, p 20); a different German examination from the early 1980s speaks of an average working time per week for managers in the economy of 50 hours (Witte et al.: 1981, pp 7-8).

In connection with the understanding of top managers regarding free time and family we must also ask whether these really long working hours concentrate on a 5-day week – whereby the individual working day would become very long – or whether using the weekends and the desk at home on weekday evenings gives rise to a more even distribution of working time:

Only 27% of all German and only 3 (from 16) British top executives keep their weekends and evenings free of work. In contrast almost two thirds in Germany and 11 from 16 British interviewees take work home with them for the weekends and evenings; 10% of Germans and only 1 Englishman go into the office quickly at the weekends.

During a manager questionnaire carried out in Germany in 1982/83 the question was asked: "Does it happen that you take your work home with you at the weeked or in the evening?". 11% answered "always", 24% "mostly", 24% "often", 31% "occasionally" and only 5% "never" (Heilmann: 1988, p 47).

Thus the majority of managers mix work and private life by the organization of their working time, that is to say they take their work home at weekends and sometimes in the evenings. We must note three things as far as this is concerned:

1. By the constant withdrawal or threatened withdrawal of the husband/father to his study at home the family is fixated more than ever on the professional situation of the manager and if we express this in a negative way we may say that the family is disciplined correspondingly.

2. Our interview partners often told us that in spite of all their good intentions to work at home at the weekends they did not always manage it. That is to say that they take their briefcase back into the office in the same condition that it was in the Friday before. This produces a permanently bad conscience and spoils the weekends in their function as a time for recuperation.

3. Linked with the latter we may continue that it is an advantage for the "psychic hygiene" to separate private life and work. A member of management of a German air and space company presented his 'model' to us:

> Basically I don't work at weekends, apart from when something catastrophic happens and that is once or twice a year. ... However I work a lot 5 days a week. On average I am in the office at 7.45 a.m. in the mornings and over the last few years I have often arrived back home at 8.00 p.m.. But this division: bringing no work home but staying longer in the office, means that when I lock my office then I also lock away business in my head. So I can never complain that things stop me from getting to sleep. ... Therefore: business dominates for five sevenths of the week (I don't see my children in the evenings, I see my wife only a little, I cannot do any hobbies), but at the weekend real private life takes place (G90, p 10).

Lee Iacocca, former boss of Ford and then of Chrysler emphasized in his autobiography that he always paid attention that weekends were free for him – except in times of absolute crisis (Iacocca, Nowak: 1982).

In this respect he is the type of clever manager with a differentiated managerial concept where he makes allowances for the amount of strain he can take and where he can withdraw himself – and this is, in the end, not only for his own good but for the good of the company.

It is a similar situation with holidays. According to the Bertelsmann study only a minority of managing directors actually make use of the full number of days holiday owing to them:

> If we compare the number of holidays per year which are actually taken with the legally fixed number of holidays which are set for managing employees and with the number of desired holidays of entrepreneurs[36], it becomes clear once again that

---

36   The question about the number of legally fixed holidays can only meaningfully

managers work hard to an above-average degree: Whilst 25% of managing employees state that they can claim more than 30 days holiday a year, only 17% actually take more than 30 days. Only 1% of the interviewed employees have the right to a legally fixed number of 20 days or less but nevertheless 11% stated that in general they do not make use of more than 20 days per year.

In answer to the question about how many days they would like to take in a year only 12% of the interviewed entrepreneurs mentioned a number less than 20 days or fewer. But in reality 48% must manage with this length of holiday. And whilst 82% dream of holidays lasting 21 to 40 days, only 47% of those interviewed actually let their dream come true (Bertelsmann-Stiftung, IWG: 1985, p 23).

To conclude let us quote a far-sighted manager from the air and space industry who states that holiday has a function of reproducing mental and physical strength not only for himself but also for his colleagues:

I take 100% of my holiday. ... I am on holiday about 5, 6 weeks in the year. I find it important that my colleagues go on holiday and I regularly check and have a look at the holiday lists in October. Of course everyone can do what he wants but he should take holiday. ... But there are always people who have 30 days holiday to come in October. I think this is wrong (G90, p 10).

We think that for the managers as well as for the staff there should be a motto which was practised about 100 years ago by some groups of hard-core workers during the process of industrialization, and in particular by the miners:

Working hard – celebrate the parties.

2.5   What do managers really do? – Regarding the understanding of the role of top executives

For the scientist working empirically to answer the question: "What do managers really do?", there arises a two-fold difficulty:

–   firstly the complexity and partly uncertainty of the managerial situation permits only difficult concepts and effective empirical methods to measure the effectiveness, rationality and professionalism of concrete management action[37];
–   secondly the working situation of managers which is often described as confidential makes the deployment of empirical methods more difficult

---

apply to dependent employees. Instead the entrepreneurs were asked how many holidays they would like to take per year.

37   See the discussion by Eberwein and Tholen (1990, pp 152- 164) regarding empirical methods.

than they are for workers at the conveyor belt and repair workers which give good results.

The concepts communication and interaction can be found in almost all examinations regarding the concrete arrangement of the top manager's working day, according to a standardized questionnaire of 1,493 top managers in Germany. The distribution of their working time is as follows (Müller-Böling et al.: 1989, p 105):

40% of working time was taken up for communication. There were from this 40%

- 8% for official meetings;
- 19% for conferences;
- 13% for telephone calls.

The managers spent 38% of their working time at their desk. From this 38% there was

- 8% post going out;
- 7% post coming in;
- 11% writing letters;
- 11% reading official papers.

The managers spent 22% of their working time "out and about". From this there was

- 5% for business meals;
- 3% on committees;
- 3% at conferences;
- 1% for lectures;
- 10% for travelling time.

If we define the position "desk" as one work block where managers work alone and if we add the travelling time (10%) to this during which the managers very often work alone, the 'rest' – 52% – of top managers' working time is characterized by communication and interaction with others.

In comparison with other examinations but also as a result of our own research experience, this number of 52% "communicative work" seems to be rather low. For example Kotter comes to the conclusion in his examinations of "General managers'" working day that they only spend 25% of their working time alone and then mostly at their own desk and the other 75% is spent in communication with others (Kotter: 1982b, p 158). George Copeman examined management methods in the United States, Great Britain and Germany and found out that on average 74% of the top managers' working day was spent in meetings (Copeman: 1972, pp 271 and 331).

The examinations of Brewer, Tomlinson (1963/64); Lawrence (1984) and Claasen (1989) confirm the predominance of communication by their description of the managerial occupation, whereby Lawrence states that this is much more informal in England than in Germany and Claasen speaks of a certain distance from the customers during communication. One manager from the German automobile industry gave us similar trends:

> As a rule I get to the office at 8 o'clock. Then according to my observations about 60% of my working day consists of meetings, coordination, conferences. 20% is working on incoming post, that means getting post done. And the other 20% is spent working on projects (G78, p 11).

This very clear distribution of working time in favour of communication and interaction with others corresponds to the requirements named by those interviewed regarding the kind of personal qualities as qualifications for company managers. Peter Drucker makes the connection between the manner of occupation (communication, interaction) and the necessary qualifications of top managers:

> The manager has a special tool: information. He does not deal with his workers; he offers them motives, he guides them, organizes them so that they can do their work. His tool – his only tool – that he has at his disposal is the spoken or written word or the language of numbers. Wherever the manager is occupied, in construction, in accountancy or in sales – his success always depends on whether he can listen and read, speak and write. He must be in a position to put over other thoughts and on the other hand to find out what other people are concerned about. ... The manager can never be successful without the ability to give impulses for performance by means of the written or spoken word or of speaking numbers (Drucker: 1974, vol. 2, pp 40-41).

The abilities of motivation, communication and integration as the most important qualities of a general manager point to the fact that management occupation has primarily to do with people and this must be integrated in the social coherence of the company.

The results of relevant examinations on the concrete action of top managers during their working day make the diversity of the managerial situations very clear[38]:

1. The working day is made up of many short episodes;
2. Superiors communicate mainly orally;
3. Contact with subordinates does play an important role but by no means the only one;
4. Managers don't have a 'fixed' place of work;
5. The working day is full of unforeseeable or unplanned contacts or events.

---

38   Summarized from O. Neuberger (1985, pp 133-136).

However such generalizing statements should be taken with care. A summary of different examinations can feign a precision amongst the readers, a precision which does not exist for the most different reasons:

–   The reports by the managers themselves about their working day are marked very subjectively and unprecisely. This depends on how serious a manager takes the report and how he actually experiences his daily work himself;
–   The situations and positions of the interviewed managers are partly very different: For example the working day of a bank manager differentiates considerably from that of a works manager in an automobile construction company; managers of the first level have quite different tasks to those in the middle level;
–   The themes of the different pieces of research differentiate considerably as well as their questions and hypotheses. The following short indications of some (by no means all) empirical research examinations shall make this last argument clear[39]:

Sune Carlson (1951) developed the diary method and examined the work of 9 Swedish managers – he was the first to actually pursue the question: "What do managers really do?".

In his book *The General Manager* (1982a) Kotter proceeds from the fact that the only two management examinations which really go into depth by Carlson (1951) and Mintzberg (1973) do not even touch 1% of the notorious tip of the iceberg. He wishes to higher this percentage in order to close the gap between conventional knowledge about management and the actual action and behaviour of managers.

Sayles (1964) describes his method as being anthropological. Moving freely in large American concerns he examined the work content of managers of the lower and middle levels.

Kurke, Aldrich (1983) model themselves explicitly on Mintzberg and try to support and make more plausible his results by means of an extensive empirical study. The result: Centrally Kurke, Aldrich reached the same results as Mintzberg.

Luthans, Rosenkrantz, and Hennessey (1985) reach the conclusion in answer to the question what successful managers do that many activities of successful managers depend on the kind of organization in which they work.

Paolillo (1987) builds on Mintzberg. He uses his concept of the roles to check his hypotheses.

Shapira and Dunbar (1977) try to check Mintzberg's set of roles in an 'in-basket' simulation test.

---

39   We orientate ourselves towards the informative summary of relevant above all Anglo-American examinations of the manager's daily work by Colin Hales (1986).

Smith (1980) emphasizes methodically the use of 'repertory grids' for the analysis of managerial work.

Marglin (1976) deviates from our theme with the question "What do bosses do?". He is more generally concerned with a definition of the functions of hierarchy in production.

Lau and Pavett (1980) use Mintzberg's model of roles. They try with the aid of this model to find out the differences of managers from private and public companies. The result: If the demands of work are not completely identical they are almost the same.

Stewart (1976) puts more emphasis on the question what makes the managers or their jobs different from each other. In an earlier study (1967a) she used Carlson's method in her 4 week observation of 160 managers of British companies and concentrated in particular on the differentiations in their work.

In spite of the heterogeneity of the examinations regarding the daily work of the managers the results of all research, also of ours, have one thing in common: The relative uncertainty of the occupations and occupation domains and the difficulty arising from that to apply criteria of efficiency on the managers' action (apart from the criteria of the annual balance which is much too global). This leads to a revision of a picture of the company manager which was widespread and was relevant in earlier scientific discussions. According to these, every action, even the smallest, in the daily work of the manager fitted perfectly and streamlined into one strategy that traced back directly to the 'big' company aims and thus determined every detail.

As a result of his timely longitudinal examinations on management action and also of his own experience as company manager the American H.E. Wrapp found a very graphic characterization for the action: "Muddling-through strategy" – however "muddling with a purpose" (Wrapp: 1967, p 95).

Others call this a situative management concept. Daniel Isenberg (1987) coined the concept of strategic opportunism: That is the ability of company managers to keep long-term aims in sight and at the same time to remain flexible enough to solve daily problems. Effective managers have such a balance at their disposal. Isenberg continues that competent management is based on incessant experiments, relecting and correcting.

> Many top managers have stated that it is not so important in which order they carry out the individual steps of strategic planning. It is much more important that they know their products and markets, that their aims are formulated clearly enough in order to direct the allocation of resources but to leave enough space for changes and that managers work suitably and in time. The constant reflection of competent managers takes place in a form which is called 'logical advising' by cognitive psychologists. Instead of waiting until they have all the information experienced managers try to analyse new problems at the outset (Isenberg: 1987, p 112).

In his famous examination of the essence of managerial work and occupation Mintzberg tried to 'uncover' the myths surrounding top management. He analysed a set of different functions and role-understanding which a manager must fulfil depending on the situation (Mintzberg: 1973, pp 54-99). According to Mintzberg, although the managers are generalists this role set may approach a definition of managers as specialists that are needed to carry out or fulfil a quite specific set of roles. The organizations do not need managers only because of some deficiencies in the system and because of unexpected changes (e.g. disruptions) in the environment but because a formal authority is needed to perceive certain fundamental regular obligations. According to Mintzberg the 10 roles concern 6 fundamental functions of a manager:

1. The securing of effective production of goods and services of organization;
2. The designing and upholding of the stability of organizational enterprises;
3. Adapting the organization in a controlled way to its changing environment;
4. Securing that the organization serves the aims of those people who have the control (the capital, capital owners);
5. To serve as key information link between the organization and its environment;
6. To convert the system of organizational status (hierarchy – status – prestige).

Mintzberg concludes from this (1975) that

1. the manager is not a systematic, reflecting planner. If he plans he does this in the context of his daily routine and not in an abstract thought process for which he must withdraw into seclusion for 2 weeks (these are also our results);
2. the manager must also carry out "compulsory tasks". He is constantly told that he should devote more time to planning and delegating and less time e.g. to customer conversations, participation in negotiations etc.. However the fact is that many of these compulsory tasks are part of his work except for exceptional cases;
3. there is no 'total' system of information according to which a company manager acts. This myth proceeded from a picture of the manager who sits at the top of a well-thought-out hierarchical system and who gathers all important information about a gigantic all-embracing management-information-system. The fact is that by the use – above all of computer supported – information systems there is indeed a better basis of information available (the plentitude of which must be worked on) but that apart from this other formal and informal, opportune and systematically planned sources of information play a great role.

Mintzberg concludes from this that management is not a profession. In our opinion he capitulates to the enormous complexity of the management situation – and he does this with false arguments and at a too early stage. The role definition and purpose description of the managerial occupation, as Mintzberg describes it, is much too standfast in the descriptive level and to a high degree is dependent on the situation, that is to say it is limited in a time and perspective sense. Furthermore the argumentation of Mintzberg is very differentiated but society as (a dependent and/or independent) variable is not considered enough in its significance for managerial action.

Rosemary Stewart tries to draw up new concepts of management work and behaviour which could perhaps lead a little further to the attempt to develop a contribution for the theory of management action (Stewart: 1983, p 96). In her model Stewart proceeds from the traditional picture of managerial behaviour and tries to develop new concepts and approaches from this:

Traditional Picture		Actual Elements
Regularity, orderliness	to	Decaying domains characterized by shortness, fragmentation, diversity
Planning	to	Reaction and instinct
Collaboration with the subordinate	to	Recognition of the significance of 'cross' relations, informal not of a hierarchically bound nature
Relying on established relationships	to	Development and upholding of mutual relationship
Use of formalized and secured sources of information	to	Use of informal speculative information
Unpolitical: only related to company aims		Understanding of the political character of the management situation in order to convince outsiders of their own aims

Like Mintzberg she also doubts the correctness of the 'classical' management function described above, which suggests a logical, orderly working process of a manager in which the different activities of the individuals can be strictly kept apart and when enough time is taken, can be planned early enough. Stewart continues that all empirical examinations show a picture of a manager who lives amongst a whirlpool of activities, who must turn his attention to the most diverse problems and people within a very short time, who must live in an unsure world with a variety of true, half-true and false information in which it is necessary to have a network of qualified and trustworthy people to help him. The top manager does not sit quietly in his managing position, but he is dependent on many people and not only on his subordinates. He must learn to act, to negotiate and to make compromises. The top manager must recognize that he lives in a political world in which he must influence people with other means instead of doing this as a result of a traditional picture of the "social coherence company" possibly with his subordinates still in the company (Stewart: 1983, p 96).

In his "capitulation" to the development of a concept of the pofessionalization of management action Mintzberg proceeds from the appropriate judgement that the management situation is very complex. But he falsely concludes from this: "If it is not even known which procedure managers use, how can their action be scientifically-analytically be described? And how can management be called a profession when the learning material of a manager cannot be specifically defined?" (Mintzberg: 1975, p 53).

But the complexity of the manager situation, the difficulties of the conceptual demarcation and the assessment of efficiency, spontaneous action of company managers and the use of a situative concept of management do not automatically mean that

a) there is no managerial professional concept – it is only defined in a different way to that of a toolmaker or doctor (see here our comments regarding "management as a profession");

b) the company manager carries out his very difficult position and situation voluntarily, without planning and without any qualifications.

Thus Mintzberg only asks about the diverse aspects of manager action; he does not examine how the managers deal with it – professionally or not.

Our interviews and the study of relevant examinations speak of extensive tendencies of professionalization in management action which are reinforced in the historical passing of time, even if we must note that company managers often have a very unclear concept of their own profession. This of course also depends on the complexity of their tasks which demands a move away from traditional professional views and classical management functions, which Rosemary Stewart initiated and which was continued by Isenberg under the concept of "strategic opportunism". A quite critical element in the development of an appropriate concept of profession, apart from practical experience and strain which was mentioned above, could be specific managerial performance ability which is founded in the successful overcoming of obstacles and as a result of which the daily work of a manager presents itself in many things more systematically to the outside observer than Mintzberg believed.

These considerations lead to the question of the understanding of the role of an industrial company manager. Basically the situation of the top manager (like every other person) is defined by a complex coherence of interaction which lies at the base of management action. This coherence is expressed in the designs of action required by the position and the perceptions of the roles of the respective actors of the instances concerned (customers, staff, supervisory board and politics) in the areas of managerial occupation (directing and arranging market relations and internal relations of the company). The ability to take over the role of the other in anticipation is essential, that is to say a mutual viewing of the perspectives of the actors and an ability to adapt to the expectations of the other actors.

To add to this there is another important aspect: the company manager must learn to handle the authority which is given to him by social institutions and as a result of his knowledge and must do this in a differentiated and liberal way. An undifferentiated use of power which very often seems despotic to the subordinates is not only counterproductive in respect of achieving company aims. At the same time it shows very often the insecurity of those who act in such a way. So this means that the company manager must always restrain himself in the apparent or actual extent of his power. This is of course no easy process of recognition for anyone but it is necessary.

Company management is ambivalent per se: on the one hand the managers are controlled in the face of capital (supervisory board) but also as a result of the compulsion, which is determined by competition, to secure the survival of the company and to proceed in a strict way against the egoistic if legitimate interests of the staff. On the other hand the need to cooperate with the staff emerges from the requirements of the 'social coherence of the company'.

The action and with this the necessary qualifications of top managers arise as the complex result of their designs of action conditioned by the position, and their perception of their role which is conditioned by the situation. Management can be seen as a bundle of strategies, structures and processes which are bound together in one complete social coherence which changes constantly (Storey: 1985).

The definition of the organizing role of the company manager is achieved by the company-related organization (e.g. by the kind of company, capital relations, the make-up and union organization of the staff), by the environment (e.g. market customers, on the side of sales as well as acquisition, State action etc.) as well as by the managers' own performance (Büschges: 1983, pp 125-130).

But the analysis of top management work cannot be exclusively reduced to the economic function. Neither can it be adequately described in concepts which are determined by the opposition of the staff against management work. And manager work cannot be understood exclusively by concepts of autonomy and the contradictory values and interests of managers. For manager work is embedded in a contradictory structure of social relations, with which and in which an institutionalized organization of capital interests is pursued compromisingly (Willmott: 1987): Firstly by systematically fixed contradictions; secondly and in connection with this by individual and collective opposition and cooperation from below; and thirdly by the managers themselves, who interpret their functional roles individually according to their own evaluations.

Precisely this inclusion of the top managers' own performance in our analysis of their roles and modes of action is necessary because the difficulty to fix the working situation and daily work of the managers in a normative way causes a basic inclarity of the aims of the managerial occupation.

H.P. Bahrdt pointed to the necessity of performance in a creative interpretation of the definition of vague role expectations (Bahrdt: 1985, pp 66-85). The person – and thus the manager – is "victim and doer" at the same time: he takes action and he is dealt with. Therefore action and position derived from the role does not mean a perfect and almost complete "external managing by spiritualization" (Neuberger: 1985, pp 50-52), by fulfilling the role expectations and position-determined interests. The case is true for top managers as well as for all other position holders (if to a different degree): on the one hand managerial action is very strongly determined by structural and institutional reasons but on the other hand it is not determined in a puppetlike way. On the contrary precisely managers – at the top of the company hierarchy – have considerable scope for action and interpretation (which they can/must fulfil by their own performance)[40]. Indeed a tendency can be found that the managerial occupation is increasingly being submitted to a process of professionalization. But this does not mean on the other hand that the managerial occupation is becoming increasingly rationalized in the sense that the work is being systematized. On the contrary, professionalization means coping professionally with the irrationalities of the working situation[41] and one's own interpretations. But in the industrial-sociological approaches in Germany in particular, company management as a rule is seen as an abstract capacity under the spell of an abstract power (of capital). In accordance with this it can only gain recognition as an objective company strategy whereby the subjective accomplishment of the situation which stands behind this and which is passed down

---

40   In their examinations of British top management Cox/Cooper presented a philosophy of management which they call "open rationality" (Cox, Cooper: 1988, p 125) and which comes very close to the complexity of the role of a top executive.

41   In the English-speaking sphere research has shown that manager action is very often intuitive as for example by R. Stewart (1983).

by the position of company management is neglected because it is not conceived as part of a social coherence.

This does not mean that for example the formal organization of the company only plays a secondary role for the managers' action, indeed the opposite is the case. It is the formal structure which determines the extent of the managers' own performance. The deviations of action from the formal organization which often arise from the managers' own performance are often only visible by the comparison with the institutional framework conditions. The latter symbolize as a foil the moments of tension of the institutionally fixed situation.

With his concept of the "duality of structure in interactions" Giddens tried to bridge the gap between objective structures – e.g. between the company and the functions within the company – and the interests and interpretations of the individuals, e.g. of the top managers:

> The communication of meaning in interaction does not take place separately from the operation of relations of power, or outside the context of normative sanctions. ... No social practice expresses, or can be exploited in terms of, a single rule or type of resources. Rather, practices are situated within intersecting sets of rules and resources (Giddens: 1979b, pp 81-82).

In our opinion the questions about perspective knowledge (knowledge that a person has above the knowledge of nothers) are just as further reaching and are linked with the research by Piaget as well as questions about the social distribution of knowledge "into which the individual grows in various moments of interaction and from which he learns to use in different ways and the fixed structures are of importance regarding the dealings with the knowledge available" (Matthes, pp 5-6). In society amounts of knowledge are distributed amongst different groups to an unequal degree. Therefore different opportunities to participate in the processes of interaction are determined from this, that is to say the people taking part in these processes have different material and immaterial resources at their disposal.

If we follow this argumentation we shall mention the relationship of the company and staff which cannot be simply reduced to a plain relationship of "top and bottom". The relationship between the top executive and staff is arranged in a somewhat differentiated way and this primarily for two reasons:

1) Parsons conceived entrepreneurial action as institutionally independent, consciously organized and economically profit-orientated action, under sharp criticism of the assumptions of classical economy (purely self-interest). With this he succeeded in explaining the objective rationality of "great industry" and of the action within industry out of the differentiation of its roles and thus its social autonomy. Consequently compulsions created by habit forming are a matter of course and motives become "fulfilling insignificances". Arnold

Gehlen described requirements and consequences of such "institutionalization" of actions in the economy in his theory of institution:

> According to its origin a labour-divided company can often be explained on the basis of rational purposes of the individuals, of the interest of the shareholders in profit and by the evaluation of a new procedure; also the cooperation of officials, employees and workers as a result of their primary interest for their living. The whole working organization revolves around its own autonomy which is called 'the company'. ... The whole system is objective, but also in the consciousness of those involved is a super-human structure, which determines the attitudes and modes of behaviour of those involved as recognition of the targets, and habitualizes these attitudes and is supported from outside. ... Therefore the 'striving for a living', as Max Weber emphasized, is not a psychological concept and not an independent psychic drive, but an attitude forced on those responsible, if they are to provide for the survival of the company under competitive conditions ... (Gehlen: 1964, pp 34-36).

Amongst other things this means that temporarily the present survival of the company is at least more important (also because of research and development costs) or becomes more important as the (short term) achievement of profit, and that the ideal of the conflict-free development of the company by avoiding drastic breakdowns in development (or even revolutionary situations) becomes dominant.

2) From the viewpoint of such a management, the relationship to the staff is characterized by a fundamental sympathy. This motivates to a policy of employment which is orientated towards stability which is enforced by the legal and tariff political development. By the formation of regular staff (segmentation) fundamental problems of the economic system, which on the social level would otherwise lead to difficult conflicts, can be treated on company level as solvable problems.

On this level management and staff/works council meet up in order to solve certain matters mutually and cooperatively.

In our interviews we could not confirm what K. Underwood stated to be the most dominating moral and human problem for (American) top managers:

> (The top manager) works in an organization, which – if it wishes to fulfil its aims within society – must work with hierarchical authority-linked structures, within which the superiors can be in command of their subordinates. On the other hand the manager lives in a democratic society which puts great emphasis on equality and personal/humanistic regulations (Underwood: 1964, pp 204-205).

We could, at least in Germany, not find this kind of legitimation crisis – perhaps the specific German development of a company constitution, which differentiates conflicts thematically and leads gradually to a solution, does not allow such problems to arise in the first place. Here company reality has become a system of unpersonal-objective relations of dominance and in modern management there is no fundamental opposition to negotiations with the staff or works council and mutual agreements.

As we will see, in Great Britain the strict rules of a partly-feudalistic class structure have not been completely overcome at least when we are dealing with the relationship of company management to their staff.

In spite of all the selective differences we may observe a process of objectivizing conflicts in both countries. This is an expression of the 'de-ideologization' of the company relations of authority. It can be seen as part of the very wide reaching process of rationalization as it was discussed by Max Weber as the progressive "de-mythologization" of all products of social life (Weber: 1979, pp 33, 66, 179).

The management definitions as well as the requirements of management qualifications arise out of these tense relations between the togetherness of institutionally determined positions and situation-conditioned role perceptions of the managers. Both are defined at the same time in the context of society which is constantly dynamically changing.

The norms of behaviour of managers should be directed towards more moral values and the social common good – also in the sense of the general company success – rather than giving free rein to the unrestrained greed for money. This is what Etzioni demands and with him a whole number of philosophers and sociologists who are particularly well-known in America under the name "Communitarians". There are two theses in particular which Etzioni links with his demand for a new economy (Etzioni: 1988):

– Man is different than the traditional thesis maintains;
– If we try to adapt the person to the ideal of the economists then economy and society will come to considerable harm.

Market economies depend on the fact that most people keep certain rules. Different to what the neo-classical theory maintains, people cannot make rational economic decisions when they are left to themselves. They can only do this when they are anchored in communities and their norms. So market economies, in Etzioni's opinion, need a re-thinking back to such communities and the social common good.

For top managers this means that they must recognize that their task is not only economic but that it also contains political dimensions. Thus we are further interested in the questions about the managers' relationship to the company, to the technology and to the market as well as about their general norms and their relationship to politics and the society.

3 Different aspects of the relations of English and German managers to the company, technology and the market

With respect to the relationship of the managers to the company and technology we proceed from the working hypothesis that this relationship in comparison to former times has undoubtedly become much closer also for businessmen. On the one hand production technology has made itself independent and on the other hand the line-organization represents this technology so that the company problems of work and technology cannot be neglected. But this means too that the planning and control of production by top management without a suitable staff of workers and without new management methods (as project management or human resource management) cannot or can only be poorly realized. There is a field of conflict possibilities, between company-orientated engineers and market-orientated businessmen, which must be conveyed by top management in a most subjective and professional way possible. The relationship to technology and to the company can in practice not be separated from the relationship to the market at a top management level. It is certainly most differently determined in the case of engineers and businessmen (organizers) and as a rule relates to several outlet, raw materials , machine and labour markets. We proceed in a general way from the working hypothesis: The relationship to the market at top management level in industrial companies is considerable for all decisions that the respective managerial occupation brings with it and therefore it is organized consciously and in a manifold way with the aim to keep those possibilities of choice on the markets relevant to the company which allow and maintain market planning and organization.

To follow we would like to present selected aspects of the relationship to the company, technology and market of English and German managers in comparison to each other[1]: We wish to present this firstly on the basis of the themes of corporate culture or corporate identity and human resource management widely discussed by English and German management.

---

1   See a comprehensive presentation of the company and market relationship of company managers by Eberwein, Tholen (1990, pp 167-239).

3.1   Human resource management in England and corporate culture in Germany – Themes of fashion or new concepts of management?

This society is not to be underestimated. It cannot get enough. It wants more cars, more air connections, more spare time, more services and above all in first place it wants more understanding: more psychologists, therapists, culture managers and survival trainers. The capitalist company is the latest candidate in the context of the rotary acceleration, of the software understanding. However it bears a different name: corporate culture or 'New German' Corporate Identity. In this case the culture question does not arise from outside the company. The problems break open from within. In relevant publications the phenomenon of 'corporate culture' is considered to be one of the most frequently discussed themes in the management levels of companies. There is some agreement here regarding the fact that management concepts from the beginning of the 'scientific way of management' can be seen as antiquated. We no longer want to view the person solely from functionalist perspectives whose motivation is shapeable (Park: 1988).

And in the *Financial Times* under the heading: "Workforce is the key to success" we read:

The quality of the workforce, and not that of the software, will be the test of companies' success in the 1990s. ... Controlling costs will always be necessary for success, but only the provision of quality will guarantee it, and that quality can only be determined by the workforce (*Financial Times*, 8.12.1990).

Thus the theme of human resource management which is as intensively discussed in Great Britain as in Germany under the theme of corporate culture is mentioned here and the *Financial Times* for example devoted a whole series of articles to this theme at the beginning of the year 1991.

But what are the reasons behind, the aims and instruments of these concepts which are often propagated as new management concepts? Are there connections between both and why is the main emphasis of the discussion in Germany on corporate culture and in Great Britain on human resource management?

First of all we may say that both strands of the discussion have roots in common with each other.

3.1.1   The origin of the new management thinkers and the aims of the discussion about corporate culture and human resource management

"Are we standing at the beginning of the culture era?": This title of an article (Müri: 1985) is characteristic of the partly very controversial discussion which was started at the beginning of the 1980s and is still carried out today. Key words as e.g. "change in values", "mediating the sense of management", "evolution in the system of work", "from the sense to profit", "culture as a factor of success" all accompany the discussion.

Different approaches of thought, interests and aims play significant roles here: but they have the common point of departure from the frequently-quoted, so-called "new management thinkers"[2], some of which came interestingly enough directly from the field of company consultancy (Peters, Waterman, Kennedy), the other four were professors of American Business Schools. Indeed in the meantime several of those companies which were identified by these 'management-gurus' as excellent have come into serious economic difficulties but for example Tom Peters has quickly readjusted to the flexibility of a qualified company consultant:

> His about-turn was declared in the memorably bald phrase 'Excellence isn't'. Instead, he argued, a company could now ensure its survival only through fast-moving change on all of its dimensions: strategy, products, services, organisation, and people management (*Financial Times*, 25.1.1991).

What is the discussion of these new management concepts all about? According to several authors the origin of the discussion leads to the Harvard professors Elton Mayo and Chester Barnard (in our opinion the origin goes back even further) who examined in the 1930s the working conditions in connection with work productivity (Hawthorne study) and became the starting point of the human-relations movement which on its part put the motivation of individuals in and with the working group in the foreground.

Thus the scientific management of Frederick Taylor was put into question. According to Taylor company success and an increase in efficiency should be improved as a result of time and movement studies, systematic labour division and company rationality. This form of performance orientation was to be replaced by a person orientation as part of human relations (Peters, Waterman: 1982, p 67). The idea of putting the human factor more strongly in the centre of company strategies has by no means been discovered through the discussions about corporate culture and human resource management. In Germany it is even older; the movement of the "Werksgemeinschaft" (works community) with its aim "the fight for the soul of the worker" had already taken hold at the beginning of the century (Hinrichs: 1981).

As part of the already mentioned discussions this idea has, of course, received a new form, possibly also a new quality. "As is so often the case in the

---

2   Ouchi (1982); Pascale, Athos (1981); Peters, Waterman (1982); Deal, Kennedy (1982); a 'British version' of *Search of Excellence* by Goldsmith, Clutterbuck (1984).

development of individual scientific theories and questions the discussion of 'corporate culture' has arisen in the United States out of the structural changes of macro-economic conditions" (Heinen: 1987, p 4).

Several factors of influence of modern time are seen by the majority of authors as the most essential or decisive factors for the discussion:

1. The implementation problems of strategies and the problems of fusions and acquisitions in companies (Holleis: 1987, p 32);
2. the increasing "farewell from technocracy" (Ulrich: 1984, p 307; Holleis: 1987, p 35);
3. the increasing influence of Japanese management methods and Japanese culture, in particular in the USA (Heinen: 1987, p 4); the article "The Re-industrialization of America" in the magazine *Business Week* (30.6.1980, p 56) can truly be classed as the beginning of the company-culture discussion within the USA; in this contribution there followed a discussion about the loss of competence in American industry on the world market;
4. the social change in values in the OECD-states of the last few years (Holleis: 1987, p 32);
5. the increasing demands of participation on staff;
6. a decreasing belief in authority within society;
7. changed and complex tasks as a result of the employment of computer-supported systems of technology and organization which on the whole need the "thinking worker" and have led to the introduction of circles of quality etc. (Malsch: 1987);
8. and finally the realization by management that a company is not only an economic-technical coherence but represents also a social coherence.

The common reference point of the management concepts and strategies arising here lies in a much stronger directing of management towards the subjectivity of employees. In our opinion these concepts may largely be understood as an increasing normative subjectivizing of work relations (Baethge: 1990). "This does not cancel out the continuing factor of distance at work but in central areas it has the effect of softening the established forms of expression and patterns of regulation within the company and questions the traditional modus of creating an identity and incorporation at and through work" (Baethge: 1990, p 1). According to Baethge there is every indication of a new social character of work which is just as distant from externally guided duty moral as from a non-committal hedonism in the face of work. With reference to Maccoby (1988) he characterizes this new disposition of motivation and behaviour in the face of work as

> the new generation primarily of employees in service professions who wish to make use of intellectual and communicative abilities ... at work in co-operative

performance, who want to be treated as a whole person and not only as someone playing a role, who refuse those conditions of authority which are not objectively well-founded, who see work as an opportunity to learn something new, to develop themselves further and to gain a feeling of competence and independence, who calculate very exactly how far they can embark on which work, who do not wish to be eaten up by work because they wish to lead a satisfying private life and, in as far as the occupation does not fulfil their expresssive needs, try to satisfy them elsewhere outside of work (Baethge: 1990, p 2).

The demand for the development of subjectivity at work is not new but the width of its dispersion and the intensity with which it is pursued in the face of the company work environment is new.

Therefore Baethge sees a new quantity and quality of subjectivizing work and stands in contrast to the much represented view that the sphere of work has a strongly decreasing significance for the creation of the personal identity. Habermas states a decreasing power of determination of the state of work, production and commerce (Habermas: 1985, p 146).

U. Beck also assumes that a change in society is taking place at the moment, a change "within whose course people are freed from the social forms of industrial society – class, stratum, family" (Beck; 1986, p 115). As part of this development the company and place of work would lose significance as a place for creating one's identity.

On the other hand Baethge represents the view that "the professional role (for large groups of employees) gains or rather has an integral function for the personal construction of an identity as well as for its stabilization" (Baethge: 1990, p 3).

And he concludes: "The positive embodiment of work in the individual construction of the identity must teach the companies to be afraid since it questions more and more their traditional instruments of regulation and control ... at least for the qualified groups of staff" (Baethge: 1990, p 3)[3].

Even if we do not follow Baethge's argumentation in all its details we may justifiably assume that corporate culture concepts as well as human resource management may be seen as attempts at overcoming the consequences of such a normative subjectivizing of work in specific and not always unproblematical ways. Thus the corporate culture concepts pursued by management have a function of co-ordination, motivation and integration.

---

3   Baethge explicitly points to the fact that this has by no means taken place as a result of a trade union oppositional power (the trade unions themselves would have to fight against the consequences of this development) but has rather arisen as a result of the normative sujectivizing of work (Baethge: 1990, p 3).

Most of the scientific authors, company consultants etc. link corporate culture and management strategy together: for example Krulis-Randa emphasizes as well as tradition, the ability to change, conditionality of time, the ability to make experiences, also the ability to learn as an important feature of corporate culture (Krulis-Randa: 1983).

Hochreutener completes these considerations when he says that corporate culture does not only consist of value concepts, norms and rules "but also of organizational structures, management instruments, selection of personnel and personnel development concepts, know-how standards, infrastructure arrangements, quality of the modernness of the works equipment etc." (Hochreutener: 1985, p 14). Ulrich demands that the top value system of managers and its philosophy should indeed be taken into consideration consistently and persistently in the top managerial decisions of the company. And: "A consistent system of aims for the company presupposes a consistent system of values for top management" (Ulrich: 1981, p 17).

If we carry on from this, instructions, indeed real 'recipes'[4] for the correct use of corporate culture by management are given. In contrast to this a minority of authors argue that culture is destroyed as a result of the instrumentalization of corporate culture which has arisen to a greater or lesser extent naturally and as a result of management strategies. Arndt Sorge writes that "an instrumentalized and narrowed cultural concept would lead to the fact that solely in the development and preservation of values, attitudes and preferences in the development of a specific way of working and thinking, the lever to increased performance is raised" (Sorge: 1989, p 206). Indeed this is not ineffective because a certain measure of cultural unity and solidarity is necessary for the functioning of a company. At the same time, as Sorge continues, especially in societies in which the rather individualistic development of oneself is specific to the general social culture (different to Japan), a narrowing, rationalization and instrumentalization of (individually determined) culture by management leads to the exclusion of significant professional, motivational and innovative qualification within the staff (Sorge: 1989, p 206). In order to avoid such narrowing and manipulation, Margit Osterloh demands that new orientations of action should be propagated only out of conviction and not as a result of a written instruction on the part of management ("discourse ethics") (Osterloh: 1982). Peter Ulrich favours "communicative company ethics" which are orientated towards "discourse ethics" and would like to leave determination of the fundamentals of company action to the "argumentative notification of all those involved or concerned" (Ulrich: 1987, p 138).

---

4   See Bennis, Nanus (1985) and above all Peters, Waterman (1982) who name the 8 basic qualities.

Nevertheless such demands – according to Deutschmann – remain very abstract as long as concepts such as power, dependence, pressure of time and norm of performance are not included in such discourse ethics – there is no unruled discourse (Deutschmann: 1989, p 384).

Similar points of departure and aims described here for corporate culture can also be found in the discussion about human resource management. Storey confirms that in the last few years organizational processes of change have taken place in a number of British companies which were often described under the concepts "decentralization", "corporate culture" etc.. The popularity of such literature as the above-mentioned *In Search of Excellence* (Peters, Waterman: 1982) is an expression of these developments (Storey: 1989, p 1).

The concept of "Human Resource Management" arose out of these connections and has only become a set category for a few years. According to Storey, in former times one preferred to speak about "Personnel Management" whereby these concepts indicate on a normative level changes in content. For a long time the personnel manager was seen as someone who was responsible for industrial relations and who in particular negotiated with trade unions. This role was not integrated in the actual happening in the company. In contrast it is the task of the human resource manager to integrate personnel management into the daily business life of a company , e.g. by planning education and training of employees, by providing participation and incentive programmmes or generally by making every effort to encourage a positive working climate (Storey: 1989, pp 4-5). Staehle attempted to find out the difference between traditional personnel management and human resource management (Staehle: 1989b, p 389):

> The reasons which are presented in literature for the change in opinion regarding the value of the personnel are manifold:
>
> – an intensification in competition (above all the Japanese Challenge)
>
> – new technologies and concepts of production (with new requirements)
>
> – problems with productivity and quality
>
> – demographic changes (age groups, employment of women)
>
> – changes in values, new lifestyles, changed expectations of the working world.

Agreement with the above mentioned reasons for the corporate culture discussion is clear. Staehle sees the specifically new factor of the debate about human resource in comparison to personnel management in

> the systematic integration of measures of personnel recruitment and development which have been seperately dealt with so far, ... in the inclusion in strategic and structural decisions and ... in the view of human resources from general manage-

ment perspective and not from a functional departmental perspective (like personnel department) as well as in the inclusion of management in the human resources
responsibility (Staehle: 1989b, p 391).

Storey points to the fact that the realization that after investing in the
development and training of staff this has a long-term positive effect for the
company, is not new. However the aspect of flexibility of human resource
management presents a change in company politics in the face of the staff and
this, in his opinion, may be seen as a change in perspectives. Personnel or
industrial relations management regarded the staff as one unified group with
whom they could negotiate via the trade union which is considered to be an
organization representing the staff's interests. In contrast to this, human
resource management tries to evaluate and pay members of staff individually.
Therefore, as Storey continues, human resource management can be seen as a
concept of individualization and we may assume that it is precisely this aspect
which makes it so attractive (Storey: 1989, p 6).

Nevertheless we must differentiate here between a "hard" and "soft" version of
human resource management. Whilst the hard version can be described as
management strategy which sees an economic and useful factor in the
development of the individual worker, as in other production factors, the soft
version is connected to the human relations school and aims primarily at the
working climate (Storey: 1989, p 6). But in any case different measures of
human resource management serve the purpose of making the working
potential of the workers more flexible as a result of education and training and
of allowing them to develop themselves to a qualitatively higher degree. But
there has been criticism from different sides of the concept of human resource
management and this is quite analogous to that of corporate culture.

Purcell (1989) differentiates fundamentally to strategic embeddings of human
resource management, firstly in a comprehensive concept of corporate culture
and secondly in a (financial) concept of control, whereby the first tries to
influence the norms, values and the image of the company by purely economic
results, whilst the second is orientated towards short-term profits. In accordance with the demands to encourage working potentials as a result of
meaningful investments in training and further education, human resource
management can only be carried out consistently within the framework of a
concept of corporate culture. In the case of British companies Purcell states the
opposite, that is to say the tendency towards short-term profits. However
human resource management is only an ideology of the entrepreneur which
should serve the purpose of increasing work productivity by intensifying and
concentrating work. The estimation by Armstrong (1989) is similarly sceptical.
Indeed he sees human resource management basically as a possibility of giving
personnel management greater significance than was so far the case within the

framework of strategic company decisions; but it is very questionable whether this possibility is realized. For either human resource management is economically a success which is written down in concrete terms by the calculating of costs or sooner or later it is banned from the company. Thus human resource management can only work within traditional spheres which would still be determined according to the calculation of costs.

But above all the possible anti-trade union intention of this concept is emphasized by critics of human resource management: "Another concern must be the failure of British management to integrate their approaches to the individual with their policies towards trade unions" (Storey, Sisson: 1989, p 173).

And Guest (1989, p 43) notes that human resource management has remained extensively limited to companies in which trade union organization is rather the exception. However we cannot conclude from this that human resource management and trade union organization exclude each other[5]. But on the other hand the intention of individualization immanent of this concept allows little scope for collective arrangements and agreements. We may fear that the decisive increase in work productivity which is strived for here may impose on the trade unions.

Human resource management is estimated in a similar negative way by different trade unions. "Unions often associate the term human resource management with an explicit challenge to their strength. They see it as an attempt by managers to bypass stewards and deal directly with workers" (*Financial Times*, 11.2.1991). For example the large Transport and General Workers Union (TGWU) warns in a film for its functionaries with contact to human resource management:

> to be wary of attempts to introduce communication and invlovement ideas such as team-briefing and quality circles, or consultation mechanisms like works councils, which do not involve unions. It also warns against easy acceptance of team-working and multiskilling.

The arguments which different trade unions bring forward against human resource management in particular are:

> First, managers will try to pursue goals through channels which bypass unions. They may encourage individual performance rather than collective pay awards; they will have team briefings rather than communicate through stewards. ...

> Second, the general improvement in the quality of people management will reduce tensions and conflicts which drive workers towards belonging to unions. ... Third,

---

5   "HRM is not necessarily anti-union. ... neither strategic integration nor quality is in any sense incompatible with trade-union activity" (Guest: 1989, p 439).

at non-union sites and in new plants, human resource management may obviate the need for unions" (*Financial Times*, 11.2.1991).

These objections are similar to those which are given in Germany from the trade union point of view against concepts of corporate culture[6]. A member of the works council of a large company told us:

> Corporate culture is a highly dangerous matter and goes against the solidarity thought of the trade unions (G37, p 7).

There are also common factors and relations in the rejection of human resource management and corporate culture. Before we make our own evaluation of the arguments we would like to throw light on the views and evaluations of the managers.

3.1.2   Corporate culture and human resource management as management ideology and as an instrument of authority or as part of a co-determined company working policy? – Experiences and views of the managers

We were posed the question whether and to what extent the discussion about corporate culture and human resource management, as it is presented in books and magazines by scientists and company consultants, by ideologically or professionally competent debaters, has entered into the way of thinking and acting of English and German managers. Therefore we asked about the significance of corporate culture for the company.

In each case a little more than half of the managers in England and in Germany stated that there was a developed and specific corporate culture in their company. Approximately a quarter of each were of the opinion that a such a corporate culture was indeed intended but still in its infancy. There was agreement so far. However almost a quarter of those English managers interviewed by us explained that corporate culture was out of the question whilst only 6% of German managers said this. In spite of this difference we may conclude that in general the consciousness of managers regarding this problem and who concern themselves with this theme is relatively high although there is a somewhat greater difference in the English group.

Is such a distance recognizable also in the different aims and functions of corporate culture concepts of English managers compared with their German colleagues? The latter described to us their aims and intentions as follows:

---

6   Compare here the argumentation by Breisig (1988), who presents corporate culture exclusively as an instrument of management and as a means of securing authority.

a) Creating the "us-feeling"[7], which can be brought about – depending on the branch of industry – by a certain policy of recruitment. A manager from the steel industry:

> It is a typical feature of the steel industry that over generations you feel closely attached to the company. ... but this is more sub-conscious than conscious. It is more the fact that the father was employed here and that he perhaps liked it here, that he felt at home here and that he was satisfied and could identify with the company (G28, p 19).

According to the top-managers creating the "us-feeling" must mean creating a board of management which can be "got hold of" or "touched". This includes a duty to inform the workers in particular of personnel politics and technical changes whose dimension may firstly remain undefined. Finally the function of harmonizing of corporate culture is mentioned here.

b) A greater scope for making decisions and taking on responsibility must be given to the worker (Keyword: delegating from the top downwards). There could stand behind this what a member of management of a large mineral oil concern outlined as his ideal: "Every worker should act as a little entrepreneur" (G68, p 22). Thus the frequently observed "inner notice of termination" of members of staff should be avoided.

Apart from the function of motivation the emphasis of the individual also comes very clearly into the foreground: The individual member of staff as participant of the "social organization works" is relieved of the corresponding collective duties (and also rights). The process of integration of the individuals is strengthened by this.

c) Since the workers are influenced quite essentially in their modes of behaviour by work and since for a great part they do this work in the company it is necessary according to the managers to take this 'socialization of work' into consideration and additionally corporate culture should also consider the respective interests of individuals.

d) However at the same time, related to what has just been said, all actions, instruments etc. must serve the good of the company. Here the demand for power and authority of management becomes clear. In comparison to the relation to the internal company organization the relation of the market of corporate culture is only regarded as being secondary by German managers.

Only 28% described corporate culture as a means of external presentation; in contrast 64% described the "identification of the workers with the company"

---

7   The contribution of corporate culture to identification of the employees with the company is very highly estimated by Meffert et al. (1988, p 12).

and 8% the "entrepreneurial way of thinking of the workers" as aims of the conception of corporate culture.

Here there is a clear difference to their English colleagues we interviewed. Indeed somewhat more than half of those were of the opinion that corporate culture should serve to the identification of the workers with their company as the following quote illustrates:

> I think it is the starting point of knowing where you are going. It is to know who you are and what you stand for. ... I think it is important for the employees as well, something for them to focus on. They need to feel a certain pride that they work for your company. ... I think that is important in any company in any industry. If people do not identify with the corporate culture then they are not going to give their best to that company (B7, p 15).

On the other hand almost half (44%) saw the essential function of corporate culture in the external presentation towards customers, business partners etc.. Thus the external function seems to gain greater significance in England than in Germany:

> Firms like to appear to the outside world to be efficient, to be contributing to the greater good of society, to be providing a quality type of service for its consumers. I think corporate identity tends to give us messages as what is this firm about to the average man on the street. He gets an impression of reliability or smartness etc. (B13, p 13).

The managers judge in a correspondingly different way the means to establish corporate culture. In the German examination group specific company guiding principles were described by the majority (42%) as such instruments – company emblems and similar things were dismissed as being inappropriate means:

> If a coat of arms, a flag, or external appearance is described in formal spheres as corporate culture, then it is a falsification of the concept culture (G66, p 22-23).

This statement represents the opinion of the majority of managers interviewed by us; the others were quite evenly distributed amongst company social politics, general rules of behaviour (work regulations), the "principle of the Open Day".

In contrast the advertising for an image was considered by the English managers to be the most important instrument of corporate culture and this was followed by company social politics and management principles. This is an order of priority which corresponds completely to the 'externalization' of corporate culture more frequently observed in our English sample.

It occurred to us in general that apart from this difference – stronger relation to the internal company organization in Germany, stronger relation to the market in England – there was a relatively greater aloofness of English managers to corporate culture given in their answers.

Indeed corporate culture is perceived also by German managers with a certain amount of aloofness in comparison to the exuberantly appearing discussion in society. Some critical points mentioned were:

a) Certain internal company habits cannot be glorified as corporate culture;
b) The discussion about corporate culture is purely a 'marketing craze';
c) The discussion about corporate culture is also a matter of fashion in the sense that it repeats those arguments as they were used in the 1950s and 1960s in the course of the discussion about the "working climate". It is indeed "old wine in new bottles";
d) The concept of corporate culture is ideologically misused. But the 'fraction of sceptics' in England was relatively greater and – what is even more interesting – brought in different arguments than their German equivalents.

The industrial relations manager of a company in the food and luxury food branch said:

> If we want them to relate to us we've got to relate to them. We want them to be proud of working for a company that is a well known, respected international company. … So we do try and encourage it not to the extent that Fiat do. There was the gentleman at Fiat who said I was conceived in a Fiat bed in a Fiat house, born in a Fiat hospital, worked and educated in a Fiat school, worked in a Fiat factory, went in a Fiat holiday camp, died in a Fiat hospital, was buried in a Fiat grave. I hate Fiat. We don't want to do that (B1, p 18).

In spite of the efforts made to gain the loyalty of the workers a certain recognition of distance between the members of staff and the company becomes clear. The manager previously quoted also sees from his point of view a limit to winning the employees over to the company.

The personnel manager of another company of the same branch argued in a similar direction:

> The idea of a corporate identity and everyone is pursuing the corporate goals etc. doesn't perculate very far down the ladder. I think you can achieve that feeling of identity and that unity of purpose etc. at the top level, but how far it cascades is another matter. I don't believe that you have got the right to demand a 100% loyalty and that they will share all the objectives that you have decided. If they have been part of the decision making in formulating the objectives then that is different. … I'm not a corporate culture man. Quite frankly, I don't know that I'd want everyone to be the same. I like to see the people as individuals. Each person needs to be treated that little differently and maybe they respond differently because they are treated differently as opposed to being herded like sheep (B3, p 21).

And an executive director of a textile company stated:

> The senior management can identify with their work. ... My labour force come to
> work for ... pounds per week. ... They wouldn't think or associate their loyalties.
> I think they feel in terms of money (B14, p 11).

Thus the English managers accept to a greater degree than their German
colleagues that the company, particularly for the worker, is not the social
totality and his work is not the sole centre of his life. Indeed we cannot suggest
that the latter is the case for the majority of German managers we asked, in the
sense of a pure resurrection of the old ideology of the works community
("Betriebs-" or "Werksgemeinschaft"):

> Here the company becomes in some way a new social centre, and indeed in the
> sense of a social, closed, structure which develops activity in all important areas of
> social life (a kind of micro-society). The objective, material differences of social
> structures like family, club, company, party etc. are disregarded in favour of a
> divorce in community structures and social structures (Braun: 1987, p 241).

But the danger of such a take-over within the framework of certain concepts of
corporate culture appears to be less known or a problem to the Germen
managers than to the English. Also the view that corporate culture is rather
something for the managers and to a lesser degree for the workers was scarcely
to be found in the German group. On the contrary in England this view was
expressed several times.

On the whole it appears to us that the comparably greater aloofness of English
managers towards corporate culture as a management strategy is an expression
of the different views on the relationship between staff and entrepreneurs/man-
agers in both countries. Whilst in Germany there dominates in principle a more
cooperative, if not conflict-free, relationship between employees and management there is in England a greater mutual distance in the way of thinking and
acting on both sides[8]. This may be a fundamental reason for the greater amount
of scepticism on the part of the English managers (and of the trade unions too)
in relation to corporate culture which proceeds rather from a harmonious
relationship between employees and company management.

The explanantion for this may be found in the fact that human resource
management concepts and strategies enjoy greater popularity in England than
they do in Germany where human resource management in company practice
is not very widely spread and where it is reserved "for exchange of thought at
management seminars" (*Handelsblatt* from 21.12.1990). Indeed human resource management is in Great Britain by no means the rule:

---

8   See chapter 4.2 for more details regarding industrial relations.

> The core of human resource chiefs is increasing its grip on British industry. Already entrenched in foreign multi-nationals and non-union companies, it is spreading in the unionised private, and even the public sector. ... Yet the growth of the terminology begs the question of how far people-management techniques are actually changing. ... Because it is easier to change the title of the personnel department than the way people are managed, it is likely that much of what passes as human resource management is simply old wine in new bottles (*Financial Times* from 3.1.1991).

But however the significance of human resource management is increasing:

> But there is no doubt that the faith is spreading among companies attracted by the search for a new day forward in the old struggle between workers and management, but one which stops short of the social partners approach of mainstream European social democracy (*Financial Times* from 3.1.1991).

Thus a comprehensive concept of corporate culture is possibly more compatible with the German view of participative industrial relations (co-determination, works council[9]) than with the industrial relations in England; and on the other hand certain human resource management strategies are obviously better suited to the staff-management relationship in Great Britain (which is less of a partner relationship) than to the German cooperative company viewpoint.

To follow we wish to see whether such tendency differences continue in a stronger technical orientation of German managers.

3.2   Technology versus finance – the "technology obsession" of the German managers and the "shopkeeper mentality" of the English managers?

> The somewhat 'de-economised' view which German managers have of the business enterprise is central. The idea that the firm is not a 'money-making machine' but a place where products get designed, made and eventually sold, with profits ensuing, tends in Germany to restrict the allure of accountants and financial controllers and to dignify the makers and those associated with them (Lawrence: 1980, p 131).

In the opinion of the British sociologist Lawrence – who has excellent knowledge of German industry and economy – industry in Germany appears almost as a purely technical arrangement of engineers where profits only in

---

9   See chapter 4.2 on co-determination and works council and industrial relations in Germany and England.

passing and in second place are gained. In contrast to this – this is a widespread opinion – there is a predominance in England of commercial workers above technicians and engineers, profits stand in the foreground of managers' thoughts whilst production technology and the products are only given secondary significance.

We were interested in the question whether there really exists a primacy of technology over economy in Germany (which comes across in such views) and on the other hand whether there is an extensive indifference towards technology and products in England. To formulate this informally, we wanted to know whether there really is a German "obsession with technology" and an English "shopkeeper mentality".

Firstly it may be confirmed that a large majority of the English managers we asked, namely 13 from a total of 16, held the opinion that their German colleagues were much more technically-scientifically orientated. In fact the other three were not of a different opinion but due to a lack of knowledge about German managers were not in a position to answer the question. A manager of a vehicle manufacturing company described this majority opinion exactly:

> In this country the engineer is not looked upon although we have professional qualifications and a professional organization. The engineer carries no status. In the eyes of the nation, the engineers in this country are somebody that deals in nuts and bolts, not somebody who is creating wealth. I could tell you where the status would be given by the public. It would be the bank manager, the solicitor and the engineer on the end would have the lowest status of all. It is the same for the manufacturing industry. There is no esteem. We find that when we talk to schools that we try to promote engineering in schools but at the stage when they are leaving school and going into careers, there is no real enthusiasm. To find an engineer, a young person who wants to be an engineer is like finding gold nuggets on the floor. ... I think the conditions and salaries are much lower in engineering than in other sorts of industries. It is sad and part of UK's problem (B10, p 10).

The industrial relations manager of a company in the food and luxury food industry formulated his opinion very drastically:

> There is this shortage of technical skills. ... What worries me is whether in Britain we are actually capable of doing it or we actually turn out to be a nation of hamburger and hot-dog sellers (B1, p 15).

The lack of technical qualifications, especially in industrial management, is also the theme of the above quoted manager:

> The few managers who are in this company, I would say that there is only one who genuinely has a technical qualification. I think they are orientated towards other qualifications. I think it is a clear disadvantage. I don't think there are enough technically-qualified and technically-orientated people. ... I don't think that in

> British industry generally there are enough people who are technically qualified in managerial positions. But it goes back to school and to the educational system. It goes back to university where it is not promoted. It is made to be less glamourous than it could be (B10, p 19).

Two reasons, which relate to each other, for the lacking technical orientation and qualification of British management were not only stated in the interviews of the two previously quoted managers but were mentioned again and again: the lack of company and social recognition of technicians and engineers and equally in a comparable way the low esteem of technical professions within the British educational system and system of vocational training. Some further excerpts from other interviews may illustrate the great extent of this view amongst English managers themselves:

> The position of technical skills is not recognized. There is no recognition (B2, p 18).

This is quoted from the managing director of a metal processing company, by the way one of the few engineer managers of our sample. But the majority of his non-technical trained colleagues shared his opinion, e.g. the personnel manager of a company in the building industry:

> I think such training and education as an engineer deserves a higher status than it gets. It deserves a higher salary (B11, p 15).

The personnel director of a chemical company sees – like many others – historical reasons for this:

> I think this is due to the fact that in the UK historically technology is classed as the poor relation (B17, p 6).

A thought which we will follow up on at a later stage. At the same time as underlining the technical deficit in England's industrial management some of those interviewed underlined their (possibly one-sided) commercial orientation, e.g. the personnel manager of a company in the food and luxury food industry:

> The problem basically stems from the inability to train for skills. With the best will in the world industry will only train for its own needs because industry in general hasn't got some wider view of society to say that we have got a moral obligation to do this, that or the other. Industrialists are hard-nosed businessmen and they will only train for the skills that they require at that given time (B3, p 18).

The executive director of a textile company emphasized explicitly:

> In Britain management is more sales-orientated rather than technical. Most have a financial background or a sales background (B14, p 8).

Millar comes to the same results in her comparative Anglo-German examination. "High status of engineers in Germany contrasts with high status of finance and marketing people in the UK" (Millar: 1979, p 63). And Armstrong pointed to the dominating role of the accountants in British industry, in particular for the guiding and control of the production process (Armstrong: 1990, p 276).

The selected quotes make clear that most managers feel this is a lack (if not a personal one) and a disadvantage in comparison to German industrial management, often linked with the reference to a better training and further training system of their German colleagues ("German management ... is better trained. You have a better structure to your training" (B8, p 14).

The opposite view of a manager from the food and luxury food industry can therefore be seen as an exception in our empirical findings and beyond this also an exception to the opinion which is predominant in professional literature and public:

> When I go to Germany people are amazed, when they know that I am a factory director, they will say which branch of engineering are you from? I am not an engineer and they say that is very unusual. So there does appear in Germany almost a straightjacket that says unless you are a formally qualified engineer you can't be involved in manufacturing management. I don't think that is as true over here. It is probably true of heavy manufacturing. I have never found it a problem, I don't believe that it has ever been a great burden to me that I wasn't a formally qualified engineer (B13, p 10).

On the whole, however, our findings prove the widespread view that in English managers' ways of thinking and acting technology has a considerably lower esteem than in the case of German managers and this is the judgement of the managers themselves. This is confirmed by an examination of the Centre for Exploitation of Science and Technology in Manchester, whose empirical basis was a number of interviews with "a total of 51 directors and senior managers of UK technology-based companies" (*Financial Times* from 23.4.1990). Those asked see a technological backwardness of English industry in comparison with foreign competition:

> Those interviewed all believe technology to be of critical importance in maintaining competitiveness, but recognize that they must innovate more frequently or make bigger leaps, to keep pace with competitors overseas (*Financial Times* from 23.4.1990).

This technological backwardness is – according to the author of the study – a consequence of the decreasing or at least low expenditure on research and development in British industry which on the other hand is an expression of a certain indifference towards production technology in English company management. The president of the British Association expressed this in very drastic terms recently:

> Britain's failure in industrial innovation is due ... to industry's lack of interest in research and development. ... Britain's industrial performance had been consistently worse than its international competitors over the last 40 years. Long-term economic growth was about the same as in the Soviet Union. If we do not pull up our socks there is the danger that we shall quickly become a third world power (*Financial Times* from 27.8.1991).

But what are in detail the reasons for the low(er) opinion of technology and production in Great Britain's industry in comparison to Germany and which consequences arise out of this for its ability to perform and compete?

The British sociologist Lawrence, quoted at the beginning, has attempted to make a systematic summary here.

First of all he states the higher "standing" of German engineers compared with their English colleagues (Lawrence: 1980, pp 79-83). This was frequently mentioned in our interviews too. This is expressed in the fact that they are represented more in German industrial management, also at the top of the company, in numerical terms much more than in England and indeed not only in the technical but also in the non-technical functions. Let us remember the corresponding numbers of our two samples as an illustration: whilst approximately half of our German managers have completed a technical or scientific course of study, only one English colleague was found to have studied in this direction. By the way the poor representation of engineers in Britain's top industrial management is not only different to Germany but also to other continental – European industrial countries like Sweden and France (Glover: 1976)[10].

As the interviewed English managers emphasized this is already a consequence of the British educational system and system of vocational training. The number of High School graduates of technical subjects of the working population in England is approximately 36% lower than in Germany although the number of employees with High School qualifications or equivalent qualifications only differ slightly in both countries from each other. Even a total of 71% is the total difference if we only include the graduates with university qualifications in the comparison (Wagner: 1986, pp 13-14). In England in 1976 only 14% of the High School graduates gained a technical or engineering qualification; the corresponding number in Germany was 26% (Wagner: 1986, p 20). Questions of technology do not play any further role in

---

10   Engineers are extremely strongly represented in company management in Russia, even dominant, as the investigations within the framework of our Russian control study have illustrated. In contrast to the West European countries we have already mentioned, this has its reasons in the special economic and social system which knew no market relations and was related one-sidedly to the technical dimension of the companies.

further management training: "The importance of technology is not reflected in the majority of UK general management programmes, in spite of the fact that it is having an increasing impact on the nature of management" (*Financial Times* from 24.7.1990).

The lower standing of British engineers is expressed in poorer payment in comparison to their German colleagues as Lawrence (1980, p 80) confirmed[11]. Furthermore in Lawrence's opinion the training to become an engineer in Germany is not only better but also socially more well-known and accepted than in England (Lawrence: 1980, p 81). But all these details do not constitute the particularity of the engineer's status in Germany. Lawrence writes with what we may assume as the clarity of a foreign observer (1980; p 82):

> It is a society in which much interest attaches to making things and this interest is widely diffused. It is a society which has a concept, 'Technik', to encompass the knowledge and skill relevant to making things and making them work. ... In all this, the engineer is perhaps best understood as the paratypical German.

Empirical investigations have discovered quite different modes of thought and behaviour of German and British engineers, within the professional group: "German engineers have more positive goals than their British counterparts: 'If he gets stuck he will fight it, but in the UK he'll leave unless you put pressure on him'" (Millar: 1976, p 58).

Technik itself has in Germany a much higher social status, precisely in the way of thinking and acting of industrial managers, yes, we can say that technology has a different cultural significance. In England, however, engineering is considered as "purely" applied science which has only a dependent and subordinate character in comparison to "real" science (Lawrence: 1980, p 96). There is not even a synonym for the German concept in Great Britain:

> It is important to grasp that Technik really does not have any equivalent in English. The English word 'technique' is not a contender. It simply means a way of doing something, and the something is not necessary technical or related to manufacture. Neither is the English word 'technology' an equivalent of the German concept of Technik. ... The corresponding word Technologie exists in German with the same vague connotations (Lawrence: 1980, p 97).

Lawrence comes to the conclusion that: "Technik exerts a pervasive influence in German firms and on German managerial thinking" (Lawrence: 1980, p 98). This is evident in the strong product relationship of German managers which has already been mentioned and was also expressed in our interviews

---

11   "According to one recent survey, the UK comes fourth from the bottom of the European league in net pay for both experienced and newly qualified engineers" (*Financial Times*, 25.2.1991).

and is in strong contrast with their English colleagues (Lawrence: 1980, p 120)[12].

But what are the consequences for the described different modes of thinking and behaviour in relation to the significance of Technik in the two countries we compare? Can we really conclude like Lawrence that Technik stands in the foreground in the considerations and actions of German managers and that therefore management strategies only stand in second place (Lawrence: 1980, p 98)? As a result of our empirical findings we cannot agree to such a critical interpretation. A professional managerial concept must provide the forming of a functioning connection between internal and external necessities of company development. Therefore it is one of the deciding tasks of top management, in spite of different priorities in the companies according to which branch they belong to and their position on the market, to avoid a purely one-dimensional pursuit of either the demands of the market or Technik.

A member of the management of an office supplies manufacturer described this quite vividly:

> Let us take a general statement of marketing people: 'You are not bringing enough products' or 'You are making too complicated constructions, the product is getting too expensive'. These are – if you like – realistic conflicts which are then settled in the corresponding committees. It is our task to get the right people for this. If we are talking about product development the marketing-man cannot sit at the table alone but the man from research and development, possibly from sales Technik must be there and if we are talking about too long periods of time for development then the toolmaker must be at the table and he must explain why it takes 6 months for a tool to be finished (G7, p 22).

But fundamentally our interviews with German managers show that the significance of production technology as technology in general has grown decisively for the managerial concepts of top management and therefore cannot be neglected in the framework of such concepts. Nevertheless this findings need some differentiations in several ways. For example modern techniques of information and communication have changed the actual working situation of the members of company management – in particular on the first level but also on the second level – to a very small degree. The member of management of a large company gave the answer which possibly appears central to this theme:

> You see, there is no terminal on my desk. The work in management directly is only shaped to a small extent by modern means of information and communication,

---

12 Such a strong product orientation of German managers has also been confirmed as being different to US-American managers, who think and act according to their orientation towards the market (*Handelsblatt*, 28.9.1990).

apart from the overhead-projector hardly anything is used. That is quite different on
levels below management. There the computer as well as communication aids, as
e.g. the network planning is strongly used. It is a question of age and self-image. I
personally think that in the near future a terminal will stand on my desk and then I
will be able to and wish to make use of it (G62, p 19).

On the other hand two thirds of managers stated that the necessity of top
management to concern themselves more with new technologies than ever
before has arisen out of the acceleration of technical change.

The results of Müller-Böling confirm this: Only 30% of German top managers
use a personal computer themselves, although a basically positive attitude
towards computer data processing predominates. Müller-Böling explains this
discrepancy between attitude and behaviour as a result of the increased age of
top managers. There is a clear increase in the personal use of computers in the
case of younger age groups. Top managers up to 40 years old use a PC or a
screen-terminal at a rate of 55% whilst the percentage of managers over 60
falls to 10% (Müller-Böling et al.: 1989, pp 107-108).

There is, on the whole, quite a contradictory relationship towards technology
in the understanding of German managers. Although the use of modern
technology is recommended and advanced it is not used in actual work. In our
opinion this is only partly to blame on the specific working situation and
structure of top management as becomes clear from the quoted comment.
Apart from that there appears to be a certain distance towards the practical use
of modern technology.

This is not only the case for the mentioned technologies of information and
communication but also for the techniques of production. As our findings
show the daily technically arranged run of production is rather a matter for
middle management (and of course for the workers) than for the managers we
asked. Here there are no serious differences between business men and
engineers in top company management; the latter also lose to a considerable
degree and as a matter of necessity the direct relationship to the practical use of
technology. There are, of course, exceptions. According to the information
given by a commercial manager of a medium-sized tool machinery construction company, the company's existence and survival to a very high degree
depends on the technical creativity of the technical manager (G119, p 22).
This is similar for the research and development departments of very big
companies in as far as they are individual managerial departments (G92,
p 19).

Finally the significance of technology for the managerial concepts of top
management are different according to their branch, product, competition
situation etc., on the whole it is very specific to the company. Thus amongst

those companies examined by us, there are those where questions of technology dominate the managerial concepts (e.g. tool machinery construction, partly automobile industry) but there are some in which these stand in the background (e.g. breweries, shipbuilding yards) where other domains are of greater significance as for example the relationship to the market. In spite of these limitations, however, a general increase in the significance of technology in the face of the growing complexity of new technologies and the increasing acceleration of technical change for the managerial conception of top management can be confirmed.

This means that the use of new technologies does not only demand changed processes of adaptation and attitude of the staff but also of the top managers. The use of the concept of "systematic rationalization"[13] demonstrates that the use of new technologies, in particular of technologies of information and communication, creates a new field of demands on company management which can also lead to great uncertainty and lack of self-confidence on the part of the managers.

Baethge, Oberbeck understand "systemic rationalization processes" as

> that by using new micro-electronically based techniques of data processing and communication, the company and external company flow of information, the communication and combination of data, the organization of company procedures and the steering of different functional domains in one administration or in one company can be newly created in one go (Baethge, Oberbeck: 1986, p 22).

Indeed the concept of the systematic rationalization emphasizes the far-reaching and thorough perspective of planning and with it also the significance of management as an instance of planning, deciding and control. But however the focus is the company use of technology which demands of management a letting go of the established functions, competencies and specializations. Here the company management is no longer only the operator, the 'subject' but also at the same time the person affected, the 'object'. Christoph Deutschmann states that the concept of systemic rationalization, in particular the extensive use of the technologies of information and communication not only "increases the uncertainty in dealings with markets and technologies, (but) ... also reduces the abilities of management to deal with them successfully" (Deutschmann: 1989, p. 375).

In as far as the concepts of the "Computer-Integrated-Manufacturing" (CIM) is concerned there is not only a technically based scepticism but also a certain

---

13   Here we do not want to go into the partly differently evaluated consequences of this systematic rationalization like e.g. those consequences regarding the aspect of qualification on the one side by M. Baethge, H. Oberbeck (1986) and on the other side by N. Altmann, M. Deiß, V. Döhl and D. Sauer (1986).

amount of uncertainty accompanied by fear. Indeed the top managers are fundamentally quite clearly informed about the necessity and fastest possible use of new technologies as we can assume from our questioning. However practicable conceptions regarding the concrete extent of the use and necessity of re-organizations are lacking. Therefore we can agree with Priore, Sabel (1985, p 22) who in connection with the introduction of Computer Data Processing confirmed that "management is uncertain as to which products are manufactured and which technologies should be employed, yes, even uncertain about how authority and competence should be distributed in the company".

A quick glance at German industrial management has shown that there is – at least it is assumed – no one-dimensional orientation towards technology. Questions regarding the market, investments and financing etc. play an important role in the way of thinking and acting of those top managers who are engineers by profession. It is the reverse for questions of production technology and product quality which are of central significance for the businessmen amongst the managers. There appears here an obvious difference to their colleagues in England. In an article in the *Financial Times* we read:

"Production management still receives scant attention. … It often pays less well than other areas of management and fails to attract the best people" (*Financial Times* from 23.7.1990). As a result of different empirical studies Lawrence (1980, pp 125-130) gives a whole list of examples for the deficits in English production management. Some of the critical points listed there are:

> Poor showing on meeting delivery dates (and a high proportion of these deadlines fixed by sales rather than production), a poor record on product innovation, too little attention paid to purchasing policy and stock control and poor coordination of the various phases of production with component batches lying idle on the shop floor for long periods (Lawrence: 1980, p 125).

Another report states:

> Production management work is … characterized by pressure, frustration deriving from industrial relations problems and a general lack of investment resulting in old plant and equipment and poorly laid out factories. Production management tends to be neglected by top management and to be staffed by 'old faithfuls' with poor career prospects. It is relatively disadvantaged with regard to pay, the allocation of company cars, fringe benefits, general promotion prospects, access to the Board of Directors and general status (Lawrence: 1980, p 126).

In comparison to this production management in Germany finds itself in a better position (Lawrence: 1980, pp 131-137). The decisive reason for this is the extensively greater social and company evaluation of technology which has already been described. Thus in Germany within production management there is, in comparison to England, a far-reaching identification with work as well as a distinct appreciation of punctuality and faithfulness to deadlines, which can be classed – as well as product quality – as a definite advantage of competition for German industry (Lawrence: 1980, pp 131, 147). This is particularly true when faced with Great Britain. An internationally comparative study which was carried out at the beginning of the 1980s found out that with regard to delivery punctuality Germany and Sweden from those countries examined were at the top of the list whilst Great Britain came bottom of the table after Italy (Lawrence: 1984, p 83).

The qualifications and company status of German production managers are better or rather higher than those of their English colleagues (Lawrence: 1980, pp 137, 148-149). Finally the regulation of industrial relations offers German production management more favourable conditions:

> The fact that the number of trade unions is small and that they are industrial unions, offering membership to all types and grades of employee in a given industry, means that demarcation disputes in a formal sense are impossible by definition. There is, in fact, no phrase in German for demarcation dispute. … One manifestation of this is the less rigid division between Production and Maintenance as functions and activities. … Another practical implication is that the German production manager has more freedom to move workers around to satisfy immediate manning needs (Lawrence: 1980, p 134).

To summarize Lawrence states (1984, pp 141-142):

> British industry has a marked financial orientation. It is strongly oriented to 'profits now'. … It emphasises financial control and budgetary surveillance, and accountants play an important part in the British system. Expenditure is closely controlled, and expenditure decisions strongly linked to hierarchical status. Capital expenditure is not a priority, and there is little enthusiasm for expenditure which do not contribute directly to profit.

Lawrence himself remarks that such modes of behaviour and action are in no way completely strange to German industrial managers but they are only less widespread and developed. These tendential differences are illustrated very vividly by the following quote:

> When British managers are asked what they are proud of they tend to answer in commercial terms with references to profitability, cost-reduction, growth of turnover or of market shares. Germans answer with references to productivity, delivery, methods and above all the presumptive quality of products. British managers think industry is about making money: Germans that it is about making three-dimensional artifacts (Lawrence: 1984, p 142).

However in spite of such tendential differences, as they have become clear in our interviews, we must also emphasize: We cannot speak of absolute dominance of technology within German industrial management. A tense relationship between economy and technology becomes evident. Precisely with regard to German top management there are signs of a certain distance to technology as we could show above. In the last example and without doubt the primate of economy counts in German industry, e.g. at least in the long run work must be economically successful. Nevertheless the appreciation of technology in the company and society is noticeably greater.

Remarkably enough this stronger orientation towards technology is considered also by British experts and managers, not only those we interviewed, to be an advantage of German industry and the more commercial orientation is considered correspondingly to be a disadvantage of British industry. In an article of the *Financial Times* (18.6.1990) we read that there is a lack of engineers "with broader business skills" since the significance of engineers or of technology in general for top management is increasing more and more. It may be possible here that in expectation of the unified market in Europe a certain amount of re-thinking in British economy and society is necessary which should begin in an increase of the appreciation of their own industry in several respects.

3.3   The British society holds little account of its own industry

In one of the first international comparisons of European managers David Granick describes the social appreciation of British industry in his own country by stating two very British examples, firstly with the help of the career planning of the 'talented young man from a good family' and secondly by looking at the obituary column of the *Times*.

To begin with the latter: A three month evaluation of this obituary in 1957 discovered that from a total of 203 deceased who were found to be worthy of consideration, only 12 came from the economy, but 34 from the Armed Forces (Granick: 1962, p 102). Here is the description of the professional motives and expectations:

> The intelligent young man from a good family, who attended an exclusive private school, then went to Oxford or Cambridge, looks for another field of occupation: the Civil Service, Foreign Service, free professions like law or medicine, or even journalism, politics ... the university career or also the State church. Apart from the free professions only the 'business branches' suitable for a gentleman, like private banking and publishing, were really considered respectable (Granick: 1962, pp 102-103).

Lewis and Stewart report from a similar case in which a young man described his way into industrial management as follows:

> My first choice was the Foreign Office, my second UNESCO, my third the BBC, my fourth the Times; then there was nothing left but teaching or business, and as I can't bear little boys it had to be business (Lewis, Stewart: 1961, p 65).

The examples can be seen as an indication of a traditional low appreciation in particular of (producing) industry by British society.

On the other hand, in a questionnaire carried out at the end of the 1950s Anthony Sampson believed to have confirmed a sensational increase in the manager's status since the end of the Second World War:

> The export crisis of the post-war period, the demise of influential posts within the Indian Civil Service or in the colonial offices, the reaction to the Civil Service with its over-exaggerated bureaucracy and the new behaviour towards the big corporations which seemed themselves to be a kind of Civil Service – all this led to a new way of looking at industry and to a new invasion of talented young university graduates in the companies (Sampson: 1963, p 457).

We were interested in how English managers valued the social status of British industry, also in comparison to other countries and other branches of economy. The answers were remarkably unanimous.

None of those managers we interviewed expressed the view that industry in Great Britain enjoys sufficient and appropriate esteem. Even so, five were of the opinion that acknowledgement had increased in the last years. Finally the view was represented by several of those interviewed that the social status of industry in other countries, especially in Germany, is significantly higher. Some selected quotes may illustrate the views of the English managers we interviewed. The personnel director of a company in the metal industry:

> Industrial management has been a dirty word for a long, long time in Great Britain. ... Status-wise, bank managers are at the top of the tree and industrial managers at the bottom (B5, p 5).

And a manager from the building industry stated:

> There is something about manufacturing in this country which people have never quite accepted. If you said to someone which is the best type of occupation, do you want to be a doctor or a lawyer or a manager? It would always be one of the old professions I think that would be quoted (B11, p 11).

The historical origin of this phenomenon was pointed to on several occasions, as for example by the following manager also from the building industry:

> I think it is historical. If we are talking at schools it is no glamour, it is better to be an airline pilot or a bank manager or a lawyer rather than be in industry and make things (B12, p 7).

These historical reasons were also given by the personnel manager of a company dealing with vehicle construction and it was connected to a criticism of (former) industrial top managers:

> I think it is true that it (the manufacturing industry) is low in the public seat. The bank manager is one of the quite highly rated occupations. It has changed a little bit. I don't think the bank manager is as high today as it used to be a few decades ago. But he is still pretty high. I think esteem has to be earned. It is not there as a natural right, is it? I think British management has been cavalier, has not demonstrated a professionalism that I believe it is acquiring today. That may be the reason why it is low in the pecking order (B4, p 3).

Lewis and Stewart described quite clearly in a comparison of English and American businessmen the distanced behaviour of certain managers (possibly of those managers who are retired) towards their own professional occupation. Even if the American manager differentiates in many respects from his equivalent in Germany there is, with regard to the quote just given regarding the social acknowledgement and identification with the professional task, no essential difference. The discovery of Lewis and Stewart applies to the comparison of German and English industrial management. But where are the reasons for such a distancing (possibly far-reaching in its consequences) of English society and also of certain managers themselves from their own industry? Are the reasons perhaps the comparably low financial incentives, that is to say income, as Granick seems to assume (Granick: 1962, pp 374-375)? We would not agree with such a narrow interpretation, especially as newer statistical data material shows that management salaries in banking and finance or in the Civil Service are by no means generally higher than in industry (*Financial Times* from 1.2.1991).

The research of the origins for the comparably low standing of British industry (as we have found out ourselves) must proceed on a wider scale and above all earlier (Lawrence: 1980, pp 163-175) as Wiener did in his examination about *English Culture and the Decline of the Industrial Spirit 1850-1980* (1981).

Wiener's hypothesis is that the crisis in which English economy has found itself since the mid-1970s has its origins above all in British history and culture. In particular the modes of thought and behaviour regarding the industrial development of the British elite are responsible for the susceptibility to crisis of the economy (Wiener: 1981, pp 3-10). This phenomenon – according to Wiener's thesis – arises from the particular course of the process of industrialization in England or to be more precise from the social structure of those persons advancing this process:

"The nation had the world's first ... essentially capitalist ruling class: the eighteenth-century landed aristocracy and gentry. What Britain never had was a straightforwardly bourgeois or industrial elite" (Wiener: 1981, p 8). This means that the social processes of change of the industrial revolution came about in accord with the dominant opinion and old elites of Victorian society. As a result of these facts the social change and modernization were not complete for essential elements of the old society lived on in the new. Wiener therefore coined the phrase: "The revolution that never was" (Wiener: 1981, p 7). According to Wiener, in Continental Europe the industrial revolution was borne by an oppositional bourgeoisie. Even if, with reference to Germany, this view must be relativized in so far as the Prussian-German bourgeoisie was by no means the motor of political radical change of the 19th century. But it is on the other hand correct that the bearers of the economic and industrial development were not or hardly ever recruited from the old management levels (Braun, Eberwein, Tholen: 1992).

In England, however the industrialists felt obliged to the traditional modes of thought and behaviour. The wealth gained within industry was used to procure a country estate or a title of nobility attached to it. The lifestyle of the old aristocracy was, where possible, copied (Wiener: 1981, p 127).

The economic development of the 19th century "threw up not one but two groups of new businessmen, with differing characteristics and different fates: one based on commerce and finance and centred in London, the other based on manufacturing and centred in the North" (Wiener: 1981, p 128). The first which is still characterized as the city was richer, more powerful, richer in tradition and settled in the centre of upper-class England, with its manifold connections to aristocracy and landed gentry and was accepted by the old elite to a higher degree than the industrial North of England. In the following period the industrial and bank elites, industry and finance separated. For this, cultural factors played a considerable role as well as economic factors (the banks invested less money in their home industry and much more in more profitable areas like the colonies). The very conservative finance elite set standards for the whole of England. At the same time there arose in bank circles a certain arrogance towards "dirty" industry. Therefore it is not surprising, according to Wiener, that the English structure of education and training took on a one-sided position in favour of the financial sector. According to the demands of English industry, support of industrial-related educational institutions were scarcely moderated. The educational elite strived for occupation in the atmosphere of the prestige-filled city and took a rather disapproving attitude to careers in industry (Wiener: 1981, pp 129- 130). As far as training is concerned, engineering was turned down by the British elite for their sons because such paths of training did not qualify them for an occupation in banking and finance and therefore were not filled with prestige[14]. Conse-

---

14   See here our corresponding explanations in chapter 3.2, "Technology versus fi-
     nance".

quently engineering developed as the domain for rising qualified industrial workers and their sons. The picture only changed a little in the years between the wars. But it was still considered the rule that the best graduates from universities almost always preferred occupations in administration and in the world of banking and finance to the way into industry (Wiener: 1981, p 132).

It was only after the Second World War that the universities changed over to industrial-related courses of study. Many polytechnics were extended after 1945 to universities. But still the hostility to industry of the universities was present in the 1960s. After asking, only Warwick University (which is in the Northern English industrial area) held a close connection to industry. The other universities orientated themselves towards the educational ideal of Oxford and Cambridge (Wiener: 1981, pp 133- 134).

Wiener stated that a managerial occupation in industry in other highly developed nations, precisely in Germany, enjoys much higher social prestige. To add to this the educational system is not averse to accommodating the educational needs of industry (Wiener: 1981, p 136). Wiener's explanation for this, namely the shock of the Second World War is in our opinion not sufficient. If we compare England and Germany on this aspect, we must assume that on the whole England had taken a continual State development.

For this reason the traditional norms and value concepts could be upheld and could really take hold. In comparison, Germany , as a consequence of two World War defeats was put and forced into the position of looking carefully through its social structures. With the collapse of traditional social structures and norms and the majority of the old management levels, national socialism brought with it a sudden modernness – of course this was without doubt not without its problems and not unbroken (Dahrendorf: 1977, pp 415-432) – which does not justify in any way whatsoever the works of the National Socialists and the catastrophic consequences of their work.

But dynamic processes of further development were set in motion in Germany which in England with its extensively unbroken traditions could not come about to such a degree[15].

The opinions of the managers quoted at the beginning express quite directly that the consequences of these different developments are still recognizable today in English industry. Various other examinations confirm this. Thus the chief executive of the time from the Chloride Group Ltd and the later chairman of British Leyland, Michael Edwards, stated at a conference in 1976 that English industry in its home country enjoyed a much lower status than other West European and North American industrial companies in their respective

---

15   See for example the latest discussion in Prinz, Zitelmann (1991).

home countries. English industry is especially effective then when it operates abroad (Fores, Glover: 1978, pp 9- 23). Lawrence expresses a similar view in his comparison of German and English industry. He names essential reasons for this situation.

"The higher standing of industry in Germany has some important general effects. It enhances industry's ability to choose the managers it wants and retain their loyalty, it raises morale and this is particularly salient in work as beset with uncertainty as management work is" (Lawrence: 1980, p 174).

Empirical examinations about the social structure of top managers of large British economic companies in the 1970s concluded that in this respect there are also very great differences between the finance sector on the one hand and industry on the other hand. Whitley comes to the result that amongst those in the finance sector there were more students from private schools; former "Oxbridge" students were represented in greater number; considerably more were members of clubs which were considered to be particularly prestigious (Whitley: 1974; as well as Stanworth, Giddens: 1974).

A newer contribution by Coates states that social admittance to the finance sector is still more exclusive than to industry, although he does make use of the above quoted material by Stanworth and Giddens (Coates: 1989, pp 28-32).

We may therefore provisionally note that the historically originated low status of English industry has indeed weakened but is still present today. The significance of this phenomenon for an industrial decline in Great Britain since the end of the Second World War cannot be quantified in detail and is certainly not solely responsible. In any case this will have contributed to a loss of industrial dynamism (Lane: 1989, p 10) which is often complained of by many politicians and scientists and which they make responsible for the present state of British industry. In recent times more and more voices have been raised in Great Britain that demand a certain amount of re-thinking within British society in respect of their own industry. In a report of the House of Lords about "Innovation in Manufacturing Industry" we read:

> The most urgent need is for a change in our culture. Unless we revise radically some of the attitudes which permeate our society we will continue to be neglected. Antipathy to manufacturing industry runs deep in our society. Industry is held in low esteem and so attracts too little of the country's talent and other resources (*Financial Times* from 7.3.1991).

With regard to Europe's future unified market such re-thinking seems inevitable in the consciousness of many English industrial managers in order to be able to remain in international competition. In their opinion a different form of industrial policy of British banks is also a part of this.

3.4   Foresighted industrial policy or short term maximization of profits – With regard to the role played by the banks in Great Britain

According to the widespread view in literature and the public, the specific relations between financial and industrial capital in Great Britain are an essential hindrance of effective and foresighted industrial policy. In 1990 the Innovation Advisory Board of the Ministry for Trade and Industry put forward a report,

> which blamed City pressures to deliver short term financial returns, for the lower growth in investment in research and development in Britain, compared with its main competitors (*Financial Times* from 26.6.1990).

The consequence is an obstacle for long term investments in necessary innovations.

Criticism from the oppositional Labour Party regarding "short-termness" of the City (and of the government) flows in the same direction as we can see from the example of Neil Kinnock who said in the spring of 1991:

> In an important speech to industrialists in Birmingham, the Labour leader pointed out that while Japanese companies took years to build scientific and technological success "British firms are forced to think and act ever more short term".Claiming that pressure to produce dividends takes precedence over long-term investment, he said that for every one pound spent in Britain on research and development, Italy spent 1.50, France 2 pounds and Germany 2.35 (*Financial Times* from 13/14.4.1991).

Christel Lane described the historical specific relationship between financial and industrial capital[16] as a crucial hindrance to foresighted industrial policy in Great Britain.

> Due to Britain's historical role of an imperial nation, financial capital developed a distinctly international orientation, and Britain remained the international banking centre even after the dissolution of the empire. … At the present time banks are not substantial investors in corporate equity. Although borrowing from banks has now become more common, credits have remained largely short-term, and bank involvement in, and control over, the internal affairs of industry has remained underdeveloped. Thus, in the highly important area of capital investment, neither the State nor the banks have been important agents of support and control, and consequently strong impulses for industrial restructuring could not issue from either quarter (Lane: 1989, pp 256-257).

---

16   See here the descriptions in the previous chapter.

In comparison, in Germany "banks are both substantial lenders and shareholders in the larger ... firms" and this "has given banks an active interest to promote the well-being of individual firms and even of whole industries" (Lane: 1989, p 259).

Even if Lane's view regarding the influence of the banks in Germany may possibly be too euphemistic it still becomes clear that, in addition to the social low evaluation of industry in England which has already been described in the previous chapter, the role of the banks drastically limits the possibilities of foresighted industrial policy which in the opinion of many is acutely necessary. The majority of the English managers we interviewed see the situation in this way too. Only one expressed the opinion that the banks would prefer a longer term security of companies. In contrast 10 managers represented the view that banks are primarily interested in a short term maximization of profits. A manager from the building industry expressed his opinion in a very drastic way and said:

> I think that bank managers in this country are extremely short-sighted and very punitive towards the small businessman. They have got the sort of mentality of dealing with shopkeepers. They see a day-to-day return. They don't look towards future development. They don't back it up. ... They don't look at any resource in the industry apart from cash (B7, pp 17-18).

The handicapping of smaller companies in particular by the banks was also underlined by the industrial relations manager of a company from the food and luxury food industry:

> Banks tend to be very unfair and very unkind on small companies that have got cash flow problems. They demand a quick return. ... Quite honestly I think the banking industry is very unreal. They will lend 3 billion to someone in South America or Africa and write it off as many of our banks do. ... Yet there is a guy down the road who owes them 50,000 pounds and they will close him down immediately. I have very little regard for the banking industry. I don't think they help industry at all really unless it suits them. They are profit-orientated (B1, p 20).

In the critical attitude of a personnel manager the Third World was once again presented as the scapegoat:

> Banks aren't big risk takers except in third world countries. They really do not get behind British industry to help you through any crisis. Yet they justify this by saying how many millions they have had to write off in Peru and places like that (B3, p 23).

Finally it was mentioned that in an international comparison the described orientations of the banks presented a disadvantage with regard to competition for British industry:

> Short-term and that is the problem. The city expects short-term results, quick results and I think this is where we differ from Japan. I don't know about Germany. Certainly Japan and maybe the US where people are prepared to be more patient. They will say OK it is a good idea and we are prepared to wait 5 years. I think in the UK people are saying that unless they get results in a year or two then they are not interested. I think this is a feature of the big banks (B11, p 20).

This is the impression of the illustrating statements and estimations of the English managers we interviewed regarding the role of the banks and the consequences for their home industry; on the whole they confirm quite vividly the short term views taken by British banks and the detrimental consequences which were also mentioned at the beginning of this chapter. The chairman of the British Glass manufacturers, Pilkington, whose company acquired a German company at the beginning of the 1980s, spoke from his direct experience with companies in Great Britain and Germany:

> The pressures on investment are not nearly so short term there. They are far more relaxed; they go for quality rather than continuous upgrading of profit margins. Earnings per share are not high on the list of priorities; they do not really understand us when we talk about that. They are driven by the long term, by products and customers, while we are driven too much by the City (*Financial Times* from 20.6.1990).

The fact that this bank behaviour weakens British industry when compared with other Western industrial countries is not only seen by some of the managers. The *Financial Times* also reported that British industry casts an envious eye on Germany (and Japan):

> UK industrialists have tended to cast an envious eye in the direction of Germany (and Japan) where the nature of the relationship between owners and management is seen to favour long-term industrial development (*Financial Times* from 24.5.1991).

In a report in front of English colleagues a German manager confirmed this: Apart from cultural and historical reasons, as for example the high evaluation of Technik (see above) and the necessity for reconstruction after the Second World War, the role of the banks in Germany is seen to be a deciding factor:

> Although the banks own just eight per cent of German companies directly, the decision of private investors (who own 20% of company shares in Germany) to allow the banks to vote their stocks gives the banks quite some voting power (and) also provides desired stability for long term investment (*Financial Times* from 24.5.1991).

However the City is all too easily taken to be the scapegoat for mismanagement in industry (see e.g. *Financial Times* from 21.5.1990). P. Marsh, the professor of management and finance at the London Business School, emphasizes that industrial managers can quite plausibly have their own motives for a short term strategy:

> When it comes to making plans for the future, managers' perceptions will be influenced by their organizational systems and contexts, including the way they are renumerated and rewarded; their time horizons within their job; the role played by the internal performance measurement and management accounting systems; and, the internal capital budgeting and project appraisal systems (*Financial Times* from 7.11.1990).

Depending on the way in which the corresponding company organization and situation is arranged there may be a short term orientation of managers and thus approaches of long term thinking and action may be prevented.

In spite of this clearly necessary differentiation, we may say that the managers we interviewed, in agreement with the dominating opinion, appraise the role of the banks and the financial sector in general in Great Britain as being negative for industry. This means that the compulsion to achieve short term profits, which may possibly be at the expense of a long term stabilization of the companies, the lack, caused by the demands and influence of the financial sector, a lack to provide foresighted industrial policy as well as of the State as of the financial capital, lead in the eyes of British industry itself to serious competitive disadvantages in the face of international competition.

With this background, what do managers expect of the future unified European market; do they look at it in hope or in fear?

3.5   Fear of Europe? The expectations of English and German managers of the united market in Europe

We asked the English managers: What are your expectations for the Common Market which will possibly be implemented in 1993? In the face of the considerable British reservations regarding this question, which have continually been heard, at least from the political (government) sector, we were indeed quite curious to hear the answers of economic managers themselves.

After all, almost half of those managers we interviewed expect positive results for the economic development from the Common Market; however only two managers emphasized explicitly that they are also prepared for this. An almost equal number of managers associated negative expectations for British industry with the key word European Market 1993 and this above all because they are not prepared for it. The language problem and too little knowledge of other cultures were also seen to be an essential hindrance to overcoming successfully the expected problems.

Only one of the managers we interviewed stated that there would be no great changes as a result of the united market:

> I think our expectations for the Common Market are not immense. I must stress that change over the next decade will be gradual rather than dramatic (B17, p 12).

However on the whole the managers expect considerable effects and as already mentioned pessimism and optimism keep an equal balance here. But let us first of all turn to the sceptics.

The personnel manager of a company for vehicle construction said:

> What people seem to hang on to in this country is the Commonwealth. ... Of all nations the British are one of the most nationalistic people. ... Deep down inside, almost every person in this country finds it extremely difficult to think European. I see what is happening in Europe and in Eastern Europe and I think of all the nations, we are the slowest. We are still messing about with a sort of protectionism or that sort of nationalism. ... That is why I have such a pessimistic view. We are so insular and so far behind. It is extremely difficult to promote a second language even in our young graduates. ... I think from that point of view we are less European. We are less equipped, less able, less prepared for 1993 than any other country (B10, pp 33-34).

The problems presented in this statement, in particular the insularity – and this is meant by no means in the geographical sense – the backward looking orientation towards the Commonwealth, the specific form of a certain nationalism and, last but not least, the widespread only slight tendency to learn foreign languages in Great Britain[17] were stated in many interviews as the main reasons for pessimistic expectations with respect to the Common Market – even if not always expressed in such a drastic form. A manager of a large company from the building industry said:

> I think with regard to Europe generally, I think it is true that many companies have not done enough. I think what has happened is that on the Continent people have always had to think of themselves as European and we haven't. It is partly the language thing but I think also we have looked to America rather than France or

---

17 This special lack was confirmed by a European wide survey of employment practices published by the Price Waterhouse Cranfield Project in June 1990. "In spite of the advent of the European market, languages received one of the lowest ratings of all, reflecting apathy in some countries such as Britain and good state provision of language training in others, such as Sweden and Germany" (*Financial Times* from 24.7.1990). A survey of 2,500 students on the Continent and in Great Britain found out that "only 52% of the British students could speak a foreign language, compared with 85% of other European students" (*Financial Times* from 3.11.1990).

Germany or wherever. It doesn't make sense. When there is some political activity in America it gets tremendous coverage here. Yet we know nothing about what happens in France. There isn't a lot of public interest. The media don't generate a lot of interest in France or Holland or Belgium and yet they are just over the water (B11, p 25).

A manager of another company from the building industry said that government politics, and above all the Prime Minister herself, were responsible (but not solely) for the insufficient preparation for Europe 1993:

I think that this country is so far behind that they are going to lose out terribly, particularly with Mrs Thatcher's attitude towards Europe. She can't afford to think of the Great British Empire because nobody else thinks of us in that way, I'm sure. I'm sure that we must appear absolutely ridiculous to other countries. Other countries have done so much more preparation for 1993 and the major problem that we have is that we are so poor at languages. We are so proud of the Great British identity (B7, p 22).

Apart from such pessimistic expectations amongst managers, there are also optimistic attitudes regarding the European Market 1993, but as a rule these are coupled with a great deal of scepticism. The personnel manager from a company in the food and luxury food industry sees a chance that the united market will force British industry to get rid of its old-fashioned customs and thus widen its horizons, but only if at the same time British industry can put away its arrogance:

I think that with the removal of the last tariff barriers that should at least put us all on an equal footing in terms of being able to compete in the market place. I think that there will be, and I hope there will be, more mobility of labour, certainly managerial labour. I think that what it will do after 1993 is to broaden the horizons of industrialists in this country. Then they will see that there are opportunities for well-organized companies within the market. But they have got an awful lot to do because we are so arrogant as a nation that we believe everybody should speak our language. ... That is going to change. It has got to change because Britain cannot survive in Europe by expecting everyone to be able to understand us. So I think that the prospects for the market and for 1993, the things that we do well we will do better. And the things that we don't do well and which we should have got rid of some time ago will go because some of our other partners in Europe with free access will come in and show us how to do it (B3, p 29).

The following manager, also from the food and luxury food industry, sees opportunities as well as risks from the European market for Great Britain and says:

It is going to mean, we believe a very much more competitive environment and that we have to be equipped and efficient in order to deal with that increased competition. So it has got many challenges, many problems but also many opportunities. At the moment we tend to concentrate on the problems because we have to get those problems sorted out before we are able to take up the opportunities. It is going to mean some fairly big changes in the ... industry (B13, p 20-21).

The selected quotes reflect the completely controversial discussion of this theme in Great Britain. Hereby the anti (united market) position is represented by the Conservative party and – after the downfall of Mrs Thatcher in a milder form – by the government. Supporter of the pro-position is above all the oppositional Labour Party which finds itself in an otherwise quite seldom state of harmony with the Employers' Associations. Nevertheless the development of these topical points of view has a long and eventful history.

In the *Financial Times* (17.10.1990) we read:

The question of sovereignty has riven British politics for more than 30 years. First it was the Labour party that was the more obviously divided. Mr Hugh Gaitskell ... said of possible British membership in 1962: 'It means the end of a thousand years of history; it means the end of the Commonwealth ... to become just a province of Europe.'

At that time, Britain was making its first application under Harold MacMillan and was vetoed by General de Gaulle. By the mid-1960s, when Mr Harold Wilson was Prime Minister, it was a Labour government that decided that Britain's future lay in Europe after all.There followed what amounted to the second French veto.

For years after, splits on Europe did as much as any other single factor to keep the Labour Party divided. ...

Yet the Conservatives have not always done much better. The Tories were never wholly the party of Europe: they just seemed more so than Labour. A significant number of Tories was opposed to British entry in the first place. ... the legislation required for accession in the parliamentary session 1971-72 went through only with the help of some pro-Europe Labour MPs. Conversely, when the Labour government held a referendum on continued membership in 1975, it was dependent on all-party support to secure a yes vote.

Thus British membership has never been quite a Tory/Labour or left/right theme. Very broadly, the centre is for it, the extremes are against. It is a long time since the central debate has been about membership itself, but the debate on sovereignty contains many of the old elements.

As already has been described, the refusal of a European federalism from the Common Market-opponents continues to be virulent. The present points of disagreement between the government and the opposition are above all the questions of a unified European currency (Ecu) and of labour and social legislation. This became very clear in the House of Commons debate about the results of the Common Market summit in Dutch Maastricht in December 1991. The Opposition leader Neil Kinnock accused the government of turning Britain into a 'downmarket economy on the fringe of Europe'. ... Mr Kinnock's onslaught focused on the optional 'optout' won by Mr Major from plans for a single European currency and on his rejection of EC-wide standards for working conditions (*Financial Times* from 19.12.1991).

In contrast to this the Prime Minister represented the view

that the deal he had negotiated would give Britain a competitive advantage over its 11 European community partners. ... to have accepted the deal with which he was originally presented would have risked a return to the 'corporatism' of the 1960s and 1970s the imposition of laws which neither employees or employers wanted (*Financial Times* from 19.12.1991).

However we must not neglect the fact that as already mentioned there are quite different positions regarding Europe also within the Conservative party. Philip Stephens wrote in an article for the *Financial Times*:

On one side are those ... who believe that Britain must not be robbed of the fruits of Thatcherism by accepting submersion in a monolithic European superstate dominated by Germany; that it can preserve its identity and authority without succumbing to, the federalist fantasies of its European partners.

On the other, there are those convinced that more than 30 years after the Suez crisis extinguished any lingering pretensions to superpower status, Britain must finally accept a modest role as a middle-ranking European power (*Financial Times* from 14/15.7.1991).

In spite of these differentiations we may confirm that on the whole the Conservative government takes on a more distanced attitude towards a united Europe or at least a more distanced attitude than many British companies and Employers' Associations. Thus the latter demand not only European training standards[18]; at the annual conference 1990 of the Confederation of British Industry (CBI) the cry for a unified European currency became loud:

Only when a single currency is established will business reap the full benefits of economic and monetary union (*Financial Times* from 5.11.1990).

A survey of the CBI of 1395 of its members had found out that almost 70% of those interviewed expected an advantage from a united European currency (*Financial Times* from 8.5.1990)[19]. As we know, the British government has not been able to agree to this view so far.

---

18   "The UK should copy France and Germany and lay down clear pathways for the education and training of 16-19 year olds, according to a survey of employers in the Thames Valley west of London" (*Financial Times* from 17.10.1990).

19   The expectations are of course not the same for all industries and companies (*Financial Times* from 3.12.1991).

In contrast we may say that employers and the Conservative government do agree on the refusal of unified European regulations regarding the co-determination of the employees (*Financial Times* from 8.2.1990). "Last week a survey of member firms by the Confederation of British Industry showed that an overwhelming majority were opposed to any EC legislation which gave workers' legal rights to information and consultation by their employers" (*Guardian* from 14.5.1991).

However on the whole British industry seems – in spite of all the scepticism which has been expressed – to be more open towards a unified European market than the Conservative government and not only in the official statements of their associations but also in practical actions. For example in 1989 for the first time in the decade British companies made more acquisitions on the European Continent than in the USA (*Financial Times* from 20.6.1990). And "EC countries were responsible for virtually half of Britain's trade ... in 1989, compared with under one third in 1973. ... There have been considerable changes, with heavy investment by British companies in Europe and vice-versa, plus many mergers" (*Financial Times* from 3.11.1990). However if we compare the future expectations of the British managers with those of their German colleagues a considerably greater optimism on the part of the latter becomes clear.

Firstly we must note that the German managers we asked consider the organization of the future Common Market to be one of the most important social-political tasks[20]. Direct economic reasons are critical here:

> Yes, I am very interested now in the European domestic market because in my opinion it promises a huge advantage for Europe. The Europeans have been forced on to the defensive by Americans, by Japanese. ... And now this domestic market is my wish from politicians, both national and European, because it is a wish I have had for so long. After Adenauer and de Gaulle it all stopped growing. But now I sense a certain drive. I sense this in our country. But I also sense it from European colleagues, competitors as well as customers. It has a high priority for me (G115, p 31).

Similarly there are economic and political considerations:

> Perhaps I look at it more from a foreign policy point of view. I think that European integration and beyond West European, a total European integration, I see it has its most important aim for economic, but if you like also for defence political reasons, so that we can prevent long-term that arising from the confrontation of the blocs in Europe, a conflict which may lead to war may ever exist (G73, p 34).

---

20 See in detail Eberwein, Tholen (1990, pp 293-301) with regard to the 'ranking list' of the social-political tasks of German managers.

And the majority of German managers feel that they are more prepared for the Common Market than their English colleagues. In particular the comparably high level of German technology and the quality of the products are considered by most to be positive points in the discussion about international ability to compete. On the negative side in their opinion there are too high wages and the too rigid rules of the deployment of workers (nevertheless trade unions and works councils are basically accepted, as we will show later).

It is therefore an impression of our interviews that on the whole there is a greater optimism in Germany with regard to the united Europe, even if German managers do not feel that they are perfectly prepared for it, as the last two quotes imply. The majority of English managers we interviewed see that other West European countries, and precisely Germany, are at an advantage as far as the opportunities of a united Europe are concerned. As the above quoted excerpts of the interviews show, the reason for this lies in their opinion in the education and training systems[21] as well as in the peculiarities of the English industrial system in general.

3.6   Interim result regarding the English system of industry: The English industrial manager – Does he really prefer to be a gentleman rather than a professional company manager?

Some time ago there was a description of the condition of the British economy which appeared in the famous German magazine *Der Spiegel*; the title of this article was: "End of an industrial nation?" (*Der Spiegel* 33: 1991, pp 92-96). At the beginning of this article we read:

> The decade of Thatcherism in which the country was to catch up with the prospering countries of the industrialized West has passed over. For the second time within one decade the United Kingdom finds itself in a deep recession. … Not one day goes by without reports of catastrophes from the economy and these bring to mind much too intensively the past which was believed to have been overcome, a past when England was the ill and weak man of Europe.

The magazine stated that amongst other things the high level of unemployment was a reason for this economic demise as well as the decline of the industrial outputs and of the turnover in the areas of trade and service and the number of bankruptcies etc.. *Der Spiegel* continued that the reason for this is above all an unsuccessful economic policy of the Thatcher government, although the Prime

---

21   See here chapter 2.2 of the examination on hand.

Minister nevertheless managed to achieve "a climate of competition amongst those many sleeping managers in Britain".

There arise many questions in the article which stand in close connection with some of the different aspects of the English and German system of industry which we have dealt with in this chapter[22]. Firstly: Is there really such a serious economic downfall of Great Britain as was described in the article of *Der Spiegel*? And furthermore: Is such a downfall the result of a long term trend or only the expression of a temporary even if especially strong, economic slump? Additionally: Can the state policy of the economy really be seen as the main reason to blame for this development? And finally: With connection to this shouldn't the question of the managers' responsibility be asked? Have the managers now remembered, as *Der Spiegel* confirms, "entrepreneurial qualities like efficiency, quickness and quality awareness" or would the English top manager – and this has been said about him for a long time – really prefer to be a gentleman rather than a professional manager?

Let us look here at the development of the economic situation in Great Britain: At the beginning of 1991 the *Financial Times* painted the dark picture of a deep, extensive recession in their annual survey of economic forecasts (*Financial Times* from 3.1.1991). According to this only minimal growth could be expected for the future. In 1990 the number of company bankruptcies had risen by 35%. At the same time the rate of inflation was still one of the highest amongst the most important trade partners. Unemployment would rise once more. However unlike the great recession of ten years ago the present crisis had affected the area of the services. On the whole the difficult recession is seen as the bitter, but necessary process of adjustment after years of excessive consumption.

A comparison of the indicators for the development of industrial production of the most important industrial countries from 1989 to 1990 shows Great Britain in last place behind Japan, West Germany, France, USA and Italy and there was a considerable gap between Great Britain and the others (*Financial Times* from 3.12.1990).

Thus we can indeed speak of Great Britain's considerable loss of importance as an industrial nation. This is seen to be the case by British authors and experts. Ch. Lane writes (1989, p 10):

---

22 The areas of industrial relations, the view of the State and the conception of the common good on the part of the managers, which are of course of great significance for the industrial system of a country, will be dealt with in the following chapter 4 regarding the relationship of English and German managers to politics and the society.

Britain entered the postwar economic race from an already weak starting position which became more evident during the 1960s and 1970s. A relatively low rate of investment, low labour productivity and an insufficient development of technical skilled manpower, allied to. … a high level of inflation, and conflict-ridden industrial relations, resulted in relatively low rates of growth or even decline in existing industries, as well as in a failure to restructure manufacturing industry towards newer and technologically more advanced branches[23].

Consequently the average rate of economic growth from 1950 to 1979 in Great Britain was 2.6% as opposed to 5.3% in Germany.

According to our estimation we may conclude that the long-term development trend of the British economy mentioned by Lane and the intensity of the economic recession presuppose and strengthen each other. The reasons for this lie partly in certain framework conditions of the British industrial system which we have already described in this third chapter of our examination.

Firstly there is the different view of the relationship between staff and entrepreneurs/managers which English and German managers uphold. There is in principle in Germany a more cooperative, if not completely conflict-free, relationship between employees and management but in England there is a greater mutual distance in thinking and acting of these two groups. This became quite clear in the light of our observations regarding corporate culture and human resource management. This appears to us to be an expression of the "conflict-ridden industrial relations" quoted by Lane which could be of less advantage to the economic development of a country than a relationship which is aimed more towards harmony between employees and managements; this will be discussed further in the chapter about industrial relations.

The lower evaluation of technology in comparison to Germany has already been quite extensively presented above and this fact is indeed felt to be a disadvantage by English industrial managers themselves. Amongst other things this is expressed in the much higher standing of German engineers compared with their English colleagues. Thus there is the consequence that in English top management engineers are not so widely represented as in Germany. This development is already rooted in the English system of education and vocational training where traditionally little value is put on a formalized technical training as compared to the German system. Lane emphasizes in her above quoted statement that this definite lack of technical qualification does not only apply to management but to the labour force in general in England[24].

---

23 J. Allen and D. Massey (1988) concern themselves with Great Britain's changed role as a manufacturing nation.

24 This situation has been openly discussed in Great Britain over the last few years. We read for example in a series of articles on this theme in the *Financial Times*

On the whole we may say that a low estimation of technology in England leads to a certain inferiority of production management in the face of the commercial dimension of the companies and enterprises[25]. Many managers complained quite strongly in Great Britain that one of the most serious consequences of this situation is the sinking or at least in comparison to foreign competitors the low expenditure for research and development which has at least partly led to technological lags in British industry.

In mutual connection with the comparably low estimation of technology there is also the low social standing of industry in Great Britain, especially in the eyes of the British elite, as we have already explained. Thus the educational elite, if they turn to the economy at all, look for an occupation in the financial sector, that is in the atmosphere of the prestige-filled city and not in the (producing) industry. In contrast, a managerial position in industry in other highly developed industrial nations, for example and precisely in Germany, is looked upon with a much higher social status. This difference has consequences for the national educational systems. According to Wiener (1981, p 136), whilst the German educational institutions are not at all against meeting the educational requirements of industry, this cannot be seen to be the case in Great Britain (with a certain exception of the polytechnics). Indeed the historically arisen status of British industry has risen but in comparison with foreign competitors it is still lower. This may be an additional reason for the loss of industrial dynamism as it was described at the beginning of this chapter.

Finally the role of the banks and finance in general in Great Britain is considered to be negative for the development perspectives of industry not only by those managers we interviewed but also by the specialized public. The compulsion to gain short-term profits, which may possibly be at the expense of a long-term stabilization of the companies, the lack caused by the demands and influence of the financial sector, a lack to produce a forward-looking policy of industry of the State as well as of the financial capital, lead in the eyes of British industry itself to serious disadvantages in the face of international competition[26]. The primate of short termism should have been intensified under the auspices of the Thatcher government.

(26.11.1990): "Britain's training compares badly with that of its industrial competitors". In this case not only the technical-related training is being referred to but a contrast to the dual system of education in Germany.

25   We have shown in chapter 3.3 that a dominance of technology in German industry does not mean that commercial matters are neglected and that the situation is completely opposite of that in England.

26   Thus the chairman of the Rover Vehicles Group demanded a national industrial strategy similar to Japan or Germany (*Financial Times*, 18.2.1992).

And last but not least there is the specifically British insularity and this is by no means simply a geographical term. There is in Great Britain a backward-looking orientation towards the Commonwealth, a connected form of a specific kind of nationalism and the widespread little tendency to learn foreign languages and these are all obstacles to a changing trend of the decline of British economy.

According to the estimation of the British professional public there appears in Great Britain to be no solution to these problems and not one of the socially relevant groups, not even the British industrial managers themselves, appear to have any conclusive concept. The latter is true in spite of the fact that according to our impressions British managers can in no way be seen as "industrial amateurs" as Granick once said (1962, pp 265-286). Since the 1960s there has been a trend to professionalize managers, in particular by better education (Mosson: 1972, pp 60-61); a tendency which was increased in the 1980s. Gans (1989) even stated a "farewell to the gentlemen". For him the type of manager who was a former "Oxbridge" student and more interested in playing golf and belonging to elitist clubs than in the efficiency of a company, belongs to the past. The MBA course of training and performance count more today than social origin. As a result of our interview findings we can follow this impression even if a general evaluation would require a broader empirical foundation. However we are able to conclude that as a result of those structural framework conditions which the managers have partly created themselves, it is difficult for British managers to prevent short-term the loss of significance of their industry.

Without doubt these framework conditions are more favourable in Germany. However there is no reason here to paint the state of the German economy in bright colours. Increasing inflation rates, long-lasting mass unemployment with an ever-increasing base of long-term unemployment, the need for housing, high State debts etc.; all this much more intensified by the process of the German reunification, are social-economic problems, for which the solution in Germany at the moment can scarcely be seen.

In comparing the industrial systems of both countries we have missed out up to now one essential aspect of the differences of German and English managers. This is the aspect of industrial relations and the way managers view society and the State. We will turn to this aspect now with reference to the relationship of German and English managers to politics and the society.

4   The relationship of English and German managers towards politics and the society

If we follow the somewhat lively public debates about corporate culture and economic ethics, we will find that precisely over the recent months the question of the manager's relationship towards the democratic process in Germany has gained significance and this is at least an expression of the considerable need of top management to present and legitimize itself. However, as Jacobi (1991, p 370) in particular has emphasized, there appears within German trade unions the widespread certainty "to know the intentions of the management anyway, and to do nothing but increase profits". But this is a much too simplified view of reality and leads to the result of "a deception brought about by oneself of the opponent and a punishable limitation of one's own strategic operations".

Here the question regarding the acting orientations of managers is mentioned from two sides. We can express this in more general terms by saying that it is the complex of a tense relationship between the economy and politics/society; of a contradictory union whose discussion has been roused since the beginning of civil society and where the division of the economy from politics bears again and again partly historically caused different evaluations.

It may be possible to conclude from the above mentioned need for legitimation that today's managers have greater political openness and rationality unlike the generation of industrial managers before them who have now mostly retired. Berghahn states the following:

> The growing into and progress of an entrepreneur/manager in a certain 'industrial culture' determines his style, modes of behaviour and attitudes in such a way that it cannot simply be unsettled in his later career, even if economic and political reality changes persistently. Even the memory of his socialization within an industrial culture, his historical awareness and the relations within the circle of colleagues with 'ideological homogenization' … and the special constraints of conformity, will at least hinder a change in behaviour and attitude if not even prevent it completely (Berghahn: 1987, p 16).

But does this stated openness mean that today there is also a structurally anchored alliance between managers and political democracy, whose absence was often complained of by Pross, Boetticher (1971, p 108)? Or is it rather an expression of a professionally and politically indifferent way of thinking and acting of managers, a way of thinking that is restricted to the function "industrial company management"?

We asked ourselves whether there is a similar topical debate about social functions and political consequences of company management in England? We were particularly interested in which systematic differences could be recognized in the political thinking and acting of English and German managers with their quite different historical-political backgrounds. Is for example the German manager more authoritarian than the English manager? How do they differentiate with regard to their attitude towards representing their employees' interests?

Which different (or) same views do they have about the obligation of the companies towards the common good, which demands and expectations do they have of the State and politics etc.?

Let us turn first of all towards the significance of ownership for the economic process.

4.1   Owner-managers or employed managers – Who can manage a company better?

"Managers are out; leaders and entrepreneurs are in" (Staehle: 1991, p 105). A summarizing essay about the topical discussion of entrepreneurs and/or managers begins with this somewhat sensational view. It is without doubt correct that as with corporate culture, there is widespread criticism of the type of professionally employed manager, who is no longer in the position to overcome urgent current questions like the Japanese challenge, the change of values in the working world and many other things. As the patent solution to this, the pursuants of this debate which is much more widely carried out in the Anglo-American sphere than in Germany, propagates the return of the "born" charismatic entrepreneur as leader[1]. Here the theories of the qualities of management, which have long been believed to have been overcome, are revived, a renaissance of the classical entrepreneur is propagated and rejection of the too scientific modern management is stated. We were interested in whether such views, which are particularly held by company consultants and therefore follow certain laws of marketing, have found expression or even agreement amongst managers themselves.

---

1   We may quote as prototype of this view Bennis and Nanus (1985, p 1) with their programmatic formulation: "Managers do things right, leaders do the right things".

We approached this theme in England as well as in Germany with the following questions: "The division of the owners and management has given rise to certain theories in literature: In your opinion do the mutual or different interests between owners and company managers outweigh each other? Could an owner-manager manage a company in a different way to that of an employed manager?".

The answers of the managers disperse widely and even fall in complete contrast to one another so that an obvious interpretation becomes difficult. This is the case for the English as well as German field of examination. However there is a striking difference in the ranking order of the answers. Whilst in Germany a relative majority of managers (in total a quarter) saw no differences between owner-managers and employed managers, the most frequent answer of their English colleagues (more than one third) was that employed managers act in a more professional manner. Does this different emphasis let us conclude that German managers see themselves to a much stronger degree as entrepreneurs than their English colleagues? Let us turn to the answers individually in order to approach this question.

As we have already mentioned, more than a quarter of the number of German managers we interviewed saw no structural difference between the managerial occupation of owner-managers and employed managers. An explanation for this which was frequently presented was that the employed manager would manage the company as if it were his own. The following quote – remarkably enough from an owner-manager – illustrates this view:

> I can withdraw and rely on my employees, because they act as if it is their own. …
> Someone who is well motivated, because work is fun and because he is given the
> possibility to fulfil his own realizations, this seems to be important for me. And
> whoever I give this possibility to, for him work is living space and therefore his
> property, even if it is not legally the case (G66, p 27).

Such a view can be found (but much more seldom) in the English examination group and we read from a manager from the food and luxury food industry:

> If I owned this company I wouldn't do the job any differently to the way I am doing
> it now (B13, p 15).

In the English group this answer stands in third position whilst in Germany it is quite clearly in first position.

However a fifth of those managers we asked see the employed manager as being at an advantage to the owner-manager. The employed manager would act more professionally in as far as he would concentrate completely on the interests of the company. In the following quote this view is expressed very pointedly:

> I think there are striking differences between whether you have a company as your own property, that is whether it has been family property for generations, which you would like to pass down to your descendants, or whether you have the other case that you only manage the company for a certain time and basically on the terms of success or not. ... I think too that precisely because everything is becoming less personal, that you have more purchasable managers, this leads to the fact that managers only look how they can get the most possible success for the company (G56, p 24).

For the English managers we interviewed this higher degree of professionalism of employed managers is by far the most important difference to the owner-manager. For example we may quote the personnel manager of a company from the food and luxury food industry:

> The employed manager would manage that company in a purely professional way. He is employed to be a professional and he is employed to produce a result. The owner may well act in a different way because he may be influenced by social factors. He may be influenced by political factors and that is not to say that the professional manager isn't going to be effected by certain factors but I think there may be a different set of factors. If the owner is a competent businessman who has been trained and educated into good business methods there is no reason why he shouldn't be a successful manager. But there is a doubt. There should be no doubt about the professional manager. That is his career, he is a professional (B3, p 23).

The opinions regarding the question of the respective scope of action of owner-managers and employed managers were very different in the English as well as the German examination group. Indeed they were sometimes contrary. Amongst the German managers there is the view that an owner-manager has less scope of action as opposed to an employed manager. Such reasons as consideration of the family, workers, customers, the community etc. were quoted here.

In contrast to this, there are almost as many judgements which say that the owners have the possibility of riskier action. The statement of an employed manager from the food and luxury food branch illustrates this as an example:

> I think that an owner-manager would surely take more risks. An employed manager must answer to another committee and mostly he does not manage alone but with 1 or 2 other people and therefore he must put more emphasis on securities than a private entrepreneur must do. The private enterpreneur can gamble much more and can take on greater risks and if they do not lead to success and that effects his purse then he must say, OK, I have miscalculated and then move on to the next theme. An employed manager cannot simply do this because there are some cases when you say, well, if this belonged to me I would do it but I can't do it in this case. It isn't my money. I can't take the risk (G23, p 29).

Apart from this there are also a considerable number of answers, and they are not only related to financial risks, which say that the owner-manager has a greater scope of action than the employed manager. This continues from the view we have already mentioned that the owner can act and take more risks and this is in complete contrast to the other assumption that the owner has only a narrow scope of action. The reason for the greater scope of action on the part of the owner-managers is, according to the managers we asked, associated with his independence of superior control organizations (like for example the supervisory board), but also with his greater autonomy within his concern in which he can at the same time act as the 'sole ruler'.

The picture in the English examination group presents itself similarly diffusely although the arguments are quite different. Here we find the view that the owner takes fewer risks:

> The fact that you are an owner-manager makes you overly subjective. If you could stand back from it a bit more, you might take more risks which might pay off (B7, p 18).

There is also the opposite opinion:

> They have a more cavalier approach to their decision making than the employed manager. They will be more conscious of the profit loss, short term profit loss than the employed manager. I think they are less patient, the owner-managers will have less patience. They would react more quickly to economic circumstances I think than the employed managers. I suppose when you put the bureaucrat in I would have to feel him being an innovator because I don't think the owner-manager is into maintenance activity to the same degree (B4, p 18).

It is assumed here that there is a greater orientation towards profit-making on the part of the owner-manager in comparison with the employed manager which could even lead to the situation where the latter acts to a stronger degree as an innovator in order to secure the existence of the company. The statement of a personnel manager goes in a similar direction. He states that the employed manager has a much greater responsibility towards the owner:

> There is a significant difference between what an owner-manager does and someone who is paid a salary to manage. You tend to find that someone who is paid a salary to manage knows that he has a responsibility towards the people who are actually employing him. Not only does he have to fulfil his particular role but he has an obligation to make sure that the trust that is placed in him is not misplaced (B5, p 30).

In complete contrast to this the following manager argues that the owner-manager is much more conscientious:

> I don't think he (the employed manager) would be so conscientious or give so much of his time (B6, p 18).

His colleague quoted here to follow, assumes the same even if with some limitation:

I think an owner-manager does have a far greater commitment unless it is one of these businesses that is about the third generation of the family. They tend to disappear because the mother is wealthy and the third generation wants to spend it. They don't have the fight, the commitment or the challenge. Generally speaking I think employed managers don't necessarily operate in the same way. They tend to be more bureaucratic, more administrative (B10, p 26).

On the whole the English as well as German interview excerpts show that the managers have a very contradictory picture of ownership themselves with regard to company management and they tend to use simplifications regarding this matter. Only very few gave a diiferentiated view as we can see from the member of management of a large chemical company who will be quoted here. As he comes from a company owner family he explained the advantages and disadvantages of the owner-manager and employed manager in connection with the company situation:

I think it is good that companies are managed by employed managers and not owner-managers. The owner-manager has a great advantage during a certain phase in the company, when he has to take on a risk according to his own responsibility and with his own money so that the first great periods of company growth can be secured. But at that moment when the company gains a certain size and becomes established in the market, the owner-manager has greater difficulties, as a rule, to manage the company successfully. There are a few exceptional cases where it is successful but by the time there is the first or second change in generation the serious problems begin. Thus there is a strong case for allowing employed managers to manage a company for a long period (G62, pp 24-25).

Thus this is the extent of our empirical findings in their contradictory nature. There is evidence of these different opinions also in the respective literature. Copeman (1972, p 332) comes to the conclusion that the owner-manager is the "better" manager as opposed to the employed manager. Goldsmith, Clutterbuck (1984, pp 132-134) see four crucial advantages on the part of the owner-managers in comparison to the employed managers: They provide continuity; they provide a long-term perspective and commitment; they have room for wider values than the norm, e.g. to provide employee benefits; it is easier for them to establish a public identity of the company. Correspondingly Staehle (1991, pp 114-115) suggests that employed managers are lacking in acting in a socially and ecologically responsible way and that they have little creativity and desire to take risks.

But on the other hand there are also supportive views for employed managers in literature. Pollard (1968) proved that in the initial phase of modern management there was something arbitrary about the owner-manager which stood in sharp contrast to the managerial requirements of big companies[2].

---

2   See Chandler (1977) for the origins of modern management; His central thesis is

There are also contrary opinions regarding the question of social responsibility. In an empirical examination of chief executives attitudes which was carried out in 42 countries the statement that owner-managers take on more social responsibility than employed managers (Peterson: 1971) was extensively rejected. Finally examinations show that when we consider the economic success of a company the owner-manager is not the better worker a priori. So for example Lawriwsky (1984, pp 223-224) has confirmed something remarkable in the small and medium-sized companies he examined: Here such companies under manager control, with regard to profitability and growth, come considerably better off than comparable companies in family possession. The finding of Pohl, Rehkugler (1987) goes in the same direction and states that owner-managers make use of modern management techniques less successfully and frequently than employed managers. Thonet (1977) gives a wider literature survey of this strongly economically orientated discussion under the title "The theory of managerialism". Some empirical findings are treated in regard to this discussion. According to this there is not one unified picture of the differences or common aspects in behaviour of owner-managers and employed managers[3].

More sociologically directed works on this theme are not so much concerned with such differences in behaviour but more with questions of the access to and the legitimation of positions within company management. But above all the social-scientific discussion deals with the question of the "Revolution of the managers". The literary point of departure and reference of this discussion is J. Burnham's book *The Managerial Revolution* which came out in 1949.

Burnham proceeds from the fact that a social revolution takes place as a result of the division of ownership and control over production means. In place of control through ownership there is a control through knowledge. The new professional managers who control the means of production by their ability and competence have taken the place of the classic owner-capitalists and have presented a new dominating class. Burnham continues that "the abolition of capitalist private ownership of production means is not a sufficient requirement and guarantee for the introduction of socialism" (Burnham: 1949, p 66). Indeed within the "managerial revolution" the ideal of a classless society has

---

that the growing complexity of the (American) company has made differentiated company management functionally necessary. The consequence of this is the development of a management profession and the employment of suitably qualified managers.

3   However within the groups of owner-managers and employed managers there are no identical patterns of behaviour and thought; see the examinations of Smith (1967) and Cooper, Dunkelberg (1986) regarding the different types of owner-managers.

not been fulfilled. On the contrary the division of class has intensified. According to tendency there is only the dominating and the dominated. The homogenous class of the managers stands opposite the wide masses of working class people.

Burnham's theses – it would be too much to speak of a "theory" of management – have been sharply criticized from another side[4]. In Germany Helge Pross pointed to the fact that these theses are neither theoretically plausible nor to be found empirically. She specifies (Pross: 1965, pp 173-176):

–   On the contrary the managers have become the keenest advocates of capitalism;
–   Their material and immaterial interests are indeed linked with the profit interests of the company;
–   The extent of the financial benefits of managers can at least be partly and indirectly calculated according to the extent of the company profits.

But the immaterial interests of the managers are also linked with the striving for company profits, whether it be the demand for prestige or the securing of the managers' own position. On the one hand the manager enjoys the highest esteem when he gains the highest profits and a constant expansion of the company is necessary for the stabilization of his own position. Pross (1965, p 176) concludes from this:

> It doesn't matter whether managers or owners control the big companies because the impulses which point in the direction of economic development remain in principle the same. Fundamentally the decisions of both groups are orientated towards the same purpose which is determined by the capitalist system. ... As long as the material and immaterial interests of the functionaries are appropriately taken into consideration, the principles of capitalist management retain their validity.

Pross continues that private ownership of production means is precisely the requirement for the autonomy of the managers.

> Neither the early capitalist economy of competition in which there were no or only a few big companies, nor an economy that only knows public ownership of means of production and that is centrally planned, offer employed managers similar chances of an autonomous disposition. In the competitive economy the entrepreneurs/managers are the masters themselves (Pross: 1965, p 170).

In contrast in a socialist society a State board of control is put in front of the manager and this board plans centrally and the manager is therefore limited in his scope of action.

---

4   Compare R. Dahrendorf (1957, pp 89-93).

In recent times John Scott (1985) put forward a differentiated consideration of the question: "Who controls the modern company?". His central thesis states that in the modern company there are three control groups that meet with each other, firstly representatives from financial institutions, secondly share-owners and thirdly managers. In many countries there is a historically founded dominance of one of these control groups; however a generalizing statement regarding company control is not suitable. In addition to this, there is also the fact that ownership shares or job descriptions are in no way identical with actual control. The fact that someone owns a large part of the shares or carries the title executive manager does not mean that he is in the position to determine the fate of a company. A title and ownership only become influential as a result of the use of strategic control. We may conclude from this that a title or ownership solely represent control potentials. Scott suggests that these groups have different motives (Scott: 1985, pp 179- 180):

– Owners: "personal interests in maintaining and enhancing their wealth";
– Financial institutions: "position as nominees of the controlling constellations";
– Managers: "structuring of their work through a managerial hierarchy".

These motives of managing do not only represent possibilities for strategic control but they also limit the control groups to certain roles:

> Corporate strategy is the outcome of the alliances and conflicts among the capitalists who make up the 'dominant coalition' of each enterprise: but the actions of this coalition are shaped by the network of intercorporate relations in which the enterprise is embedded and, beyond this, by the actions of the state and other political agencies and by both organized and unorganized workers.

If we summarize in total our empirical findings and the selected results of the appropriate literature we may conclude that it is not possible for definite to determine empirically fundamental and systematic differences of behaviour. Furthermore we may assume that structural demands of the economic process like dependence on the market, competition with other sellers etc. lead to adaptation of the behaviour of owner-managers and employed managers. This is the case to the same extent for England and for Germany.

However, fundamental changes have occurred as a result of the process of the division of ownership and control. Firstly the admission requirements for the position of the company manager have been displaced. This was mentioned at an earlier stage[5]. Secondly the significance and function of ownership in the economy and society have changed according to tendency. In our opinion capital ownership in industrial companies has been considerably de-emotionalized, even relativized, in its significance for industrial company management

---

5   Compare chapter 2.2.7.

by the development of a no longer ownership concentrated 'professional' and 'scientific' management.

It is possible to conclude from the statements of managers we interviewed that German managers feel more strongly bound to ownership and that they think that they act and think like an owner. In contrast to this their English colleagues underlined the professional side of the managerial occupation[6]. But these differences do not appear to be so striking that it is possible to deduce far-reaching differentiating interpretations from them.

On the contrary the division of ownership and control must be seen as a common structural feature of modern industrial societies, whose consequences – at least in England and Germany – can be defined as identical. Even if the common features dominate here, when we look at the following aspect to be dealt with, the relationship of the manager towards the society and politics, the managers' conception and view of the respective system of industrial relations, we cannot see many common features.

4.2   "Industrial relations" – Victorian class barriers in England and open social structures in Germany?

The British sociologist Peter Lawrence that we have already quoted a number of times has pointed to the fact that "Germans are particularly given to the view that their country has become a classless society and German managers especially like to draw the foreigner's attention to this happy state of affairs" (Lawrence: 1980, p 106).

On the other hand it was only recently that Ralf Dahrendorf, who has proved himself to be a connoisseur of both the British and German society, spoke of "peculiarly English ... " class structures "(that in reality are rather corporative caste structures)" (Dahrendorf: 1992, quoted in *Die Zeit*, 27.3.1992). And Anthony Sampson, one of the most well-known and critical 'anatomists'[7] of British society, describes the class difference as the longest-living and most British(!) of all differences (*Die Zeit* from 10.4.1992, p 44).

---

6   It is possible to say that shortly after the First World War a New Thought movement developed with the concept that management should be a professional occupation. A scientific method of company management was to replace autocratic company management which was based on ownership rights (Child: 1969).

7   Sampson (1963) developed, as we have seen in the subtitle, an anatomy of British society.

But can we really speak of an open society in Germany and a class society in England as the title of this chapter asks? It is our impression and we agree here with Ulrich Beck that

> in Great Britain social class affiliation is still clearly perceivable in daily life and is the object of much more conscious identification than in Germany. This affiliation is bound to the style of language (accent, style of expression, vocabulary), to forms of eductaion, to the sharp class division of housing areas ('housing classes'), to clothes and all that can be summarized under the title 'lifestyle' (Beck: 1986, pp 121- 122).

However Beck's statement points to a difference in external perception. Whether this difference can be seen in the internal structure of both societies, is to be examined on the basis of the respective industrial relations. In order to do this a short characterization of the different systems of industrial relations is necessary.

4.2.1   The different systems of industrial relations in England and Germany[8]

According to Jacobi (1989, p 43), the institutional backbone of the collective system of negotiation in Germany is

> the dual structure of representing the employees' interests and this characterized by
>
> – the division of institutions in trade unions and works councils,
>
> – the division in the representation of trade union members' interests by a tariff monopoly and the representation of staff interests by company regulations
>
> – the division of spheres of influence and means of power in a non firm based market of negotiation which has the right to strike and a staff oriented market of negotiation directed at achieving company peace free of work conflicts.
>
> The dual system is recognizable by its flexible solving of problems and great ability to make compromises and ensures that the manufacturing place of goods or services is not a place for conflicts but remains an undisturbed arena of production.

The most important institutions of this system are the trade unions, the works constitution with its fundamental and essential form, the works council, as well as co-determination at company level.

In the main the trade unions are organized according to a principle of (political) united trade union and industrial branch, so that the following motto applies, at least on the whole: One company – one trade union. The company

---

8   This introduction can and shall only mention the essential structural features of both systems in a sociological perspective; more detailed presentations can be found by Mielke (1983).

connections for the trade unions are the shop stewards who are elected by the members of the trade unions in the companies.

The works councils are at least formally independent of the trade unions although there are in fact a lot of mutual points and collaboration between them. The members of the works council are elected by the whole staff of a company whose interests they are obliged to represent. But they must also serve the good of the company. In the Works Constitution Act their position and function have a legally fixed foundation.

In addition to this, there is also co-determination on company level which should allow company or external representatives of the employees to act on their behalf in the organs of supervision and management in the company. For this, there are legal foundations for the Co-determination Law for the Montan (iron, coal and steel) industry (Monatsmitbestimmungsgesetz from 1951), the Works Constitution Act (Betriebsverfassungsgesetz from 1952) and the Co-determination Law (Mitbestimmungsgesetz from 1976). These institutions are embedded in a developed network of work and socially legal regulations which form for Germany the distinct system of industrial relations. This system has taken shape in a longer-term historical-social process[9], that shows elementary continuity in spite of all breaks and differentiations[10] and has not been put into question by the conservative-liberal government coalition which has been in power for several years. And so we have the key word for the short description of the English system of industrial relations. Whilst in Germany there is not "Kohlism" as such, if perhaps only as an expression, "Thatcherism" in England has a considerable influence on the state of industrial relations. But let us proceed step by step.

One important difference of the English system of industrial relations to that of the German system is the lacking functional and institutional division in tariff autonomy and works constitution "so that one single system of representation of employees' interests dominates" (Jacobi: 1989, p 46).

As a rule there is not a counterpart to the German works council in British companies. Instead staff interests are represented by shop stewards, that is to say company representatives of the trade unions who represent a mixture or a combination of works councils (Betriebsrat) and trade union spokesmen (Gewerkschaftliche Vertrauensleute) in Germany. In addition to this the shop stewards of a firm or company do not belong to a single union as in Germany. But the shop steward committee is made up of several or of many trade unions. The reason for this is that the English trade unions, different from those in

---

9   See Braun, Eberwein, Tholen (1992) on the history of the German company consti-
    tution.
10 With the exception of the Nazi period.

Germany, are not mainly structured according to the industrial branch principle. Apart from industrial unions there are craft unions and general unions. This leads to the fact that several unions are represented in one company. Impressive proof of the heterogeneity of British trade unions is the fact that according to R. Hoffmann (1989, p 353) there are approximately 370 individual trade unions in Great Britain of which 83 are members of the main federation the TUC.

Jacobi says that "the tendency of British companies to works or company agreements" corresponds to the company-centred trade union structures. Compared with the Federal Republic of Germany there lacks at the same time an "orienting and correcting influence on company processes of negotiation by central management institutions ... . The consequences are that the places of production are always direct places of conflict and the point of view of the company negotiators can be narrowed down and become company-centred" (Jacobi: 1989, p 46). An expression of this circumstance is the great frequency of strikes in England, which bears the name "the British disease"[11].

The German regulation of co-determination at company level does not exist in England. And finally there is not the extended network of further work and social legal regulations as in Germany. Thus the organization of industrial relations in Great Britain was embedded for a long time in a social self-understanding which is marked by different authors as a post-war consensus. In its most general view it consisted in the aim of full employment and the Welfare State connected with State intervention to fulfil these aims (Prigge: 1991, p 28). This consensus was withdrawn by the Thatcher conservative government and legitimized with the comment that there exists a certain backwardness of British trade unions. The collective work relations were changed and indeed in a legal way, especially by the Employment Acts of 1980 and 1982 and the Trade Union Act of 1984. The basic intentions of these measures were (Kastendiek: 1988, pp 175-176):

- to weaken the trade unions in the face of the companies, e.g. by forbidding most forms of sympathy and solidarity strikes;
- to strengthen the members and unorganized in the face of the trade unions, e.g. by the rule of strike ballots about closed shops, strikes etc.;
- to restrict certain forms of action of the trade unions by binding them to civilly legal obligations of liability or even to penal findings.

---

11 However the frequency of strikes in England is not as great as is generally assumed especially if we consider their significance for managers (Lawrence: 1984, p 62-63). And in Germany strikes are by no means completely ruled out, as e.g. the conflicts in the spring of 1992 have shown.

By the way much of this is an essential part of industrial relations in Germany. Whether an assimilation of the systems of industrial relations in England and Germany has taken place, above all how managers in both countries evaluate the respective systems and possibly consider an adaptation to be worthwhile shall be examined in the following chapter. Let us first of all turn to the trade unions.

4.2.2   Trade unions – A stabilizing factor or opposing power?

The question as to whether the German trade unions are more a social stabilizing factor and the English trade unions are an opposing power has played a considerable role in the discussion about character and social significance and has always found controversial expression[12]. But at this point we are primarily interested in clarifying the view of the managers. The two expressions of stabilizing factor and opposing power do indeed cover the range of answers given by the managers in reply to the question regarding the tasks and functions of trade unions. However there were different points of emphasis in both countries.

The comments made by a member of the board of directors of a large chemical company is symptomatic for many similar views of German managers:

> The trade unions have the task of articulating the interests and wishes of employees and of being a partner in communication with company management, the employer. As such the unions should be accessible and capable of negotiation. It is very difficult to speak to one's workers without a trade union, without a works council because as a rule they are not easily accessible on their own. You cannot speak directly with 5,000 workers and you cannot make agreements with them. For the majority of German companies, for the German economy, I think the trade unions and the way they fulfil their tasks is a good thing (G62, p 25).

On the whole the answers of the German managers document a high acceptance of the trade unions. 116% of the answers (several answers were possible here) consider the unions to have an important function in the economy and society[13]. 70% of these consider the trade unions to be a necessary representative of the employees' interests in society. 28% see trade

---

12   Compare the book of the same name by E. Schmidt (1971); Also look at the debate about "Cooperatives versus conflicting trade union politics" by Bergmann, Jacobi, Müller-Jentsch (1976).

13   Ulrich and Probst came to a similar conclusion in their examination of evaluating managers. 76% of those who were interviewed consider trade unions to be extensively or at least partly an indispensible part of the market economy (Ulrich, Probst: 1982, p 31).

unions above all as stabilizing factors, that ensure stability in society and at work. 12% appreciate their role as partner in communication for management. And 6% even classify them as a positive factor for the industrial location Germany.

In contrast, only 45% of the answers of the German sample were critical of trade unions. Only 10% of these expressed a clear refusal of trade unions and attributed a too great political influence to the unions and even considered them to be superfluous or harmful. 35% of the answers classed trade unions as being unmodern or wished for stronger limitation to pure (not political) representation of interests.

How can this mostly positive picture of German managers of trade unions be explained? The statement quoted at the beginning already gives one answer. A large part of managers see the essential function of trade unions to be putting together employees' interests and by doing this become an authorized and competent partner for company managements. Some managers even assess the fulfilling of this function as an advantage in competition for the location of the Federal Republic of Germany. This function of trade unions is emphasized in particular by a member of the board of directors at an international concern:

> Surely the most important thing is to represent the employees, because the individual, however much he is seen by the employer he remains too small, and so the putting together and registration of all in a trade union has been a splendid idea and has its own significance. ... This is surely the great responsibility and the great success of this concept. ... That this can lead to situations where the employer and shareholder come into conflict with the opinion of the representatives of the employees is quite naturally to be expected and is perhaps even wished for (G74, p 24).

A manager of the automobile industry pointed quite pronouncedly to the function of trade unions:

> Trade unions have manifold functions. For me they have a politically stabilizing function in our society. Furthermore they have the function as industrial unions to maintain the peace at work which is the reason why the company is so strongly interested in trade unions, that is to say as reliable partners of negotiation with whom we can make agreements. It can not be our interest to destabilize trade unions. ... We want to have strong and reliable unions. We see them as a stabilizing internal company factor (G78, p 22).

The quoted views emphasize clearly the character of trade unions as stabilizing factors. In this function the work of the unions is very closely linked with representing employees' interests and has this task even as a condition. However representing these interests is given not so much an original but more an instrumental significance. In other words: the aspect of the opposing power remains mostly in the minority. Only very few managers emphasized the opposing character of the trade unions as for example a member of management of a large chemical company who said:

> For me it is an unrenouncable part of our democratic system. Just as the government party needs an opposition, so the company needs something like an opposition. I don't know whether I can say a matter of control. But a force, that takes the other side sufficiently into consideration (G61, p 30).

The manager of a mineral oil concern, who stressed the functions of representing and protecting employees' interests from a trade union also represented a minority position:

> The trade unions are absolutely necessary, because the entrepreneur or the manager ... the employer in the classical sense is of course inclined, and this is completely legitimate and quite reasonable, to get the maximum from his production means in order to fulfil his aims. And there must be an institution who makes the limits so that it does not happen that they work 16 hours, when it is necessary and perhaps that they do monotonous work. Then they would become crazy etc.. This doesn't interest the entrepreneur at all. He would never think that this cannot be reasonably expected of someone, because of course he has other things on his mind and therefore the trade unions have for me a 100% justifiable right to exist (G75, p 30).

Without ignoring the views that criticize trade unions we can say that there is a high degree of acceptance of the trade unions amongst German managers. That the managers look more closely at the character of trade unions as an stabilizing factor arises from their concentration on economic company interests.

But how do the English managers judge 'their' trade unions who are more strongly obliged to the model of an opposing power than their German counterpart?

Firstly we may confirm that those English managers we interviewed accept the trade unions but only in a small majority. About half see the trade unions as necessary representatives of employees and/or as important partners in communication for company management and/or as a meaningful corrective that forces management to a more rational form of politics. At the same time the number of 'trade union critics' amongst the English managers is clearly greater than amongst their German colleagues. The main reasons for this were that the trade unions concerned themselves too little with representing interests and too much with politics and that they were too bound up to the classic conflict between capital and work and on the whole too unmodern and not in the position to make use of new influence like technical change, changed structures of employees' needs etc.. Interestingly enough only one of the interviewed managers mentioned the too great an inclination towards industrial actions as an argument to criticize trade unions. Only 10 years earlier an examination of British managers by Poole et al. (1981, pp 80-88) – with a different emphasis however – gave a somewhat different picture. According to this examination almost 80% of managers considered the legal regulation (in the sense of limiting) of strike actions to be the most important task of State intervention. More than 80% considered the role of trade unions to be harmful for national economic interests. And even more than 50% agreed to the thesis that trade unions had more power than management. Possibly the fewer answers criticizing trade unions from the managers we interviewed are an expression of the success of the (anti)trade union politics of the conservative Thatcher government. A manager from the food and luxury food industry said:

> I think that some of the labour legislation that has come in has diminished or changed the role of the trade unions. ... the role and the function of the trade unions in this country is diminishing (B3, p 24).

Today it is easier for the managers than in former times to accept these politically tamed trade unions and in relation to management to grant them positive functions as the following answer illustrates:

> I think the most important contribution they make is that they make management manage properly. If you have a trade union organization you may well have to justify the decision you have made. Therefore it makes managers manage in a logical way (B17, p 9).

As in the case of the German managers an instrumental way of looking at trade unions is linked with a positive evaluation as we see in the following quote:

> Without trade unions I think British industry would be worse. My job is easier with trade unions than it would be with fragmented associations, people getting together in small groups. It is much better where I can talk to one group of people. I think they are essential and the way that they are organized is the criticism that one could make and management's responsibility for recognizing them and accepting them has played an important role. You can either use them or fight them. My attitude has always been to use them. I think industry would not be so good without their contribution (B10, p 27).

Thus there are two examples of a positive attitude towards trade unions. But a manager from the food and luxury food industry gives the opposite view:

> I totally disagree with the role trade unions played in the past. I think they brought politics into the work place and there are politics, but I've got my own personal politics, but I keep them to myself. I got sick and tired of listening to trade unionists spouting that they have got socialist views and they automatically assumed that I am a conservative. I think that clouds their judgement. What they ought to be doing is working on a professional basis and looking at their members and what their members ought to be achieving. ... Our trade unions are political because they formed the labour party and you can't escape it. The contribution they made to society, I think they make very little, quite frankly. I think they are 50 years behind

the times. They still talk the same kind of language they did in the 1930s. They still talk about the working class and they put everything in class terms (B1, pp 21-22).

The reasons for a negative behaviour towards trade unions will be summarized once again and brought into context. Apart from this the statement has one aspect which in our opinion is marked by a central difference in viewing trade unions by English and German managers: It is the task of trade unions to be "looking at their *members* and what their *members* ought to be achieving". In contrast to this German managers consider it the most important task to represent the interests of the *employees*. In our opinion this different way of looking at trade unions, on the one hand employees' interests and on the other hand members' interests is not purely coincidental and has not only formal significance. Let us look at some comments from the English group. In reply to the question regarding the most important task of trade unions there was the following comment by a manager from the vehicle industry:

> To protect the interests of their members. That means looking after them as individuals in personal grievances but also collectively in the areas of wage negotiations and pensions. I think they have a legitimate area of activity and an important area of activity is looking after the members' interests as they relate to the employment contract (B4, p 19).

A manager from the food and luxury food industry said concisely:

> The role the trade unions play is the traditional role of negotiating conditions and terms for their members (B13, p 15).

Another manager from the same industry went into more detail:

> The most important functions of the trade unions are to afford some protection to their members. That protection can be a number of ways. Firstly because we don't have a statutory minimum wage policy, they have got to guard against exploitation by unscrupulous employers. They are not always successful in that but at least, if they can set the yardstick for a certain industry where they do have influence, then the terms and conditions that apply within that industry will obviously in some ways be spun off into other industries, because of the need to attract labour (B3, pp 23-24).

As we have already said, the relation to the employees (in Germany) and only to trade union members (in England) is in our opinion more than a formal or language difference. It is much more an expression of a different understanding of the trade unions (with respective differences for individual trade unions). German managers view trade unions (as real and symbolic representatives of the employees) as an essential part of a social-mutual model of conflict and negotiation. In this model we must proceed from different interests of the employers and employees but at the same time the opponents are obliged to work for the common good. This assumes a willingness from both sides to understand the position of the opponent and even to anticipate this when acting. The English attitude is quite different: Here we are talking about "purely representing interests". The trade unions represent the interests of their members, the management represents the interests of the company or the capital owner – and this happens without the inclusion of those aspects which go beyond these particular interests. There is a bargaining process between the opponents, (and there is logically enough a greater distance between the two parties than in Germany) and this process determines which interests are enforced.

A few of the English managers we interviewed think that the German trade union system, or at least elements of it, is better than the English and in particular the industrial branch principle and the greater willingness to cooperate on the part of the trade unions. One manager from the building industry said:

> Yours (trade unions) are industry based. ... We have about six unions on one site. From what we see, I think that the German system is more cooperative than the British system (B12, p 6).

And another manager of the same branch commented: "I don't think they see management as an enemy" (B11, p 21). But such a type of trade union as in Germany would need to be embedded in a more extensive model of cooperation within industrial relations as was mentioned above, and in particular on the level of the works constitution. Therefore there is the question whether elements of such a model in England are available and whether such a model would be considered to be desirable by managers (and trade unions).

4.2.3   The cooperative model in Germany and conflict model in England – The views of the managers regarding the works constitution

As we have presented in chapter 4.2.1 the institutions of works and company constitution in England and Germany are very different. There are no regulations in England regarding co-determination at the company level or works councils. To follow we will outline[14] the view by German managers regarding co-determination and works council and finally we will give a presentation of the English managers.

The American sociologist Clark Kerr – an expert on the German system of industrial relations – had described the German regulation of co-determination as "a sheep in wolf's clothing" in the 1950s. By turning around this expression Kerr made clear in an appropriate way that co-determination

---

14   A more detailed presentation can be found in Eberwein, Tholen (1990, pp 258-268).

was not an institutionalization of "socialist foreign management" of the companies, as its strongest critics assumed, but that it was a completely system conform regulation that approached at best in a "class conflict disguise".

We were interested in the managers' views about co-determination. Do they share Kerr's standpoint or do they see co-determination from the opposite side namely as "a wolf in sheep's clothing" that has a paralysing effect on the company and hamper the chances of competition of the German economy on the world markets? We will concentrate on co-determination at company level as it may be found in the Co-Determination Act of the coal, iron and steel industries in 1951, in the Co-Determination Act of 1976 and partly in the Works Constitution Act of 1952. An expression of these regulations are the employee representatives on the Supervisory Board and the Labour Director on the Executive Board of the companies[15].

Regarding our question about their opinion of co-determination, the German managers gave clearly more critical answers than when talking about trade unions. Is it really "the wolf in sheep's clothing"? Is it considered to be a disturbing factor within the managerial main departments, in economic decisions? Let us look at the answers a little more closely: After all 34% of the managers see co-determination as a necessary element in a pluralistic society. We may quote the member of a board of directors from a large chemical concern to illustrate this view:

> Co-determination is a great thing. And all those who maintained that it would not work or who started all kinds of actions in fear of it have in my opinion been proven wrong. ... Co-determination does work. ... It is nonsense to expect a genuine democracy. But thinking things through together leads to an improvement of the result (G68, pp 25-26).

Thus this manager accepts completely the limitation of entrepreneurial 'self-glory' through co-determination but at the same time makes an essential reservation: This co-determination does not bring real democracy and it should not bring this. Instead co-determination is seen as being functional, namely as a means to improve the result. Nevertheless it is linked with genuine participation on the part of the employees (representatives) according to this opinion and it is in no way a particularly perfidious manager trick to integrate the employee in the company purposes. Co-determination is viewed in a positive way by a further 9% of the German managers we interviewed who connect the carrying out of important decisions with it. However the functional aspect of co-determination is emphasized here. All other managers – and that is well over half of those we interviewed – consider co-determination in a

---

15   In the chapter Industrial Democracy Lawrence gives a short introduction in English on the regulations here (1980, pp 42-50).

more negative way. The lack of professional competence and special knowledge of those involved in co-determination were given as the primary reasons for this. This applies for different reasons also to the trade union representative on the works council:

> In certain areas I think co-determination is not justifiable because professional competence is really lacking. I think it is dangerous for the trade unions to try and bring functionaries on the supervisory board within the framework of co-determination because they are just as removed as the others, like the actionaries and only wish to carry out social politics through the company (G23, p 30).

It is also true of the company employee representatives:

> Employees in works council meetings. What I have experienced is that you just sit there because you haven't got the information like company management. What are they supposed to do? In my opinion it is a farce in medium-sized companies (G24, p 31).

Finally a considerable number of managers expressed the view that they would accept co-determination only if there was a possibility for the employees to take on responsibility. Apart from the fact that the German trade unions have historically been and still are willing to bear responsibility for society as a whole (contrary the English trade unions) there still arises the question about the content and consequences of such responsibility. For we must not forget that employed managers and a large number of shareholder representatives in the supervisory boards are not liable to the extent of their own property.In respect to the question of the responsibility for securing jobs which comes more and more into the public it is not possible to assume that the employee representatives in the organs of co-determination act carelessly.

The reference of lacking liability on the part of employee representatives by some of the managers must therefore also be viewed as a rejection of co-determination on company level.

However, in spite of the critical estimations about co-determination, we may confirm that: if we look at the relevant empirical examinations, co-determination has proved itself on the whole, at least and above all in large concerns. There are indeed completely different points of emphasis in the employment of co-determination laws[16], but on the whole co-determination contributes considerably to an arbitrary-peaceful way of solving conflicts and this is characteristic of the German system of industrial relations. In this way co-determination in the way it is perceived and experienced is possibly less important for the individual company. But for society on the whole it may be

---

16   Compare here U. Bamberg et al. (1987, pp 58-84).

seen as the central expression of general recognition of the principle of dialogue and negotiation.

The works council in general is seen as the most important organ of company representation of employees' interests. In answer to our question "Is the works council important for you?" a manager from the second management level of an international mineral oil concern said:

> Yes, I think if we didn't have it, we would have to invent it very quickly, because an organ that is constructed to get rid of internal company troubles and matters of conflict is something only other countries could wish for. I have made the experience that with the works council, if you take it to be as important as it should be and employ it in processes that you have, can bring with it ideas very quickly as a transformation instance into all staff departments. And this, I will call it dual system, that we have, so that we say, we must work with the works council together in order to solve difficult processes in cooperation because it is not a model of confrontation with the works council (G73, p 31).

The comment: "If there weren't a works council we would have to invent one" was heard often. From the managers' point of view the works council is quite obviously the most important and useful institution in the system of industrial relations. Only a very small minority of 4% of managers considered the works council to be superfluous, even harmful for a conflict-free run of the company. There were two fundamental reasons given for this: lacking qualifications and or ideologically founded confrontation thinking of the works council. One manager described the works council as a second centre of power in the company (G78, p 22). This thought can already be found in Dahrendorf's work (1977, pp 226-250): There is the danger within works councils that there is a tendency for them to become an addition to the company structure of authority, whereby – as H. Schelsky maintained – staff representation takes on the position of an institutionalized hierarchy within the company. As part of the official company structure of authority the works council is shown to be a bearer of authority and indeed at the side of management as member of the managing group in opposition to the staff as the subordinates. In this way by constructing works councils (according to the German model) a change in the industrial management structure is achieved that at the same time smooths the way for new industrial class conflicts by building up a new authority. Consequently the works council could not fulfil its (integrative) function of alleviating class conflicts – so far Dahrendorf.

Apart from the fact that these statements can hardly be proven empirically – and our findings also speak against them – a formal equation of the roles of authority of management and staff representatives forms the basis of Dahrendorf's evaluation of the position and situation of the works council. It is obvious that these are not the same either in their establishment, content and range. On the other hand the managers are very interested in a strong works council:

> I would like a strong works council. Only a strong works council, strong in the sense of employees, can be a works council, that can really have some effect in a company. Personally I would like to have works councils where one or two strong personalities are represented, who can stand up together for a front of understanding (G79, p 26).

With this we come to the majority of managers (96% of those we interviewed) who see the works council in a very positive way. The most frequent reason given here was that the works council is important as a partner in communication with company management. The works council brings together the individual employees to one staff whose interests, conceptions and wishes are easier to handle and to overcome by management. This conception of the works council is linked with representing interests. The latter is indeed a requirement so that the works council in its function can be taken seriously as a central partner in communication.

This function of representing employees' interests is particularly emphasized by those managers who consider the works council to be important for articulating the interests of the staff. One manager of the air and space industry expressed himself in a particularly clear and perhaps exaggerated way by saying:

> I am still convinced that 80% of the workers are really in a weak position from my own company and in other companies, even if they belong to a trade union. It makes the work of company management easier and at the same time more difficult to speak with the staff and to formulate positions and then indeed to reach an aimed agreement, or any agreement at all. I would see what I have said as positive (G72, p 28).

Here again we see the functional interest of the managers in the works council: the works council enables staff actions to be calculated and thus to be planned. In connection to this we may also categorize the role of the works council as mediators of information between company management and staff; let us look at a manager of a middle-sized steel construction company:

> Yes, basically the works council should be the mouthpiece of the staff, should be a filter for problems so that employees can get rid of problems through the works council so that company tasks are not hindered by questions of all kinds and trivialities. It is important that the works council sees from its inner conviction that the company behaves itself in a fair way – this is a flexible concept of course – and that it pays in a social way so that it can continue this behaviour in the company in a positive way. The works council should also ensure that the worker who is not informed about all things should get the feeling that the company thinks in a social

and positive way and that fundamentally the works council continues and reflects this positive attitude (G67, p 18).

The possibility of perceiving the interests for the staff is open to the works council as long as there is a competent and skilled politics on the council's behalf and even if the council is seen under a functional aspect by company management. A manager of an automobile concern expressed this in very clear terms:

> It must still be found out if free scope is left in the company that the works councils can fill (G108, p 30).

However there are only a few managers who judge the works council exclusively according to instrumental viewpoints. The works council is brought in as an extended arm of company management or as part of the personnel department. The answer of a managing director of a middle-sized company of the metal industry illustrates such an attitude:

> … and they can support us in essential matters in managerial work. And I must say that this is practised here. If we have to complete an order in a very short time, then we speak to the works council and say, tell your people that we have to do overtime and tell them why this is necessary and the works council can bring this across to the employees much better than we can. In this respect they have a very important task within the company (G112, p 23).

It is our preliminary result that on the whole the works council is accepted and viewed in a positive way by industrial company managers to a very high degree. Of course there are different forms and types of relationship between works council and company management in different companies. Our empirical findings prove such differentiations too. In his examination about works councils and company management H. Kotthoff has developed a typology of participation models in the industrial company which covers "the ignored works council" as well as "the works council as a cooperative opposing force" (Kotthoff: 1981, pp 46-89). Kern and Schumann also point to corresponding differentiations in their famous study *Das Ende der Arbeitsteilung?* (Kern, Schumann: 1984, p 325). But in general the works council can be seen as a central element, recognized by the majority of managers, within the system of industrial relations in the Federal Republic of Germany.

In a comparison of German and English managers P. Lawrence confirms an almost total acceptance of the works council by German managers (Lawrence: 1980, pp 49-50):

> It is also noticeable that (managerial) acceptance of the Works Council is just about total. … No one can imagine life without the Works Council. The first time the author asked a senior manager about the company's attitude to the Works Council the laconic reply was, 'The Works Council Act is a piece of legislation like any

other: we implement it.' That this matter of fact acceptance exists is important because there are grounds for regarding the Works Council as the central institution of the co-determination system, and as one having some positive effects from management's standpoint. The practical importance of the Works Council, in the context of running companies, is that it provides for the regulation of many issues in an agreed, institutional way, and does so in advance. To put it the other way round, it is unlikely (though not impossible) that there will be strikes or disruptions of normal work about, for instance, canteen prices, appointments, promotions and transfers, because all these issues are regulated by the Works Council. And it is understood on both sides that the Works Council will regulate these affairs, and that it will do so before the event, not after a crisis has become manifest.

The statement by Lawrence contains an evaluation of the German works and company constitution from the British point of view and he emphasizes precisely those points which are particularly striking for a foreign observer. We asked English managers for their evaluation of the German system of works constitution and co-determination. Almost half of those we interviewed stated that they did not know the German system (or at least not well enough). Even a part of those managers left only had a general knowledge of the character of industrial relations in Germany rather than detailed knowledge of the relevant regulations. But with this backgound in mind we may classify the answers to our question. About half of them thought the German system was better. Only one manager was of the opposite opinion. Approximately one third admitted that the German system was good for Germany but not transferrable to England.

Two selected quotes are possibly more conclusive than this distribution of answers and they show very clearly the difference between the English and German system. One manager from the building industry noticed that in England neither staff nor management is really interested in co-determination regulations as they are to be found in Germany:

> In the 70s there was a movement to have workers on the board here. It didn't honestly work. A few companies tried it but generally they found that there wasn't a lot of enthusiasm from the workers and not much from the directors. They would say, you are the managers, you are the directors of the company, you are supposed to be leading us and making the right decisions. Tell us where we are supposed to be going. Don't try and share the responsibility by having us on the board, because it is not our job. That is your job. These are the sort of arguments that one heard (B11, p 22).

From this statement we can see very clearly the English conflict model as it was described above. The much stronger awareness of difference between management and staff was underlined by a manager from the food and luxury food branch:

> In the UK there has been too much of a 'them and us' situation (B16, p 13).

The same is true of the statement of a manager from the vehicle construction branch who faces this model very critically:

> It seems that you have got a better system than we've got. … it seems to me you have attitudes amongst workers and amongst management, which encourage cooperation to a much greater degree than we have here. Whether it is history or what I don't know, but it is rather sad. It seems to me that we regard competition and conflict as important ingredients in life instead of emphasizing the cooperation and cooperative element, that is more important (B4, pp 19-20).

In her Anglo-German comparative examination Millar stresses the difference between the English conflict model and German model of cooperation:

> A striking aspect of Works Council functioning was their dual interest; firstly, as representative of the workforce who elected them but, secondly, their concern with the welfare of the company as a whole. This contrasts with an exclusively Union form of representation where interests tend to be more partisan and sometimes directed towards outside pressures rather than the interests of the company as a whole or even of most of its workers (Millar: 1979, p 61).

She concludes from this that "the Works council is a more effective form of representation at plant level than the Union representation through shop stewards" (Millar: 1979, p 57). And she continues: "The conflict model in the UK may be more virile but conflict models are often not well adapted for solving problems, exchanging information in a non heated situation and making balanced compromises" (Millar: 1979, p 64).

Our own findings do not permit any direct conclusions regarding the effectiveness of different works and company constitutions. But in a final result we may attempt to evaluate in a summary the different systems of industrial relations in both countries.

4.2.4   Industrial managers and industrial relations – A conclusion

Let us turn again first of all to German managers. As we could show from our findings, the majority evaluate the system of industrial relations in a positive way even if they have different motives for doing so. It is striking but obvious that the evaluation of the fundamental elements of this system are directed strongly towards functional, partly instrumental standpoints. Therefore we may say that in the awareness of the managers the gradual introduction and fundamental recognition of a staff and employee co-determination in its different forms has not removed and should not remove the socially required and functionally necessary relationship between company management and staff. Co-determination has rationalized company management (which is not categorized as such by managers) in the sense that in principle it is limited to all that is functionally necessary within a capitalist market economy. And for this reason it receives its functionality within the framework of the economic process. Therefore we cannot speak in a strict sense about a democraticization of firms and companies. In spite of the move away from authoritarian styles of management the managers refuse a change of sovereignty similar to people's sovereignty, that is to say they refuse any infringement of the autonomy of company management. Nevertheless the liberalization and rationalization of industrial relations is evidence of the considerable ability to compromise and process of company managerial relations. Within the institutional framework of the industrial-capitalist economic and social system this has proved to be much more far-reaching than was assumed[17].

Within this framework there is employee's interest representation with differentiated claims for information, participation and co-determination which make an extendable basis for perceiving the work and company interests of the employees and staff. Problems regarding work can be discussed; there is a safeguard to prevent arbitrary authority being carried out. And the consideration of social matters in management practice has been enforced. In modern management there is no basic resistance against negotiations or mutual agreements. The establishment of communicative relations within this framework make the development and employment of a conflict regulation possible which does justice to the changing requirements of existence and functioning in the industrial company in general.

Such a conflict regulation has the character of a compromising balance between the different interests involved, that is of the employees and trade unions and management. The liberalization of industrial relations can be explained by this. Within this framework the class contrasts (in Marx's sense of the word) are rubbed out and 'changed' into a 'difference in competence' between management and staff. On the other hand we do not proceed from interest identity within the company but from differences in interests (Fox: 1973, pp 192-199). These constitute a complex of tensions and competing demands which must be worked on and mutually discussed in order to uphold a cooperative structure which is able to exist and within which every individual and group can pursue their demands. Rights and laws are implemented for this purpose. In this case it is at least implicitly presumed and expected that the different interests can be bridged over by negotiating compromises. However this presupposes the assumption that normative differences between competing groups and individuals are not so fundamental that they cannot be settled by forming a compromise.

---

17   This idea can be found in Giddens (1979, p 356): "Capitalism has proved itself to be an elastic economic system, which can bear greater modifications without producing the revolutionary collapse expected by Marx".

Therefore every group must limit its own demands and claims to such an extent that the respective contrahent feels that it is tolerable. The existence and continuation of cooperation can only be possible in this way. Within the framework of such a compromising balance of different interests there is the possibility for employees to have certain rights of participation and a certain kind of autonomy. These are expressed in the various possibilities of the staff and their representatives to participate and work in co-determination. As Fürstenberg (1958) has already found out, the works council takes on a clear position in the intersection of expectations of three groups – staff, company management and trade union. Nevertheless these rights are limited so that in the end they do not cancel out the entrepreneurial autonomy of management and do not put this autonomy into question but put it under a certain amount of control.

The corresponding strategy of management can be described as being rational to the extent that it tries to take into account the changed requirements of existence and function of the industrial company through a specific and systematically adequate regulation of conflict. The differences in interests between staff and management cannot be denied and the conflicts arising from these are neither suppressed nor ignored. The conflicts in their strategic intention, that is to say with the aim of upholding a cooperative relationship between staff and management, are settled systematically with the participation of the staff or their representatives. The liberality and rationality of such a management strategy can be seen here. A. Fox has described this connection in simple terms as follows (Fox: 1973, p 195): "In current circumstances their best chance of being able to control events lies in their being ready to share that control with the groups they are seeking to govern".

This does not mean of course that we are talking about a strategy of solving problems and conflicts, which is free from the exercise of power. It appears that here social realism (conflicts are not denied), political liberalism (every interest group can and should bring with it claims and expectations) and pragmatic-rational conflict solving (with the help of mutually fixed and/or accepted ways of carrying out conflicts) are linked with each other. On the whole we may conclude that the process of the rationalization and liberalization of industrial relations moves fundamentally within industrial-capitalist market relations and requirements of processing and does not exceed its limits.

Thus the German system of industrial relations is an essential element of the thematically differentiated and gradual regulation of social conflict potentials. According to M.R. Lepsius (1979) it is a typical form of presenting and settling interests in modern industrial societies of the parliamentary-democratic type. Industrial relations form an extensive network of institutions to overcome and settle social conflicts. The effect of this institutional network is that socially conditioned conflict content is taken apart, specified and differentiated or rather taken apart, divided up and treated on different levels. Therefore conflicts are robbed of an explosive force which goes beyond the system and can as "dismantled complexes of problems" be given different solutions: "As a result of the institutionalization of social conflicts there is a number of specific regulation problems in place of diffuse and valuable 'fundamental questions' and a number of pragmatic 'questions in procedure' in place of 'constitutional questions'" (Lepsius: 1979, p 194).

Within such an institutional network such matters of conflict can and may only be carried out within the framework of the works constitution and which can and are implemented on this level. A works constitution which functions in this way needs a supplement through and embedding in more extensive labour and social laws and an extended possibilty for tariff contracts which the German labour movement has historically been working for.

As a result of the fact that only such problems are negotiated within the works constitution that can be solved in the company, and others are treated on other levels, 'a division of labour' between works constitution that is works council, trade unions and political parties has arisen and this division allows a relatively pragmatic attitude towards solving conflicts between employees and employers. Precisely for this reason is the system of industrial relations accepted and supported by the majority of managers.

This great capacity to solve conflicts in the German model is also viewed in a positive way by some of the English managers we asked and we heard from a manager from the food and luxury food industry who said:

> I think the advantage it has is its symmetry. ... The German system is the new world (B13, p 16).

A manager of the vehicle construction industry can even be described as a real 'admirer' of the German model and would very much like to transfer it to England:

> I think the two tier bargaining structure is something that we should adopt fully. We know about it and how it works. It is a process of change and it is extremely difficult to get people to adopt it. I think it is an excellent way of operating. ... Over here it is much more fragmented although in this company we do attempt to adopt the local style. We try to adopt the German structure (B10, p 28).

But the following manager from the chemical industry pointed to the fundamental difficulty of such an approach in England:

> I believe it works in Germany because Germany tends to be rather more disciplined in society and they have a more disciplined approach than the UK. If we introduced a similar system in the UK, there would need to be massive education. The trade union officials we have in the company have no enthusiasm really for being

involved in co-determination. They see their role as responding to management
(B17, p 10).

In our opinion we must add that learning processes would be necessary on the
part of management if the German model were to be employed in England.
Poole et al. point in their somewhat older examination to the fact that British
managers refuse participation and industrial democracy and instead prefer a
"unitary frame of reference" (Poole et al.: 1982, pp 288-305).

Independent of the fact whether such an adaption would be meaningful and
desirable we must underline one other point: The ability to settle conflicts
pragmatically is much more represented in the German system of industrial
relations than in the English system. According to Jacobi (1989, p 45), the
collective bargaining system in Great Britain possesses a "low capacity of
effective self-regulation of labour relations". This system of trade union and
negotiation is "out-of-date in the sense of political and social steering of
capitalist democracies" although it would be wrong to make the "unreasonable" trade union movement the scapegoat for the economic demise in Great
Britain (Jacobi: 1989, pp 45-46).

At times the pragmatism of solving the conflicts in Germany is equated with a
lack of democracy and an excess of authoritarianism in industrial relations. We
consider this to be completely wrong. Not only our own findings, that prove a
general acceptance of the participation of employees by German managers,
support this. But different Anglo-German comparative examinations come to
the same conclusion. We may also see in J. Millar's Anglo-German comparison, that has been mentioned several times, that German management – as
opposed to British management – takes employee participation very seriously.:

> Both on the management level and shop floor a more traditional view of relations
> was apparent in the UK, also with respect to participation. There was still a 'one
> way' view of influence in the UK. For example, on consultation one top manager
> stated, 'Everyone is given the opportunity to express his opinion – we may then
> take the decision we intended to take anyway.' One of the more striking aspects of
> attitude in Germany ... was the view that one should go to participative meetings
> without preformed opinions, that one should listen and respond. Otherwise
> consultation becomes a 'front', a form of Tokenism (Millar: 1979, p 58).

Jürgens emphasizes that in Germany, as opposed to Great Britain, works
councils and trade union representatives are in a position to develop their own
concepts and alternatives of organization for work within the framework of a
cooperative model of solving problems (Jürgens: 1991, p 208).

Finally Lane comes to the conclusion that the picture of the authoritarian
German and democratic British manager is wrong. British managers practice a

kind of pseudoparticipation (Lane: 1989, pp 107-114) (see here the above quote from Millar: 1979). Nevertheless there are areas in which British employees have greater influence than Germans (Lane: 1989, p 247). By the way Hofstede's examination confirms that German managers are more partcipative than British managers (Hofstede: 1984, p 258).

Let us return to the provacative question we asked at the beginning of this chapter: Class barriers in England and open society in Germany? Our findings and considerations show that neither of these descriptions are suitable. In the end England as well as Germany are both industrial-capitalist market economies of Western style and show similar social structures with all their differentiations in detail. We could show that the fundamental difference in the field of industrial relations is not in the structure of social conflicts but in the form and solution of these conflicts. For many managers (in Germany) and for some (in England) the German model is seen to be more pragmatic and effective with respect to a social common good. To follow we would like to look at the matter of whether such mutualities and differences continue in the question of a possible orientation towards the common good by the managers.

4.3   Regarding the tense relationship between the company good and the common good as seen from the managers' point of view

We asked the managers, "Is there something like an obligation of a social common good on the part of company managers? What does this consist of in your opinion? In which relation does this 'common good' stand to the 'company good'?".

More than half of the German managers seemed to be of the opinion that the company contributes automatically to the social common good whether it be because of its share in the whole economy (social product) or by its mere existence as the source of jobs and income and producer of practical values. Representing many answers we will quote here the words of a member of the board of directors from the food and luxury food industry:

> I would like to ask an opposing question there. It is obvious that every prospering company influences the common good in a positive way, otherwise not so many communities would support the establishment of new firms. ... You see, a person is satisfied when he has sufficient income and is content in his profession. A company offers both these things in one form or another. So, here perhaps self-interest becomes common interest or however you would like to describe it. Of

course they have a function of the common good, without influencing this directly (G9, p 27).

Behind this view there is an appraisal like that which was experessed in a similar way, if in another connection, in the 18th and 19th century by the English utilitarian Jeremy Bentham and the 'forefather' of the liberal market economy, Adam Smith. According to this appraisal, the primarily egoistic pursuit of individual interests (here of the company) becomes in the end the wealth of the nation and is increased to everybody's benefit (Smith) and in this way becomes the 'greatest fortune for as many people as possible' (Bentham).

A German manager from the automobile industry reinforced the validity of this old principle for today's terms by saying:

> The obligation towards the common good of the company means that first and foremost it remains able to compete and to perform and that does not mean a minimum of performance ability and a minimum of competition ability but a maximum of both. Because in international competition only top performance is appreciated (G78, p 24).

More than half of the English managers we interviewed shared this view: A company fulfils automatically a common good function as a result of its mere existence and its economic occupation and implications. The following quotes can illustrate this widespread view. Here are the words of a manager from the building industry:

> ... helping the company to be more successful and more profitable, that means prosperity for the local community and I think that ought to have its own rewards in being well regarded by that community (B11, p 24).

The manager of a company in the vehicle construction industry expressed a similar view:

> I think to generate profit, which is then seen as investment and as regeneration of business and wealth has to be looked upon as a social act. Creating wealth and security of jobs for an area (B10, p 30).

This answer pattern is represented equally amongst German and British managers.

Approximately one fifth of the German managers see a common good obligation of companies or managers to be fulfilled through certain additional activities. Company social politics was described as an internal company instrument, from company sports facilities to lunch vouchers. The most important external company activity in this connection is the 'sponsoring' of sports clubs and events, art etc. which has obviously come into fashion to a high degree in recent times and works according to the motto: "Do good and talk about it" (e.g. G68, p 30). In England the corresponding share of these answers was somewhat smaller (a seventh).

Let us summarize the statements of company managers made so far. We may say that almost three quarters of German managers and two thirds of their English colleagues see an unproblematical connection between common good and company good and therefore see also – in different forms – a considerably frictionless compatibility between the two. Nevertheless the quoted comments point to the fact that the managers we interviewed make use of a formal concept of common good. Basically they view society as a number of individuals whose social connection is created through discussion and negotiation. This presupposes materially a private and really prepolitical (even moral) connection to a philosohy which in practice in society does not exist because the society is interwoven with structural differences in interest and contrasts. But it is precisely this last point that is negated by the majority of managers.

A significant number of managers represent another view here:

Approximately a fifth of those interviewed in both countries is of the opinion that company good and common good do not simply merge a priori and we see here the example of a German manager from the food and luxury food industry:

> I believe however that every company is obliged to see itself as a part of this country and not to manage their affairs according to the motto: Why should I be interested in a clean river Rhine? Or why should I be interested in a clean world? As long as it is allowed I will do it. But every company or every action has consequences somewhere for others and we should proceed according to the motto to disturb the the spheres of others as much as necessary but as little as possible (G25, p 33).

His English colleague from the vehicle construction industry argues in a similar way:

> I think there has to be a balance between the responsibility for your community and society and the pure unadulterated pursuit of profit (B10, p 31).

The automatic union of company good and common good is not presumed here. But these managers see the tension between the two not in an antagonistic way. On the contrary this could be taken into account by (most) companies from the very beginning and could therefore be defused. The manager quoted above from the food and luxury food industry described in a very abstract and general way what such a 'defusing' could look like. The quote makes very clear that the managers in this answer category have a similarly formal concept of the common good as those in the majority who see the connection of company and common good as unproblematical from the outset.

Finally there is a number of approximately 10% (in Germany) and considerably more (in England) interviewed managers who maintain the view that the
obligation towards the common good in comparison with the company good is
of little importance and that there is not such an obligation for companies. In
reply to our question on this theme a member of the managing board of
directors of a large concern said:

> I find it difficult to say yes to the question of a common good obligation on the part
> of companies because the company comes into great conflicts at the moment when
> the interest of the company is demanded on the one side and the interest of the
> community and society is asked for on the other side. I think it is obvious to push
> the interest of the company into the foreground and to say that you must decide in
> the company according to this interest, and to make it clear to every individual in
> the company that he is a citizen in a society and that he must carry out certain tasks
> within this society. The company manager must be sure in this double responsibil-
> ity, which consequences a company decision, which is good for the company, may
> have for society and whether as a member of this society he can really make this
> decision. And then he must really make up his mind for one or the other. But in his
> thoughts and comments he should separate the two because all other attempts are in
> my opinion relatively dishonest or lead to a disguising of the connections and to a
> dishonest statement (G62, p 27).

Here the possible discrepancy between the common good and company good
is made very clear in a differentiated consideration and not as a moral deficit of
the individual managers[18], but as an opposing structure. One of his English
colleagues stated briefly:

> The shareholders who own the company are interested only in profit and dividend
> and a return on their investment. They are not really interested in welfare (B17,
> p 11).

Our empirical material does not give any clear idea whether German or
English managers are more or less orientated in their thoughts and actions to
common good requirements. There is an assumption that in Great Britain
social concepts of the common good play a smaller role. Margaret Thatcher
had even maintained that in Great Britain there was no society but only
individuals (and their families) (*Die Zeit* from 30.11.1990). Harvey et al.
(1984) suggest that English managers, or at least some of them, treat their
social and political environment like the weather. Anthony (1986:
pp 193-199) demands a stronger social and morally-political responsibility on
behalf of managers. But as we have already said, we cannot trace any
systematic difference of the common good relationship of German and English
managers from our findings. It appears to us that the field of tension and
conflict between the company and common good is determined in the same

---

18   R. Jackall (1988) appears to reproach US managers for this.

way in both countries by the economic and social structure. But the question becomes interesting when we think about whether managers in England and Germany possibly have different perceptions of working in this field of conflict.

We find one first indication of this in the following comment by a manager of a company for energy supply:

> It is quite simply the task of politics to convert demands for the common good into economically calculable dimensions through legal regulations. It is impossible just to preach insight, moral and ethics. We must make economically relevant dimensions out of the need of the common good through laws and decrees (G22, pp 16- 17).

Here the indication of the task of politics in this connection is interesting and indeed a number of managers in Germany – fewer in England – made such a claim in connection with matters regarding environmental protection. They were quite willing to accept certain regulations from the government which should however be valid for everyone in order to prevent any disadvantages in competition. On the other hand the managers hope for a reliability and predictability of future developments which would make strategic action easier for them.

This leads us to the question which views and expectations managers in England and Germany have of the government and politics.

4.4   The view of the managers regarding State-political action

Some time ago the managing director of a British company wrote in a report for the Financial Times that

> the German experience clearly shows that in some areas of business activity 'more state', not 'less state', is needed. ... Perhaps it is time for some new thinking in the boardrooms with some serious consideration being given to where the best interests of business really lie. There is plenty of evidence that unbridled free-for-all capitalism may no longer be the best way; and that what business in Britain needs is the kind of managed economy that has, for example, served Germany so well" (Financial Times from 28.11.90).

With this the relationship between State/government and economy is mentioned or becomes critical: the question whether and to what extent State intervention is allowable or even necessary in the economic process. The quoted manager obviously proceeds from the fact that in Germany such a relationship is closer and in the end more fruitful than in England where the government and the majority of managers supported a strict separation of economy and politics. Some time ago the Chancellor of the Exchequer at that time said in apt words that "the business of government is not the government of business" (*Observer* from 25.10.87, quoted in Lane: 1989, p 256).

We were interested in the extent of such differences amongst the managers' viewpoints. Let us come at once to one important result: In both examination groups there was only a minority of managers who demanded (to a lesser or greater degree) total economic State abstinence (in the German sample about 30 and in the English 20% of the answers).

This answering behaviour of the managers is surprising in two respects: Firstly the supporters of the principle "More market – less State" amongst the English managers was in no way more frequently represented than amongst their German colleagues, indeed it was rather the opposite that was the case. Secondly on the whole you can describe these findings as a blow in the face to the neo-conservative supporters of a 'night-watchman State' according to an economic-liberal pattern. It was only seldom that we found an ideologically motivated request for the retreat of the State and an unlimited effectiveness of the market mechanismas it is described in the following statement of a German manager from a mechanical engineering company:

> I would not consider it to be good to interfere with the matters of the company in a strongly regulating way. I am a very strong supporter of this free market economy with social suggestions. I mean, you see that has been a philosophy for me for a long time. I mean, something starts working out successfully when a certain amount of independence is maintained as well as the possibility to develop one's own ideas, concepts and is least of all regulated (G38, p 30).

Several managers criticized a certain mentality of subsidy from the State as well as from the economy, which would work out to be contraproductive in the end; a manager from a mineral oil concern in Germany said:

> It is my opinion that precisely as far as economic politics is concerned, he should be less committed and should withdraw himself from all those things because through such State commitment in some fields we are turning into a museum. That is quite bad. You only need to look at a subsidy report and see where the tax money is going. It is the agricultural sphere, it is the railway, coal, steel and the shipyards etc.. And in these cases structures that are artificially kept alive cost enormous amounts of money for our national economy. But if they allowed the money to flow freely, of course within certain framework conditions, so that the companies could manage their affairs and if it was not stored then in my opinion they would have more employment (G75, p 35).

With the promotion of economic-political abstinence the function of the State and its fixing of certain framework conditions is mentioned here.

On the whole it is our impression that the majority of company managers in England as well as in Germany are aware of the 'organized' character of their position in as far as the immeasurably social and also State framework conditions and intervention are a precondition of their action. In their opinion continual and planned company development and politics is (more or less) dependent on direct or indirect State intervention (e.g. armament agreements, monetary policy, political climate, on the whole economic and political framework conditions). Thus in the German sample more than 60% and in the English sample about 50% of the answers we were given emphasized the task of the State to fix framework conditions for the economy. The following manager of a German air space company gave a typical answer in this sense:

> The State has the task of creating, pursuing consistently and of sanctioning certain framework conditions. ... It is my view that the State must create clear framework conditions, in competition law, monopoly law, cartel act, in tax law and in social legislation. But this framework which the State fixes, must have validity and should not be changed or re-designed every 1 or 2 years, so that a certain stable framework of external data is created for the company (G87, p 37).

Two aspects become particularly clear in this comment. On the one hand the manager demands that the observance of State framework conditions should be put through by sanctions. Secondly the stability and continuity of State framework conditions was to be secured with the aim of making the conditions for the company calculable and plannable. An English manager demanded of State politics: "To put forward a policy of stability for industry" (B2, p 28). Approximately a third of the answers in the German sample and half of the answers in the English sample asked for an active influencing of the State in the economic process in addition to the fixing and guaranteeing of framework conditions. This could occur as a result of an active policy of technology or in general as a result of aimed allocation of subsidies.

In this connection a manager from a German air and space company described any withdrawal of the State out of the economy as a catastrophe – an evaluation which has originally to do with the conditions of his industry[19]:

> Let us take technology. ... It originates from basic research and you cannot separate the two. Here the State has a task, that is completely obvious. ... I would even like to see in our country that the State should engage itself more intensively with the cultural domain ... and here with basic research ... (G101, p 23).

Two of his English colleagues went even further in their plea for State commitment in economy. This is partly linked with clear criticism of their own industry:

---

19   See the topical discussion about the European Fighter Aircraft (EFA).

> I think it should be stronger because I don't believe you can rely on British
> industry. They are not likely to invest in plans that might generate a profit in the
> future. ... I just don't think you will get long-term investment on securing the
> future of people from British industry. You need government legislation and you
> have got to force them to do it (B10, p 32).

Another English manager described himself as:

> Advocate of a mixed economy, but I do feel that within a mixed economy there are
> certain industries and certain aspects of the economy, which cannot or shouldn't be
> left to the free market. I think the basic utilities for a start should be controlled,
> centrally controlled. I'm not in favour of a free economy (B3, p 28).

On the other hand the company managers do not see the State as a 'repair shop
of capitalism'. One typical answer in this sense was given by a manager from
the car industry in Germany:

> The State is not an entrepreneur, but it is also not a repair shop. It must try to be
> something inbetween. I am not of the opinion that the State is an entrepreneur in the
> sense of nationalization or something similar. I refuse that completely. But I also
> refuse the State when it thinks it must withdraw itself completely from every
> company (G108, p 33).

On the whole we can see that the majority of managers appreciate State
commitment in the economy and would not like to do without it. This is the
case for our findings in Germany as well as in England. In the face of the
widespread opposite picture this is a surprising result for England. It may be
possible that a change in the managers' views has taken place here. At the
beginning of the 1980s Poole et al. had confirmed that the managers preferred
a policy of "neo-laissez faire" (Poole et al.: 1982, p 297). We consider it
conceivable that after a decade of Thatcher's economic policy the weaknesses
of such a policy have become clear to the managers in particular when we
think about the almost non-existent forward-looking industrial policy (cf. here
chapter 3.4) and the concepts of regional development. The quote from the
beginning of this chapter is further proof of this[20].

As well as their function as economic actors the managers are of course also
citizens and fathers. As such they expect the State to get involved with
economic processes in a regulating way and this became particularly obvious
in the case of the problems of ecology; here we hear from a manager in
Germany from the air and space industry:

> As far as ecological mechanisms are concerned it should commit itself more,
> because the self-regulating powers of social behaviour are not sufficient. ... And
> in the meantime we know that extensive damage has been caused and that we

---

20   This does not alter the fact that most of the English managers still prefer the Conser-
     vatives to the Labour Party.

cannot continue in this way so the State must join in. It is of course painful to take away any liberties that you view as being your own, it is very difficult. And on a voluntary basis this would occur too slowly. ... The processes would be sooner there than the time it takes for the last one to become aware that we are really talking about a catastrophe (G69, p 23).

An English managing director from the textile industry answered in a similar way:

Legislation should control all aspects of any manufacture that could damage our environment, the atmosphere. I believe strongly in that it has to be controlled. Everything is worth protecting, our life, our future, our children (B14, p 16).

In general we may say that in the eyes of the managers "With State" or "Without State" do not come into question. The economic process is developed in interaction between private economy and democratically legitimized State.

With this we will turn to our next question complex. Which social problems and political aims linked with these do the managers, in their role as company managers and as citizens and social individuals, consider to be the most significant or of prime importance? We asked the managers which social-political problem or task they would put at the top of their personal list.

As we have already seen there were no significant differences regarding the question about State intervention in the economic process between English and German managers but in this question there were considerable differences in opinion. Let us look first of all at the 'national lists'.

German managers mentioned the four most important social-political tasks in this order:

- fight against unemployment;
- environmental protection;
- organization of the Common Market (EG'93);
- upholding of the social peace.

And now their English colleagues:

- fight against inflation;
- environmental protection;
- fight against unemployment and strengthening of the industrial location of Great Britain.

The relatively high value for the managers of the fight against unemployment is surprising for us and possibly for the reader: It took on first place in Germany and third place in England. Some excerpts from our interviews, especially in Germany, may illustrate this. One manager of a food and luxury food concern said:

> I think it is right that the general opinion states that unemployment that we have had now for years is perhaps the greatest social problem we have and if you are manager of a significant company you are perhaps directly called upon to do something against it in person. ... And you do not really know what to do from the viewpoint of a company (G19, p 32).

The manager of a company from the building industry argued in a similar way:

> Unemployment ... is a big problem for the family. When a person is at home for a long time then we all know what happens. It ends in alcohol problems when he is fed up at home. And so something must be done. Only I think, that this problem is often taken too lightly in public and I say this quite consciously. We cannot say with simple formulas: Now I will fight aginst unemployment (G31, p 27).

Both statements say that unemployment is not only perceived and taken seriously in its economic but also in its social dimension. At the same time it becomes clear that both managers neither have conclusive concepts nor practical contributions to fight unemployment and this was the case for the majority of managers we interviewed. Thus the following English manager from the building industry may be seen as one of the few exceptions:

> Unemployment is a particular area of my concern. I never look to recruit outside an area of unemployment now (B6, p 21).

Hardly any other manager expressed such far-reaching conceptions and suggestions for fighting against unemployment as the member of the board of directors of a large chemical company who said:

> I consider higher flexibilization to be a good means. The question of filling a position with two people is certainly a very interesting question. This should be discussed much more intensively. And the question of creating purely weekend jobs, in order to make better use of capital intensive things and then perhaps to arrange for the workers who only work at the weekends to have 28 hours per week with a corresponding wage nevertheless, all this is very interesting. I think we should use a large part, larger part of our time for further education. I could imagine a 40 hour week where 5 hours a week could be used for further education and training and 35 hours spent on the job. All these are things that exist in a stronger flexibilization of our working time and they would give us greater possibilities to employ more people and to solve future problems in the employment of workers (G62, p 24).

Without wishing to evaluate these suggestions individually: It is our opinion that by linking work with further education there is an attempt to make working time more flexible and this concept could do justice to the productivity interests of the companies as well as to the professional interests of the employees and at the same time the companies would not be relieved of their responsibility. As we have already said, such or similar conceptions were rather the exception amongst the managers we interviewed. Most of the managers face the problem of unemployment like 'private people', i.e. not with the economic competence of their manager role but as 'people like you and me'. This is all the more remarkable when we consider that social unemployment is directly or indirectly created by the companies. But here we neither want to speak of one-sided blame nor of hasty patent solutions. But it remains to be said that a majority of managers in this matter exempt themselves from a certain subjective role division of social responsibility – an individual solution which is politically quite easy[21].

As already mentioned, the problem of unemployment in both samples has a considerable if not quite different value. The first place which unemployment had in the German sample was filled by another theme in England; namely, inflation. Increasing at an almost double-figure rate, this was a very topical theme at the time of our interviews. Thus it was placed in such a high position for reasons of topicality. Contrary to this the problem of social mass unemployment in England and in Germany has been a long-term structural problem that will continue to be of considerable social-political significance. That this has a lower value in the eyes of English managers is probably a result of greater individualism which was introduced in the Thatcher era in the sense of egoism in British society. In both samples environmental protection was put in second place. Are we talking about an action-relevant inner conviction or about extensively fruitless lip service?

Let us look at one example from a manager of an air and space company:

> Now it is my personal opinion that at the very top and I put this high on the list, this is environmental protection. We must succed in stabilizing environmental protection today, or let's say in the next 5 years. This must be done with enormous orders from the legislators (the industrial companies will not do it voluntarily). They will talk about it but they won't do anything. If there is a necessity to have environmental protection then in Germany, one of the most densely-populated countries in the world, and in Europe. If we do not succeed in this then the succeeding generation will have lots to bear (G72, p 32).

We have the impression that the comments about environmental protection made by the managers must be taken seriously. However they see contradictions between the logic of pure economic company interests and the demands of ecology[22]. Therefore as a rule, they ask for State directives for companies in

---

21   We find no signs in our interviews to show that company managers approve of or even promote social unemployment in the sense of an industrial reserve army.

22   G.E. Famulla (1989) presented in a differentiated observation that there are not only contrasts between capital logic and ecological aims.

order for them to carry out ecological principles. This becomes even clearer in the comments of a car manager and he says:

> Government must determine what the environment will look like beyond the economic interests. That is an original political task and they must all comply to this. ... Government must work to ensure economic peace again and again and we must ask or challenge them to new efforts so that no more damage will be done to the ecological sides. However we must recognize again and again that with the open borders that we have, all these measures only strangulate us to the extent that they do not make us unable to compete. That is a field of tension. But we are tackling the problem and I expect this of the government (G108, p 34).

Different to the question of unemployment here State intervention is asked for – and with good reason. The English manager we quoted before argued in a similar way. On the other hand this possibly points to the fact that managers see the ecology problems much more as a private person than in their role as bearer of an economic function that contributes to a more or less enduring degree to the destruction of the environment.

In this case the company managers do not greatly differentiate from other groups of the population for whom the problem of ecology has a great significance. We cannot find from our empirical findings an important difference between English and German managers although questions about environment in England are generally not as deeply embodied as they are in Germany.

We may confirm as an interim result that in both central social problem areas the managers stay away from political responsibility in spite of all their de-emotionalization and professionalization in that they refer to their role as private person, father etc.. But precisely in these matters their economic competence would be needed to a special degree.

In Germany managers put the question of organizing the Common European Market in third place of those social-political tasks. This was stated with a clear distance from the next point although we must add that at the time of our interviews the German unification was not a topic for discussion. Directly economic reasons as well as economic and political considerations are critical here:

> I think European integration and beyond West European, total European integration, as the most important aim for economic or if you like defence political reasons to avoid a conflict which could arise from the confrontation of the blocs in Europe on a long-term basis which could possibly lead to war (G73, p 34).

In England it was interesting to see that the organization of the Common Market as a political task was not mentioned at all. Without wanting to emphasize this finding too much we can say: in our opinion the divided relationship to the European Market that is widespread in Great Britain, is reflected here. On the one hand only a minority of English managers feel that they are adequately prepared for the Common Market (see here our comments in chapter 3.5). On the other hand it does not appear to them to be a political problem. In this case perhaps we are dealing with repression or the mental isolation of England from the Continent goes so far in the case of the managers that they only attach secondary importance to preparation for the Common Market.

Of equal rank with the fight against unemployment English managers mentioned the strengthening of Great Britain as industrial location in third place as political task. This point was mentioned by their German colleagues but with less emphasis. The Germans put keeping social peace in fourth place and this was placed much lower down the list by the English. Only very few of the managers we interviewed referred particularly to the democratic process as e.g. a German manager from an air and space concern:

> I consider the most important State political task is to uphold a certain minimum level of democracy in our State, that means that to a certain extent we must remain an open society in which democratic change can take place. I consider that to be the essential and most important task of a State. I see the second essential task to be that this State in the system with trade unions, companies, political side, justice of the individual inhabitants, that this State gives the members of this community an adequate, economic basis where basically certain material needs and also cultural needs are satisfied. I consider these to be the two essential functions of a functioning State. And apart from this, what I see as democratic conviction is a certain freedom to exchange opinions, a certain freedom to travel and a certain amount of education. And above all what is essential for me, because I have experienced it as being positive in my career is a certain equality of opportunities so that people who are materially not as affluent as others, at least have the chance to receive a reasonable education and can develop accordingly. I would see this as being a fundamental principle of a democratic State. And thus I am of the opinion that parties, companies and trade unions should be obliged to the same extent. For me that is a central point of a democratic common good (G87, p 35).

Here essential principles of a democratic system are outlined in their political as well as economic significance. But as we have already mentioned the relationship to the democratic process was only mentioned by a small minority. But we cannot simply conclude from this that the political democracy is of no importance for the managers. This question can only be answered in the complete connection of the relationship of industrial company managers to politics and the society.

4.5   Top managers and the democratic process

It is hardly possible to answer the question about the field of tension of economy and politics to an adequate degree and in its full scope by using our empirical material as the basis. However it is possible to outline the industrial managers' relationship to the democratic process in a summary and in connection with the whole question complex regarding their relationship to politics and society.

Willmott (1984) worked on the "political element" of the management occupation in a very readable essay. He stresses that most of the theoretical and empirical approaches towards "managerial work" exclude the political dimension of managers' work and consequently see management as being politically neutral[23]. In contrast to this Willmott represents the view that managerial work – and this is especially the case for the occupation of top managers – is political in two respects.

> Managerial Work is political not only in the sense of employing interpersonal skills to get things done through the agency of others. It is also political in the way it is involved in the production and reproduction of institutions that appease the conflict between labour and capital (Willmott: 1984, p 363).

Even if the political implications of managerial occupation do not directly relate to the conflict between capital and work, there is in a general sense a political relevance of managerial action by the fact that different (by no means all) decisions affect directly or indirectly the working and living situation of a more or less large number of people[24]. A personnel manager of the vehicle construction industry specified this:

> It is more important that the manager behaves in the correct way because he has the greater ability to influence the destiny of others than the shop floor worker (B4, p 21).

How do managers behave towards their social responsibility mentioned here and has a change taken place in comparison with former manager generations?

Let us look first of all at the situation in Germany:

In an examination carried out in the mid 50s the American political scientist G. Almond stated that there was an opportunist relationship of company managers towards the democratic process. According to this politics would be closely

---

23   This is by no means the case for all theoretical views on management; cf. the literary discussion in chapter 1.1. and here in particular the comments about the "Labour Process Debate".

24   See our corresponding explanations in chapter 2.4.1 regarding the power and influence of top managers.

understood as interest politics. On the whole responsibility for political development was not accepted. Neither was there any inclination to rational deviating views on including political discussion etc. (Pross, Boetticher: 1971, pp 115-116). Almond even explained: "... the fragility of the democratic institutions in today's Germany cannot be separated from the spiritual poverty of German business people and academics" (Almond: 1955/56, quoted by Berghahn: 1987, p 184).

Compared with that, we assume – we take care in our interpretaions – that on the whole the actions and views of company managers related to planning, organization, management and control of industrial companies show that a transition from the former 'opportunist' behaviour towards society and democracy has taken place. Today's member of top management is aware of the 'organized' character of his position to such an extent that unpredictable social framework conditions direct his action.

However there is still a certain distance to the State and to the democratic process and its economic and works representatives (trade union, works council etc.). This distance is expressed in a rather instrumental or functional view. It arises from the work-related orientation towards the good of the manager's own company or companies which excludes a democratically autonomous definition of the common good by which the State must orientate itself. Such an objective distance towards politics exists in spite of a developed awareness of the dependence of one's own action on political allowances and framework conditions. This situation definition can be interpreted sociologically as an expression of the position of every company management in a bourgeois society, that has set the economy socially and autonomously by the guarantee of ownership and by the free use of private people of production means. With this they have created economic dynamism, within which every distance to politics was institutionalized in a legal State environment, and of which our interviews give a lasting impression. This not only corresponds to the orientation towards lawfulness and legality of their own action in a negative sense but also to the willingness to allow their own action to be restricted by general rules. One example of this is the attitude of many managers regarding questions on environmental protection. The reduction of the right of ownership which is connected to this dynamic to a kind of right of control and initiative sets the responsibility but it brings the entrepreneur or manager into the foreground that sets about the progressive mediation of production factors by means of the management apparatus. Therefore today it does not appear to be chance or compulsion that today's industrial company manager does not derive his legitimation from ownership but from his performance, that is the 'managing' of complex company units.

On the basis of our findings it may be assumed regarding the social self-locating of German top managers that company managers see themselves at the same time as "trustees of the industrial potential of society" and in this sense lay claim to a considerable political competence of action for themselves. They take the legitimation for this from their economic function which is central for society or of performance however it may be defined. In general they seem to claim that their occupation represents top form of a modern rationality which is able to differentiate and integrate the economic-political system and can lay claim to objective sovereignty.

Company managers have accepted that the community gives them directions (State framework conditions of the economic process, trade union, works council etc.), as a result of and within which they direct their action. In this sense and in our opinion we can speak of a liberalization, objectivization and democraticization of top industrial management. This differentiates today's managers quite clearly from the classical entrepreneur of the bourgeois society but also from the industrial managers of the first post-war generation of the Federal Republic of Germany, which can hardly be found in companies today.

As a result of the very different historical-social developments there has not been this latter type of manager in England. Does this mean that the English top managers are more strongly attached to the democratic process than their German colleagues? Or can the reverse situation be found today?

To come straight to the point: Our empirical material does not allow any clear differentiations. It can scarcely be possible in research practice to find out whether English or German managers think and act 'in a more democratic sense'. There are some indications for both interpretation possibilities. However it is our impression that the location of managers in the democratic process in both countries is marked fundamentally and in a very similar way by the structure of the economy and society. However we may take the opportunity here to get rid of a prejudice: we cannot assume that German managers have a priori a greater inclination towards politically authoritarian patterns of thought and action than their English counterparts. Our findings suggest this for industrial relations as well as for the common good and opinions of the State in England and Germany. Conversely we can no more state the thesis that English company managers have in general a stronger 'commercial mentality' because of their more commercial, less technical orientation[25] than the Germans whereby business and morals stand only in an instrumental relationship to each other: Morals are upheld as long as profits are gained. Further-reaching perspectives for the future do not play a role here

---

25   See here chapter 3.2.

(Hansen: 1992). We found such a viewpoint neither amongst the English nor amongst the German managers.

But on the other hand top managers are not those socially responsible managers who think completely politically and who commit themselves as political activists outside the company. There is possibly a contradiction in the mentality of the managers who on the one hand feel they are trustees of the industrial potential but on the other hand dispense with political responsibility in the fact that they see social mass unemployment, the ecology problem as "private people" and not in their roles as company managers. But in fact it is precisely these managers that have the economic competence and potential to solve these problems.

Is such a type of company manager thinkable and desirable for the future, a manager, who orients his action in the sense of Max Weber towards being "ethically responsible", that is he acts according to the maxim that "he has to be responsible for the (foreseeable) consequences of his action" (Weber: 1968, p 175)? This would mean that the managers would be obliged not only to fulfil their economic function by keeping the laws and considering possible negative consequences. The taking on of responsibility when solving social problems would be a much more suitable obligation.

5 Conclusion: Regarding the transferability of national models – What can German and English managers learn from each other?

Some years ago Wiener (1981) presented the view in his much respected and controversially discussed book in Great Britain that "in the world's first industrial nation, industrialism did not seem quite at home. In the country that had started mankind on the 'great ascent', economic growth was frequently viewed with suspicion and disdain" (p IX). And he found out that the structural weakness of the British economy "is rooted deep in the nation's social structure and mental climate" (p 3)[1]. Consequently he demands, and quotes Dahrendorf that "an effective economic strategy for Britain will probably have to begin in the cultural sphere" (p 4).

We could say in a somewhat casual way that the American Wiener traces the weakness of British economy in origin to a decline in the entrepreneurial spirit in Great Britain. It is easy to imagine that this thesis was received by politicians and business people in Great Britain either in a consenting or dismissing manner but that in any case this thesis found great resonance. Wiener's book was especially discussed and looked at in academic circles. The thesis of an attitude towards entrepreneurship that has changed since the end of the last century was rejected because such a generalization of historical trends would not do justice to the reality (Hannah: 1990). Above all this criticism was directed against the statement that British managers are hostile towards universities and on the other hand that the British system of education and further education would not meet the international standards of managerial training.

Our findings, which we have presented in a comprehensive way do not give a final answer to these questions. The comparative analysis of the working and professional situation (including the social situation) of English and German managers supports partly Wiener's argumentation and partly that of his critics, depending on the problem. However it is remarkable in this connection that the

---

1 See Mathias (1983) regarding the economic and socially historical explanation of the economic situation and structure of Great Britain.

English executives we interviewed are inclined to Wiener's view in questions on the education and further education of managers as well as on the social status of industrial company managers.

On the other hand it seems that the question is still open as to how far-reaching (national) cultural influences are for the working and professional situation and the modes of thought and behaviour of managers[2]. It is our impression that this scope is very great in certain fields. This is true for example for the system of education and further education, the relationship to Technik, industrial relations etc., where the differences between Germany and England are considerable and the mode of thought and action of the company managers is correspondingly different. As we have already shown, this becomes clear partly in certain linguistic expressions.

But there are also some fields in which our findings do not point to specifically national differences but to structural mutualities of the working and profes-sional situation of German and English company managers. This is true in the case of the daily work, working time and the management situation which has generally become more complex, the directly work organizational features of the manager occupation which are very similar in industrial companies in England and Germany. Finally the mutualities of English and German managers prevail regarding the question "owner-manager or employed man-ager" and surprisingly enough with respect to the company managers' view of State-political action. This may be to blame on the fact that in the case of the German and English society we are dealing with developed industrial-capitalist market economies of similar calibres.

But let us go back to the differences: Linked with this, there is the question as to what extent national models or special features in certain domains between the countries are transferrable and thus to what extent German and English managers can learn from each other. As a result of his empirical examinations in companies in 40 different countries Hofstede came to recognize that "International organizations such as ... the European Common Market by definition cannot fall back on one dominant national culture". On the other hand "organizations can function only if their members share some kind of culture – if together they can take certain things for granted" (Hofstede: 1984, p 273). Two things become very clear here: Firstly a functioning organization needs something like a common culture, secondly in international organiza-tions this culture cannot be dominated by one (or several) nation in the face of the others so that no culture imperialism can take hold. This does not only arise out of the necessity of a democratic legitimation but also of an economic and organizational functioning.

---

2   Compare here the extensive discussion in chapter 1.2.

Herewith the difficulties of a transferring of one national model to another are mentioned and they have been thematized by several authors. Lawrence (1980) confirms for example that a simple transferring of German models to another cultural circle is not possible. And Lane (1989, pp 293-294) states "the highly problematic nature of such borrowing and hence some scepticism about the success of cultural transplants". Two reasons in particular made the transferring of one culture to the other very difficult:

> The first can be described as consisting of the fact that industrial culture/institutions have long historical roots and that the resulting patterns are, therefore, so deep-seated in national consciousness and practice that they cannot be uprooted without destroying the whole fabric. ... A second formidable problem to the social engineering of industrial change is presented by the tightly interwoven pattern of institutional structures and cultural values and the interaction between the various elements.

Nevertheless Lawrence and Lane emphasize that a change in the industrial structures and views in Great Britain is necessary in order to prevent a colonization of British industry by foreign companies (Lane: 1989, p 296). Here certain elements of the German model are worth thinking about without the consequence that "features of German business organization should be slavishly copied" (Lane: 1989, p 298).

Which elements are involved from the British point of view? Lane and Lawrence agree that these are the German system of professional training and the system of industrial relations. According to Lane these lead to a technically highstanding and cooperative works culture. Within this framework the investments of the companies in training and further training paid off by a high degree of work productivity and willingness to work on the part of the employees. To secure the cooperation between staff and company management an institution like the works council is particularly of advantage (Lane: 1989, pp 298-300).

In a similar way Lawrence points to the high level of peace at work, the emphasis on the product and Technik, the foundation of the manager's authority from his own experience and performance and the far greater standing of industry in Germany. As a conclusion of her Anglo-German comparison Millar suggests the adaption of the German works council and of the German system of professional education and further education (Millar: 1979, pp 64-65). And David Marsh, then German correspondent for the Financial Times, adds long-termism in the relationship between industrial companies and banks as well as regional politics (decentralization) in Germany as being beneficial elements for the economy (*Financial Times* from 15.4.1991). But he also gives a very clear warning: "Wholesale introduction of expensive and bureaucratic German-style consensus into land unprepared for

it, can have disastrous consequences – as East Germany is finding out"
(*Financial Times* from 15.4.1991).

As the German example shows this warning cannot be taken seriously enough.
It is true of course in the other direction, that is the possible adaption of
English elements in the German model. Nevertheless we proceed from the
assumption that by respecting their specific traditional feature and independence national cultures are neither theoretically nor practically insuperable
obstacles for the adaption of other cultural and social norms as it is stated from
one part of culture-comparing management research.

In our opinion we may expect (and perhaps hope) that national cultures will
lose significance in their separating function in the future (key word: EG
1993). In the past these national cultures have been overestimated, perhaps
because it is easier to push something foreign away than to cope with it
objectively. It is known that changes in one's own behaviour are the most
difficult to realize. Additionally there was politics. National cultures have
often (and negatively) been mobilized in times of crisis by different, mostly
dominating political groups.

But the intransingency of national cultures is not as big as is often assumed. In
our opinion culture significance is regionally anchored but these regions must
by no means be identical with nations. To say it casually: it is possible that the
cultural difference between a Prussian and a Bavarian (or between an
Englishman and a Scot) is greater than that between a Briton and a German[3].

In other words different modes of behaviour and thought are possible and
meaningful within specific national cultures. This is because culture is only
one of several factors of influence for the thinking and acting of individuals
and groups.

This all points to the fact that at least within Europe and by upholding national
and cultural independence we could learn much more from each other (and in
future we must do this) than is the case at present.

In relation to our theme, we must attribute considerable significance to the
eductaion and further education of managers (international management, Euro
managers) now and for the future (*Financial Times* from 21.1. and 9.4.1991).
These processes of education should not solely be left to the (international)
companies because otherwise a colonization of the weaker by the stronger
economies cannot be disregarded.

---

3   See the latest study by Kotthoff and Reindl (1990, pp 324-353) about the influence
     of the region on the relationship between staff and management.

We hope that this book has not only put questions forward but that it has made the reader's judgement easier about which of the respective national conditions and solution possibilities could be more suitable.

References

Allen, J., Massey, D.: *The Economy in Question*, London 1988.

Almond, G.A.: The political attitudes of German business, in: *World Politics* 8, 1955/56, pp 157-186.

Altmann, N., Deiß, M., Döhl, V., Sauer, D.: Ein "Neuer Rationalisierungstyp" – neue Anforderungen an die Industriesoziologie, in: *Soziale Welt* 2/3, 1986, pp 191-207.

Anthony, P.D.: *The Foundation of Management*, London, New York 1986.

Armstrong, P.: A comment on Murray and Knights. Critical perspectives on accounting, in: *Accounting, Organizations and Society* 9, 1990, pp 275-281.

Armstrong, P.: Limits and possibilities for HRM in an age of management accountancy, in: J. Storey (Ed.): *New Perspectives on Human Resource Management*, London 1989, pp 154-166.

Aron, R.: *The Industrial Society*, London 1967.

Baethge, M.: Arbeit, Vergesellschaftung, Identität – Zur zunehmenden normativen Subjektivierung der Arbeit, in: *SOFI – Mitteilungen* 18, December, 1990, pp 1-11.

Baethge, M., Oberbeck, H.: *Zukunft der Angestellten. Neue Technologien und berufliche Perspektiven in Büro und Verwaltung*, Frankfurt/M, New York 1986.

Bahrdt, H.P.: *Schlüsselbegriffe der Soziologie*, München 1985.

Bamberg, U., Bürger, M., Mahnkopf, B., Martens, H., Tieman, J. (Eds.): *Aber ob die Karten voll ausgereizt sind ..., 10 Jahre Mitbestimmungsgesetz 1976 in der Bilanz*, Köln 1987.

Barnard, Ch.: *The Functions of the Executive*, Cambridge, Mass. 1938.

Bate, P., Child, J.: Paradigms and understandings in comparative organizational research, in: P. Bate, J. Child (Eds.): *Organization of Innnovation. East-West Perspectives*, Berlin, New York 1987, pp 19-49.

Baumgarten, R.: *Führungsstile und Führungstechniken*, Berlin 1977.

Bavelas, A.: Leadership: Man and function, in: *Administrative Science Quarterly* 4, 1960, pp 491-492.

Bechtle, G.: Strategieanalyse eines multinationalen Konzerns als Methode – Methode als Strategie, in: M. Heidenreich, G. Schmidt (Eds.): *International vergleichende Organisationsforschung*, Opladen 1991, pp 130 -141.

Bechtle, G.: *Betrieb als Strategie*, München 1980.

Bechtle, G., Lutz, B.: Die Unbestimmtheit post-tayloristischer Rationalisierungsstrategie und die ungewisse Zukunft industrieller Arbeit, in: K. Düll, B. Lutz (Eds.): *Technikentwicklung und Arbeitsteilung im internationalen Vergleich*, Frankfurt/M, New York 1989, pp 9-91.

Beck, U.: *Risikogesellschaft*, Frankfurt/M 1986.

Beck, U., Brater, M., Daheim, H.: *Soziologie der Arbeit und der Berufe*, Reinbek 1980.

Beck-Gernsheim, E.: Von der Liebe zur individualisierten Gesellschaft, in: J.Berger (Ed.): *Die Moderne – Kontinuitäten und Zäsuren*, Göttingen 1986, pp 209-233.

Beck-Gernsheim, E.: Vom "Dasein für andere" zum Anspruch auf ein Stück "eigenes Leben". Individualisierungsprozesse im weiblichen Lebenszusammenhang, in: *Soziale Welt* 3, 1983, pp 341-374.

Beishon, R.J., Palmer, A.W.: Untersuchung von Managerverhalten, in: L. Zündorf (Ed.): *Industrie- und Betriebssoziologie*, Darmstadt 1979, pp 183-209.

Bell, C.: *Middle Class Families*, London 1968.

Bell, D.: *The Coming of Post-Industrial Society*, London 1974.

Bendix, R.: Manager-Ideologien im Industrialisierungsprozeß, in: F. Fürstenberg (Ed.): *Industriesoziologie III. Industrie und Gesellschaft*, Darmstadt und Neuwied 1975, pp 261-279.

Bendix, R.: *Work and Authority in Industry*, New York 1956.

Bennis, W., Nanus, B.: *Führungskräfte – Die vier Schlüsselstrategien erfolgreichen Führens*, Frankfurt/M, New York 1985.

Berghahn, V.: *Unternehmer und Politik in der Bundesrepublik*, Frankfurt/M 1987.

Bergmann, J., Jacobi, O., Müller-Jentsch, W.: *Gewerkschaften in der Bundesrepublik*, vol. 1, 2nd ed., Frankfurt/M 1976.

Bertelsmann-Stiftung, Institut für Wirtschafts- und Gesellschaftspolitik (Eds.): *Die Arbeitsmotivation von Führungskräften der deutschen Wirtschaft. Ergebnisse einer Umfrage bei Unternehmern und leitenden Angestellten*, Gütersloh, Bonn 1985.

Bessant, J., Grunt, M.: *Management and Manufacturing Innovation in the United Kingdom and West Germany*, Aldershot 1985.

Bleuel, H.P.: *Die Stützen der Gesellschaft*, München, Wien 1976.

Bowey, A.M.: *Handbook of Salary and Wage Systems*, 2nd ed., Aldershot 1982.

Braun, S.: *Die besseren Zeiten kommen nicht von selbst. Festschrift zum 65. Geburtstag von Siegfried Braun*, Bremen 1987.

Braun, S., Eberwein, W., Tholen, J.: *Belegschaften und Unternehmer*, Frankfurt/M, New York 1992.

Braun, S., Fuhrmann J.: *Angestelltenmentalität*, Neuwied 1970.

Braverman, H.: *Die Arbeit im modernen Produktionsprozeß* Frankfurt/M, New York 1977.

Breisig, Th.: Die Herrschaft dritten Grades, in: *Angestelltenmagazin* 4-8, 1988, pp 3-5, 15-21.

Bretz, H.: Warum Unternehmen charismatische Manager brauchen, in: *Harvard-Manager* 1, 1990, pp 110-119.

Brewer, E., Tomlinson, J.W.C.: The managers's working day, in: *The Journal of Industrial Economics*, vol. XII, 1963-1964, pp 191 -197.

Brose, H.-G. (Ed.): *Berufsbiographien im Wandel*, Opladen 1987.

Budde, A., Child, J., Francis, A., Kieser, A.: Corporate goals, managerial objectives, and organisational structures in British and West German companies, in: *Organization Studies* 3/A, 1982, pp 1-32.

Büschges, G.: *Einführung in die Organisationssoziologie*, Stuttgart 1983.

Büschges, G.: Organisation und Herrschaft, in: G. Büschges (Ed.): Organisation und Herrschaft, Reinbek 1976, pp 14-28.

Burnham, J.: *Das Regime der Manager*, Stuttgart 1949.

Burns, T.: Management in action, in: *Operational Research Quarterly* 2, 1957, pp 45-60.

Burns, T., Stalker, G.M.: *The Management of Innovation*, London 1961.

Bynner, J., Roberts, K. (Eds): *From School to Work: Transition to Employment in Two European Countries*, London 1990.

Caird, S.: What does it mean to be enterprising, in: *British Journal of Management* 3, vol. 1, 1990, pp 137-145.

Calori, R., Lawrence, P.: *The Business of Europe*, London 1991.

Carlson, S.: *Executive Behaviour*, Stockholm 1951.

Carroll, S.J., Gillen, D.J.: Are the classical management functions useful in describing managerial work?, in: *Academy of Management Review* 1, vol. 12, 1987, pp 38-51.

Chandler, A.D.: *The Visible Hand. The Managerial Revolution in American Business*, Cambridge, Mass. 1977.

Child, J.: *British Management Thought. A Critical Analysis*, London 1969.

Child, J.: Management, in: S.R. Parker (Ed.): *The Sociology of Industry*, 3rd ed., London 1977, pp 35-55.

Child, J., Fores, M., Glover, I., Lawrence, P.: A price to pay? Professionalism and work organzation in Britain and West Germany, in: *Sociology* 1, vol. 17, 1983, pp 63-78.

Child, J., Kieser, A.: Organization and managerial roles in Britain and West German companies – an examination of the culture-free-thesis, working paper 7/75, Institut für Unternehmensführung der Freien Universität Berlin, Berlin 1975.

Claasen, D.: Konferenz ist alles, in: *Wirtschaftswoche* 47, 17.11.1989, pp 74-75.

Clegg, S.R.: *Frameworks of Power*, London 1989.

Clements, R.V.: *Managers. A Study of their Careers in Industry*, London 1958.

Coates, D.: Britain, in: T.Bottomore, R.J.Brym (Eds.): *The Capitalist Class. An International Study*, New York, London 1989, pp 19-45.

Cooper, A.C., Dunkelberg, W.C.: Unternehmertypen. Ergebnisse einer empirischen Studie, in: *Internationales Gewerbearchiv*, 1986. pp 269-277.

Cooper, C.L.: Chief executive lifestyle survey, Centre for Business Psychology/Manchester and Cooper & Lybrand Deloitte 1990.

Copeman, G.: *Der Top-Manager. Eine vergleichende Untersuchung der Managementmethoden in den Vereinigten Staaten, Großbritannien und Deutschland*, Zürich 1972.

Cox, Ch.J., Cooper, C.L.: *High Flyers. An Anatomy of Managerial Success*, Oxford 1988.

Crocket, G., Elias, P.: British managers: A study of their education, training, mobility and earnings, in: *British Journal of Industrial Relations* 1, 1984, pp 34-46.

Dahrendorf, R.: *Der moderne soziale Konflikt*, Stuttgart 1992.

Dahrendorf, R.: *Gesellschaft und Demokratie in Deutschland*, 5th ed., München 1977.

Dahrendorf, R.: *Soziale Klassen und Klassenkonflikte in der industriellen Gesellschaft*, Stuttgart 1957.

Deal, E., Kennedy, A.: *Corporate Cultures. The Rites and Rituals of Corporate Life*, Cambridge, Mass., 1982.

Deutschmann, Chr.: Reflexive Verwissenschaftlichung und kultureller "Imperialismus" des Managements, in: *Soziale Welt* 3, 1989, pp 374-396.

Drucker, P.F.: *Neue Management-Praxis*, 2 vols., Düsseldorf, Wien 1974.

Dubin, R., Spray, S.L.: Executive behaviour and interaction, in: *Industrial Relations* 2, 1964, pp 99-108.

Düll, K.: Gesellschaftliche Modernisierungspolitik durch neue "Produktionskonzepte"?, in: *WSI-Mitteilungen* 3, 1985, pp 141-145.

Easterby-Smith, M., Thorpe, R., Lowe, A.: *Management Research. An Introduction*, London 1991.

Eberwein, W., Gelbert, A., Tholen, J.: *Kommentierte Bibliografie zur Arbeits- und Berufssituation industrieller Unternehmensleiter*, Bremen 1992.

Eberwein, W., Tholen, J.: *Managermentalität – Industrielle Unternehmensleitung als Beruf und Politik*, Frankfurt/M 1990.

Etzioni, A.: *The Moral Dimensions: Towards a New Economics*, New York 1988.

Famulla, G.E.: Umweltorientiertes Management, in: W. Fricke, K. Johannson, K. Krahn, W. Kruse, G. Peter, V. Volkholz (Eds.): *Jahrbuch Arbeit und Technik in Nordrhein-Westfalen*, Bonn 1989, pp 31-47.

Fayol, H.: *General and Industrial Management*, London 1949.

Fletcher, C.: The end of management, in: J. Child (Ed.): *Man and Organization*, London 1973, pp 135-157.

Fores, M., Glover, I.: The real work of executives, in: *Management Today* 11, 1979, pp 104-108.

Fores, M., Glover, I. (Eds.): *Manufacturing and Management*, London 1978.

Fox, A.: Industrial relations. A social critique of pluralist ideology, in: J. Child (Ed.): *Man and Organization*, London 1973, pp 185-233.

Fürstenberg, F.: *Das Aufstiegsproblem in der modernen Gesellschaft*, Stuttgart 1969.

Fürstenberg, F.: Der Betriebsrat – Strukturanalyse einer Grenzinstitution, in: *Kölner Zeitschrift für Soziologie und Sozialpsychologie*, 1958, pp 418-429.

Gabele, E., Hirsch, W., Treffert, J.: *Werte von Führungskräften der deutschen Wirtschaft*, Frankfurt/M 1977.

Galbraith, J.: *The New Industrial State*, Harmondsworth 1967.

Gallie, D.: Probleme kulturvergleichender Sozialforschung: Ein Beitrag aus britischer Sicht, in: M. Heidenreich, G. Schmidt (Eds.): *International vergleichende Organisationsforschung*, Opladen 1991, pp 71-79.

Gans, F.: Abschied von den Gentlemen, in: *Manager Magazin* 11, 1989, pp 398-413.

Gans, H.J.: *The Levittoners*, London 1967.

Gehlen, A.: *Urmensch und Spätkultur – Philosophische Ergebnisse und Aussagen*, 2.rev. ed., Frankfurt/M 1964.

Giddens, A.: *Die Klassenstruktur fortgeschrittener Gesellschaften*, Frankfurt/M 1979 (1979a).

Giddens, A.: *Central Problems in Social Theory*, London 1979 (1979b).

Giddens, A.: Elites in the British class structure, in: Ph. Stanworth, A. Giddens (Eds.): *Elites and Power in British Society*, London 1974, pp 1-21.

Glover, I.: Executive career patterns: Britain, France, Germany and Sweden, in: M. Fores, I. Glover (Eds.): *Manufacturing and Management*, London 1978, pp 157-178.

Glover, I.: Executive patterns: Britain, France, Germany and Sweden, in: *Energy World*, December, 1976.

Goldsmith, W., Clutterbuck, D.: *The Winning Streak. Britain's Top Companies Reveal their Formulas for Success*, London 1984 .

Gottschalch, D.: Kehrtwende zum Privaten, in *Manager Magazin* 11, 1982, pp 159-163.

Gowler, D., Legge, K. (Eds.): *Managerial Stress*, Essex 1975.

Granick, D.: *Der europäische Manager*, Düsseldorf, Wien 1962.

Granick, D.: Why managers perform differently in different Countries: France, Britain, USA, USSR, And East Germany, in: J.J. Boddewyn (Ed.): *European Industrial Managers, West and East*, New York 1976, pp 543-557.

Granovetter, M.: *Getting a Job. A Study of Contacts and Careers*, Cambridge, Mass. 1974.

Grochla, E.: *Unternehmensorganisation*, Reinbek 1972.

Gröh, W., Trost, S.: *Anforderungsstrukturen und Angebotsprofile auf dem Arbeitsmarkt industrieller Führungskräfte*, Bremen 1991.

Guest, D.: Human recource management: its implications for industrial relations and trade unions, in: J. Storey (Ed.): *New Perspectives on Human Resource Management*, London 1989, pp 41-55.

Gutenberg, E.: *Einführung in die Betriebswirtschaftslehre*, Wiesbaden 1958.

Habermas, J.: *Die neue Unübersichtlichkeit*, Frankfurt/M 1985.

Haire, M., Ghiselli, E.E., Porter, L.W.: *Managerial Thinking: An International Study*, New York 1966.

Hales, C.: Management processes, management divisions of labour and management work: Towards a synthesis, paper presented on the 6th Conference of the Labour Process Debate, 23rd – 25th March, 1988, Aston University, Birmingham.

Hales, C.: What do managers do? A critical review of the evidence, in: *Journal of Management Studies* 23:1, January, 1986, pp 88-115 .

Halsey, A.H.: Educational systems and the economy, in: A. Martinelli, N.J. Smelser (Eds.): *Economy and Society*, London 1990, pp 79-101.

Hamer, E.: *Die Unternehmerlücke*, Stuttgart 1984.

Handy, Ch., Gordon, C., Gow, I., Randlesome, C.: *Making Managers*, London 1988 .

Hannah, L.: Human capital flows and business efficiency. Sense and nonsense in the Wiener thesis, unpublished paper, London 1990.

Hansen, K.: *Die Mentalität des Erwerbs – Erfolgsphilosophien amerikanischer Unternehmer*, Frankfurt/M, New York 1992.

Harbison, F., Myers, Ch.: *Management in the Industrial World*, New York, Toronto, London 1959.

Hartmann, H.: Arbeit, Beruf, Profession, in: Th. Luckmann, und W.M. Sprondel (Eds.): *Berufssoziologie*, Köln 1972, pp 36-52.

Hartmann, H.: *Der deutsche Unternehmer. Autorität und Organisation*, Princeton 1959.

Harvey, B., Smith, S., Wilkinson, B.: *Managers and Corporate Social Policy*, London 1984.

Heidenreich, M., Schmidt, G. (Eds.): *International vergleichende Organisationsforschung*, Opladen 1991.

Heidenreich, M.: Problems of generalisation in cross-national studies of organisations, in: *International Sociology* 2, vol. 6, June, 1991, pp 181-200.

Heilmann, W.: Büro im Wandel. Vom Ort der Arbeit zum Ort der Kommunikation, in: *Office Management* 5, 1988, pp 46-48.

Heinen, E.: *Unternehmenskultur, Perspektiven für Wissenschaft und Praxis*, München, Wien 1987.

Herzberg, F., Mausner, B., Snyderman, B.: *The Motivation to Work*, New York 1959.

Hickson, D.J., Mc Millan, Ch.J. (Eds.): *Organization and Nation*, Farnborough 1981.

Hinrichs, P.: *Um die Seele des Arbeiters. Arbeitspsychologie, Industrie- und Betriebssoziologie in Deutschland 1871 – 1945*, Köln 1981.

Hochreutener, P.E.: Grundlage für ein wirkungsvolles Management sind Unternehmens-kulturleitbilder, in: *Management-Zeitschrift* 1, 1985, pp 14-18.

Hoffmann, R.: Gewerkschaften in Großbritannien, in: *Die Mitbestimmung* 5/6, 1989, pp 352-355.

Hofstede, G: *Culture's Consequences*, London 1984.

Hofstetter, H.: *Die Leiden der Leitenden*, München 1980.

Holden, P.E., Pederson, C.A., Germane, G.E.: *Top Management*, New York 1968.

Holleis, W.: *Unternehmenskultur und moderne Psyche*, Frankfurt/New York 1987.

Iacocca, L., Nowak, W.: *Iacocca – Eine amerikanische Karriere*, Berlin 1982.

Isenberg, D.J.: Strategischer Opportunismus, in: *Harvard-Manager* 4, 1987, pp 108-112.

Jackall, R.: *Moral Mazes: The World of Corporate Managers*, New York 1988.

Jacobi, O.: Der Einfluß von gewerkschaftlichen Organisationsformen auf die wirtschaft-liche Entwicklung, in: *Gewerkschaftliche Monatshefte* 1, 1989, pp 42-50.

Jacobi, O.: Die Gewerkschaft und ihr Beitrag zum Projekt der demokratischen Moderne, in: *Die Mitbestimmung* 5, 1991, pp 368-371.

Johnson, G.: Managing strategic change. The role of symbolic action, in: *British Journal of Management* 4, vol. I, 1990, pp 183-200.

Jowell, R., Witherspoon, S., Brook, L.: *British Social Attitudes. Special International Report*, Aldershot 1989 .

Jürgens, U.: Wandel des betrieblichen Arbeitseinsatzes in der Automobilindustrie, in: M. Heidenreich, G. Schmidt (Eds.): *International vergleichende Organisations-forschung*, Opladen 1991, pp 190-210.

Jürgens, U., Naschold, F. (Eds.): *Arbeitspolitik, Leviathan Sonderheft* 5, 1983, Opladen 1984.

Kastendiek, H.: Zwischen Ausgrenzung und krisenpolitischer Konditionierung. Zur Situation der britischen Gewerkschaften, in: W. Müller-Jentsch (Ed.): *Zukunft der Gewerkschaften. Ein internationaler Vergleich*, Frankfurt/M, New York 1988, pp 160-190.

Keep, E.: Corporate training strategies: the vital component?, in J. Storey (Ed.): *New Perspectives on Human Resource Management*, London 1989, pp 109-125.

Keller, E. v.: Die kulturvergleichende Managementforschung, unpublished dissertation, Bern 1981.

Kern, H., Schumann, M.: Industriesoziologie als Katharsis, in: *Soziale Welt* 1, 1988, pp 86-96.

Kern, H., Schumann, M.: *Das Ende der Arbeitsteilung?*, München 1984.

Kocka, J.: *Unternehmensverwaltung und Angestelltenschaft am Beispiel Siemens 1847 – 1914. Zum Verhältnis von Kapitalismus und Bürokratie in der deutschen Industrialisierung*, Stuttgart 1969.

Kotter, J.P.: *The General Manager*, New York 1982a.

Kotter, J.P.: What effective general managers really do, in: *Harvard Business Review*, November – December 1982b, pp 156-167.

Kotthoff, H.: *Betriebsräte und betriebliche Herrschaft*, Frankfurt/M, New York 1981.

Kotthoff, H., Reindl, J.: *Die soziale Welt kleiner Betriebe. Wirtschaften, Arbeiten und Leben im mittelständischen Industriebetrieb*, Göttingen 1990.

Kruk, M.: *Die großen Unternehmer*, Frankfurt/M 1972.

Krulis-Randa, J.S.: Die menschliche Arbeit als Bestandteil der Unternehmensstrategie, in: *Die Unternehmung* 2, 1983, pp 140-146.

Kurke, L.B., Aldrich, H.E.: Mintzberg was right! A replication and extension of the nature of managerial work, in: *Management Science* 8, vol. 29, August, 1983, pp 975-984.

Lane, Ch.: *Management and Labour in Europe. The Industrial Enterprise in Germany, Britain and France*, Aldershot 1989.

Lange, E.: *Akademiker in der Privatgesellschaft*, Stuttgart 1981.

Lau, A.W., Pavett, C.M.: The nature of managerial work: A comparison of public – and private – sector managers, in: *Group and Organization Studies* 5, December, 1980, pp 453-466.

Laub, G.: Das Märchen vom Streß der Leitenden, in: *Die Zeit* 3, 1974.

Lawrence, P.: *Management in Action*, London 1984.

Lawrence, P.: *Managers and Management in West Germany*, London 1980.

Lawriwsky, M.L.: *Corporate Structure and Performance. The Role of Owners, Managers and Markets*, London, Canberra 1984.

Lepsius, M.R.: Soziale Ungleichheit und Klassenstrukturen in der Bundesrepublik Deutschland. Lebenslagen, Interessenvermittlung und Wertorientierungen, in: H.-U. Wehler (Ed.): *Klassen in der europäischen Sozialgeschichte*, Göttingen 1979, pp 166-209.

Lessem, R.: The adaptive manager, in: M. Devine (Ed.) *The Photofit Manager. Building a Picture of Management in the 1990s*, London 1990, pp 161-177.

Lewis, N.: Changes in socio-legal structures: The British case, in: B. Jessor, H. Kastendiek, K. Nielsen, O.K. Pederson (Eds.): *The Politics of Flexibility. Restructuring State and Industry in Britain, Germany and Scandinavia*, Aldershot 1991, pp 195-216.

Lewis, R., Stewart, R.: *The Managers*, New York 1961.

Lipset, S.M., Bendix, R.: *Social Mobility in Industrial Society*, London 1959.

Locke, R.R.: *The End of the Practical Man: Entrepreneurship and Higher Education in Germany, France and Great Britain, 1880 – 1840*, Greenwich, Conn., 1984.

Luthans, F., Rosenkrantz, St.A., Hennessy, H.W.: What do successful managers really do? An observation study of managerial activities, in: *Journal of Applied Behavioral Science* 3, vol. 21, 1985, pp 255-270.

Lutz, B.: Die Grenzen des "effet societal" und die Notwendigkeit einer historischen Perspektive. Einige Bemerkungen zum vernünftigen Gebrauch internationaler Vergleiche, in: M. Heidenreich, G. Schmidt (Eds.): *International vergleichende Organisationsforschung*, Opladen 1991, pp 91-105.

Maccoby, M.: *Why Work. Motivating and Leading the New Generation*, New York 1988.

Malsch, Th.: Die Informatisierung des betrieblichen Erfahrungswissens und der "Imperialismus der instrumentellen Vernunft". Kritische Bemerkungen zur neotayloristischen Instrumentalismuskritik und ein Interpretationsvorschlag aus arbeitssoziologischer Sicht, in: *Zeitschrift für Soziologie* 2, 1987, pp 77-91.

Manager-Magazin 6, 1988, pp 276-282.

Mansfield, R.: Who are the managers? in: M.J.F. Poole, R. Mansfield (Eds.): *Managerial Roles in Industrial Relations*, Aldershot 1980, pp 12-20.

Mansfield, R.: Career and individual strategies, in: J. Child (Ed.): *Man and Organization*, London 1973, pp 107-132.

Mansfield, R., Poole, M.: *International Perspectives on Management and Organization*, Aldershot 1981.

Marginson, P., Edwards, P.K., Purcell, J., Sisson, K.: What do corporate officers really do?, in: *British Journal of Industrial Relations* 2, 26, July, 1988, pp 229-245.

Marglin, S.A.: What do bosses do? in: A. Gorz (Ed.): *The Division of Labour: The Labour Process and Class Struggle in Modern Capitalism*, Brighton 1976.

Maslow, A.: *Motivation and Personality*, New York 1954.

Mathias, P.: Entrepreneurship and Economic History: The State of the Debate, in: M.J. Earl (Ed.): *Perspectives on Management*, Oxford 1983, pp 40-54.

Matthes, M.: *Interaktionistische Soziologie*, no place no date.

Maurice, M., Sellier, F., Silvestre, J.-J.: *La production de la hierarchie dans l'entreprise. Recherche d'un effet societal*, Aix-en-Provence 1977.

Meffert, H., Hafner, K., Poggenpohl, M.: Unternehmenskultur und Unternehmensführung – Ergebnisse einer empirischen Untersuchung, working paper 43, Wissenschaftlichen Gesellschaft für Marketing und Unternehmensführung e.V., 1988.

Mielke, S. (Ed.): *Internationales Gewerkschaftshandbuch*, Opladen 1983.

Millar, J.: *British Management versus German Management. A Comparison of Organisational Effectiveness in West German and U.K. Factories*, Farnborough 1979.

Mintzberg, H.: *The Nature of Managerial Work*, New York 1973.

Mintzberg, H.: The manager's job: Folklore and fact, in: *Harvard Business Review*, July-August, 1975, pp 49-61.

Mosson, T.M.: Management and its environment in Great Britain, in: J.L. Massie, J. Luytjes (Eds.): *Management in an International Context*, New York 1972, pp 39-63.

Mülder, J.B., and Partner: *Wege zur Unternehmensspitze*, Berlin 1982.

Müller-Böling, D., Klautke, E., Ramme, I.: Manager-Alltag, in: *Bild der Wissenschaft* 1, 1989, pp 104-109.

Müri, P.: "Stehen wir am Beginn des Kulturzeitalters?" Kritische Gedanken zum neuen Trend, in: *Io Management-Zeitschrift* 4, 1985, pp 205-208.

Naschold, F. (Ed.): *Arbeit und Politik*, Frankfurt/M, New York 1985.

Neuberger, O., Kompa, A.: Serie Firmenkultur, in: *Psychologie Heute* a-d, 1986.

Neuberger, O.: *Führung*, 2nd ed., Stuttgart 1985.

Newcomer, M.: *The Big Business Executive, the Factors that Made Him 1900 – 1950*, London, New York 1955.

Nichols, T., Beynon, H.: *Living with Capitalism*, London 1977.

Osterloh, M.: Unternehmensethik und Unternehmenskultur, discussion paper 42, Lehrstuhl für Allgemeine Betriebswirtschaftslehre und Unternehmensführung der Universität Erlangen, Nürnberg 1982.

O'Thoole, J.: Corporate and managerial cultures, in: C.L. Cooper (Ed.): *Behavioral Problems in Organization*, New Jersey 1979, 71-79.

Ouchi, G.: *Theory Z. How American Business Can Meet The Japanese Challenge*, New York 1982.

Oyen, E. (Ed.): *Comparative Methodology. Theory and Practice in International Social Research*, London 1990.

Pahl, J.M., Pahl R.E.: *Managers and their Wives*, London 1971.

Paolillo, J.G.P.: Role Profiles for Managers in Different Functional Areas, in: *Group and Organization Studies* 1, vol. 12, 1987, pp 109-118.

Park, W.: Führen durch Umherwandern, in: *Die Tageszeitung*, 8.10.1988.

Parsons, T., Smelser, N.J.: *Economy and Society*, 2nd ed., New York 1969.

Pascale, R.T., Athos, A.G.: *The Art of Japanese Management. Applications for American Executives*, New York 1981.

Peters, T.J. Waterman, H.: *In Search of Excellence. Lessons from America's Best-Run Companies*, New York 1982.

Peterson, R.: Chief executives' attitudes: A cross cultural analysis, in: *Industrial Relations* 2, vol. 10, 1971, pp 194-210.

Pohl, H.-J., Rehkugler, H.: Das Management mittelständischer Unternehmen, in: Statistisches Landesamt Bremen (Ed.): *Statistische Monatsberichte* 11, 1987, pp 258-269.

Pollard, S.: *The Genesis of Modern Management*, Harmondsworth 1968.

Poole, M., Mansfield, R.: (Eds.): *Managerial Roles in Industrial Relations*, Aldershot 1980.

Poole, M., Mansfield, R., Blyton, P., Frost, P.: Managerial attitudes and behaviour, in: *British Journal of Industrial Relations* 3, vol. 20, 1982, pp 285-307.

Poole, M., Mansfield, R., Blyton, P., Frost, P.: *Managers in Focus*, Aldershot 1981.

Priewe, J., Weber, D., Lamparter, D.: Branche im Zwielicht, in: *Management Wissen* 3, 1988, pp 82-104.

Prigge, W.-U.: Wirtschafts- und Sozialpolitik während der Regierung Thatcher, in: *Aus Politik und Zeitgeschichte* B28, 5.7.1991, pp 27-36.

Prinz, M., Zitelmann, R.: *Nationalsozialismus und Modernisierung*, Darmstadt 1991.

Priore, M., Sabel, C.F.: *Das Ende der Massenproduktion*, Berlin 1985.

Pross, H.: *Kapitalismus und Demokratie, Studien über westdeutsche Sozialstrukturen*, Frankfurt/M 1973.

Pross, H.: *Manager und Aktionäre in Deutschland. Untersuchungen zum Verhältnis von Eigentum und Verfügungsmacht*, Frankfurt/M 1965.

Pross, H., Boetticher, K.W.: *Manager des Kapitalismus*, Frankfurt/M 1971.

Pugh, D.S. (Ed.): *Organization Theory. Selected Readings*, 3rd ed., London 1990.

Purcell, J.: The impact of cooperate strategy on human resource management, in: J. Storey (Ed.): *New Perspectives on Human Resource Management*, London 1989, pp 67-91.

Reed, M: *The Sociology of Management*, London 1989.

Robertson, J., Iles, P.: Approaches to managerial selection, in: *International Review of Industrial and Organizational Psychology* **, 1988, pp 159-211.

Rosenstiel, L. v., Nerdinger, F.W., Stengel, M., Spieß, E.: *Führungsnachwuchs im Unternehmen*, München 1980.

Sachse, Ch.: Manager im Urlaub, in: *Management Wissen* 8, 1988, pp 88-92.

Sampson, A.: *Wer regiert England? Anatomie einer Führungsschicht*, München 1963.

Sayles, L.R.: *Managerial Behavior*, New York 1964.

Scase, R., Goffee, R.: *Reluctant Managers, Their Work and Lifestyles*, London 1989.

Schelsky, H.: *Auf der Suche nach Wirklichkeit. Gesammelte Aufsätze*, Düsseldorf, Köln 1965.

Schienstock, G.: Managementsoziologie – ein Desiderat der Industriesoziologie?, in: *Soziale Welt* 3, 1991, pp 349-370.

Schmidt, E.: *Ordnungsfaktor oder Gegenmacht? Die politische Rolle der Gewerkschaften*, Frankfurt/M 1971.

Schmiede, R., Schudlich, E.: *Die Entwicklung der Leistungsentlohnung in Deutschland*, 3rd ed., Frankfurt/M, New York 1978 .

Schumpeter, J.A.: *Kapitalismus, Sozialismus und Demokratie*, 5th ed., München 1980.

Scott, J.: *Corporations, Classes and Capitalism*, 2nd ed., London 1985.

Shapira, Z., Dunbar, R.L.M.: Testing Mintzberg's Managerial Roles Theory Using an In-Basket Simulation, International Institute of Management – Wissenschaftszentrum Berlin, Discussion Paper Series, March 1977.

Silver, M. (Ed.): *Competent to Manage: Approaches to Management Training and Development*, London 1990.

Smith, M.: An analysis of three managerial jobs using repertory grids, in: *Journal of Management Studies*, vol. 17, 1980, pp 205-213.

Smith, N.R.: *The Entrepreneur and his Firm: The Relationship between Type of Man and Type of Company*, East Lansing, Mich. 1967.

Smith, P.B., Peterson, M.F.: *Leadership, Organizations and Culture*, London 1988.

Sorge, A.: Organisationskulturen: Realer Hintergrund und soziologische Bedeutung der Modewelle, in: *Kultur und Gesellschaft, 24. Deutscher Soziologentag 1988 in Zürich*, vol. 1, Frankfurt/M, New York 1989, pp 193-210.

Sorge, A.: The management tradition: a continental view, in: M. Fores, I. Glover (Eds.): *Manufacturing and Management*, London 1978, pp 87-103.

Sorge, A., Warner, M.: *Comparative Factory Organisation*, Aldershot 1986.

Spiegel, Der: Ende einer Industrienation: in: *Der Spiegel* 33, 1991, pp 92-96.

Staehle, W.: Unternehmer und Manager, in: W. Müller-Jentsch (Ed.): *Konfliktpartnerschaft*, München, Mering 1991, pp 105-121.

Staehle, W.: *Funktionen des Managements*, 2nd ed., Bern, Stuttgart 1989 (1989a).

Staehle, W.: Human Resource Management und Unternehmensstrategie, in: *Mitt* AB 3, 1989, pp 388-396 (1989b).

Staehle, W.: *Management*, München 1980 (1980a).

Staehle, W.: Menschenbilder in Organisationstheorien, in: E.Grochla (Ed.): *Handwörterbuch der Organisation*, Stuttgart 1980, pp 1301-1313 (1980b).

Stanworth, Ph., Giddens, A.: An economic elite: A demographic profile of company chairmen, in: Ph. Stanworth, A. Giddens (Eds.): *Elites and Power in British Society*, Cambridge 1974, pp 81-101.

Statistisches Bundesamt (Ed.): Datenreport 1989. Zahlen und Fakten über die Bundesrepublik, Bundeszentrale für politische Bildung, vol. 280, Bonn 1989.

Stewart, R.: *Choices for the Manager*, Englewood Cliffs 1982.

Stewart, R.: *Contrasts in Management*, Maidenhead 1976.

Stewart, R.: Managerial behaviour: how research has changed the traditional picture, in: M.J. Earl (Ed.): *Perspectives on Management*, Oxford 1983, pp 82-98.

Stewart, R.: *Managers and their Jobs*, Maidenhead 1967 (1967a).

Stewart, R.: *The Reality of Management*, London 1967 (1967b).

Stewart, R., Duncan-Jones, P.: Educational background and career history of British managers, with some American comparisons, in: *Explorations in Entrepreneurial History* 1, vol. 9, 1959, pp 61-71.

Stewart, R., Smith, P., Blake, J., Wingate, P.: *The District Administrator in the National Health Service*, London 1980.

Stöber, A.M., Binding, R., Derschika, P.: *Kritisches Führungswissen. Emanzipation und Technologie in wissenschaftssoziologischer Sicht*, Stuttgart 1974.

Storey, J. (Ed.): *New Perspectives on Human Resource Management*, London 1989.

Storey, J.: *Managerial Prerogative and the Question of Control*, London 1985.

Storey, J., Sisson, K.: Looking to the future, in: J. Storey (Ed.): *New Perspectives on Human Resource Management*, London 1989, pp 167-183.

Stout, R.: *Organizations, Management and Control. An Annotated Bibliography*, Bloomington 1980 (1980a).

Stout, R.: *Management or Control? The Organizational Challenge*, Bloomington 1980 (1980b).

Strasser, D.: *Abschied von den Wunderknaben*, München 1985.

Streich, R.: Konfliktdeterminanten von Führungskräften aus Interaktion von Arbeit und Freizeit, in: J.C. Brengelmann, L. v. Rosenstiel, G. Bruns (Eds.): *Verhaltensmanagement in Organisationen. Ein Kongressbericht*, Frankfurt/M, Bern, New York, Paris 1987, pp 220-224.

Thonet, P.J.: Managerialismus und Unternehmenserfolg, unpublished dissertation, Saarbrücken 1977.

Ulrich, H.: *Management-Philosophie für die Zukunft*, Bern, Stuttgart 1981.

Ulrich, H., Probst, G.: *Werthaltungen schweizerischer Führungskräfte*, Bern, Stuttgart 1982.

Ulrich, P.: Die Weiterentwicklung der ökonomischen Rationalität – Zur Grundlage der Ethik der Unternehmung, in: B. Bievert, M. Held (Eds.): *Ökonomische Theorie und Ethik*, Frankfurt/M 1987, pp 122-149.

Ulrich, P.: Systemsteuerung und Kulturentwicklung in: *Die Unternehmung* 4, 1984, pp 303-311.

Underwood, K.: On the pinnacles of power – The business executive, in: P.L. Berger (Ed.): *The Human Shape of Work. Studies in the Sociology of Occupations*, New York, London 1964, pp 181-210.

Wagner, K.: *Die Beziehung zwischen Bildung, Beschäftigung und Produktivität und ihre bildungs- und beschäftigungspolitischen Auswirkungen – ein deutsch-englischer Vergleich*, Berlin 1986.

Wald, R.M., Doty, R.A.: The top executive – a firsthand profile, in: *Harvard Business Review*, July-August, 1954, pp 45-54.

Warner, M.: Industrialization, management education and training systems: A comparative analysis, in: *Journal of Management Studies* 24, 1987, pp 91-112.

Warner, W.L., Arbegglen, J.: *Karriere in der Wirtschaft*, Düsseldorf 1957.

Watson, W.: Social mobility and social class in industrial communities, in: M. Gluckmann, E. Devons (Eds.): *Closed Systems and Open Minds*, London 1964, pp 112-135.

Weber, M.: Der Beruf zur Politik, in: J. Winckelmann (Ed.): *Soziologie – Weltgeschichtliche Analysen – Politik*, 4th ed., Stuttgart 1968, pp 167-185.

Weber, M.: *Die protestantische Ethik I. Eine Aufsatzsammlung*, 5th ed., Gütersloh 1979.

Weber, M.: *Wirtschaft und Gesellschaft*, 5th ed., Tübingen 1972.

Weber, W.: Defizite internationalen Management Trainings – Zur Bedeutung interkultureller Kommunikationsprozesse, unpublished dissertation, Universität Bremen 1990.

Weltz, F.: Die doppelte Wirklichkeit der Unternehmen und ihre Konsequenz für die Industriesoziologie, in: *Soziale Welt* 1, 1988, pp 97-103.

Weltz, F., Lullies, V.: Das Konzept der innerbetrieblichen Handlungskonstellation als Instrument der Analyse von Rationalisierungsprozessen in der Verwaltung, in: U. Jürgens, F. Naschold (Eds.): *Arbeitspolitik, Leviathan Sonderheft 5*, 1983, Opladen 1984, pp 155-170.

Whitley, R.: The city and industry: The directors of large companies, their characteristics and connections, in: Ph. Stanworth, A. Giddens (Eds): *Elites and Power in British Society*, Cambridge 1974, pp 65-80 .

Whitley, R., Thomas, A., Marceau, J.: *Masters of Business. The Making of a New Elite?*, London, New York 1981.

Whyte, M.: *Payment Systems in Britain*, Aldershot 1981.

Whyte, W.M.: *The Organization Man*, Harmondsworth 1965.

Wiedemann, H.: *Das Unternehmen in der Evolution*, Berlin 1971.

Wiener, M.J.: *English Culture and the Decline of the Industrial Spirit 1850- 1980*, Cambridge 1981.

Willmott, H.: Studying managerial work: A critique and a proposal, in: *Journal of Management Studies* 24,3, 1987, pp 249-270.

Willmott, H.: Images and ideals of managerial work: A critical examination of conceptual and empirical accounts, in: *Journal of Management Studies* 21,3, 1984, pp 349-368.

Witte, E., Kallmann, A., Sachs, G.: *Führungskräfte der Wirtschaft*, Stuttgart 1981.

Wrapp, H.E.: Good managers don't make policy decisions, in: *Harvard Business Review*, September-October, 1967, pp 91-99.

Yates, B.: *The Decline and Fall of the American Automobile Industry*, in: Der Spiegel, Nr. 35/1983, pp 126-136.

Young, M.: *The Rise of Meritocracy*, Harmondsworth 1961.

Zapf, W.: Die deutschen Manager, in: W. Zapf (Ed.): *Beiträge zur Analyse der deutschen Oberschicht*, München 1965, pp 136-149.